Portugal to Waterloo
with Wellington

Portugal to Waterloo
with Wellington

The journal of a British Commissariat
officer during the Peninsular War and
the Campaign of 1815

John Edgecombe Daniel

LEONAUR

Portugal to Waterloo
with Wellington
The journal of a British Commissariat
officer during the Peninsular War and
the Campaign of 1815
by John Edgecombe Daniel

First published under the title
Journal of an officer
in the Commissariat
Department of the Army

Leonaur is an imprint
of Oakpast Ltd

ISBN: 978-1-84677-922-0 (hardcover)
ISBN: 978-1-84677-921-3 (softcover)

http://www.leonaur.com

Contents

Introduction	7
Journal	11
1811	20
1812	38
1813	90
1814	131
1815	166
1816	225
1817	227
1818	228

Introduction

introduction to the ensuing *Narrative* it may be useful here
rief outline of what occurred in the War of the Peninsula,
arrival of the author in that country; not so much with
fording fresh information, as to enable the reader to
grand chain of events which led to the glorious and
ted.

1808, Buonaparte (then in the zenith of his pow-
e, King of Italy, Protector of the Confederation
peace (if not in alliance) with all the northern
the Pyrenees with his army, and after beat-
nish forces assembled to oppose his march,
nth of December, where he caused his
'ged king of Spain—Ferdinand the 7th
een made prisoner and conveyed to

d
ro-
the
ered
r the
Alava
e vic-

become
from Lis-
ke), to aid
tion, how-
d ceased, so
r the painful
lthough con-
ce of a French
o the, most seri-
engagement on
killed,
leaving with his
nder the Marshals
eep the country in
occupied by the
till occupied by the
rotect this new order
7th, at his restoration in
rogated the laws thereby
them.

nd extraordinary measures, Na-
y of a few of the Spanish no-
ating military force brought
aniards to submit for the
national spirit remained
e found men who were
native dynasty: these
ne Junta, retired to
on with England;
feated and dis-
ds under their
ntains, from
nemy's forag-
off their suppli

in every quarter, causing great terror and distress; and although in this they became little better than brigands or freebooters, often regardless whether they plundered friends or foes, yet it served to keep the spark of resistance alive, until the councils and arms of England could be effectually exercised for their relief.

In the Spanish Government abuses of the most serious nature had long prevailed, insomuch that the most loyal Spaniards, perceiving that this had paved the way to the enemy's success, thought they should equally serve both their king and their country by introducing a form of government upon the basis of a constitution, likely to promote and secure the true interests and liberties of both. The Junta accordingly applied themselves to the task, and having framed such a constitu-tion as the nature of circumstances would allow, they solemnly boun themselves to observe its laws.

As the arms of the allies subsequently prevailed, the same was p claimed in every part of Spain, and received by the people with utmost demonstrations of loyalty and affection. On the day we en Madrid in 1812, it was proclaimed there, with great pomp, und immediate auspices of the two Spanish generals Don Miguel d and Don Carlos de Espana, and was then styled the fruits of t tory of Salamanca [1].

No sooner had the policy of Buonaparte against Spain known in England than a British force was ordered to march bon (which had already been liberated from the French y the cause in Spain. Before they could reach the scene of a ever, all efficient resistance on the part of the Spaniards h that Lieutenantenant-General Sir John Moore was und necessity of ordering a retreat upon Corunna, which ducted with the most judicious skill and courage, in f army very superior in numbers, subjected our troops t ous privations and losses, and terminated in a severe the plains of Corunna, in which General Moore wa

Buonaparte now returned in triumph to Franc brother a very large portion of the French army, Soult, Mortier, Jordan, Victor, and Bessieres, to l subjection, reduce Cadiz and other fortresses s patriotic forces, and, finally, to consolidate and t

---

1. To the surprise of every reasonable man, Ferdinand the
-814, rejected the whole of the above named articles, ab
 red, and punished the parties concerned in framing

Introduction

As an introduction to the ensuing *Narrative* it may be useful here to give a brief outline of what occurred in the War of the Peninsula, prior to the arrival of the author in that country; not so much with the view of affording fresh information, as to enable the reader to contemplate the grand chain of events which led to the glorious and happy results narrated.

In the autumn of 1808, Buonaparte (then in the zenith of his power as Emperor of France, King of Italy, Protector of the Confederation of the Rhine, &c and at peace (if not in alliance) with all the northern powers of Europe) passed the Pyrenees with his army, and after beating in succession all the Spanish forces assembled to oppose his march, arrived at Madrid in the month of December, where he caused his brother Joseph to be acknowledged king of Spain—Ferdinand the 7th having previously, by stratagem, been made prisoner and conveyed to Paris.

In the execution of these bold and extraordinary measures, Napoleon had been aided by the treachery of a few of the Spanish nobles, which, together with the preponderating military force brought against their country, obliged the loyal Spaniards to submit for the moment to the new order of things; yet the national spirit remained unshaken, and in the legislative assemblies were found men who were firmly resolved to adhere to the ancient and native dynasty: these forming themselves into a court, called the Supreme Junta, retired to Cadiz, and maintained an alliance and communication with England; while, on the other hand, the military, although defeated and dispersed in the field, formed themselves into guerrilla bands under their own chieftains, and retreated into fortresses or to the mountains, from whence they carried on a desultory warfare against the enemy's foraging parties and other detachments, by which they cut off their supplies in every quarter, causing great terror and distress; and although in this they became little better than brigands or freebooters, often regardless whether they plundered friends or foes, yet it served to keep the spark of resistance alive, until the councils and arms of England could be effectually exercised for their relief.

In the Spanish Government abuses of the most serious nature had long prevailed, insomuch that the most loyal Spaniards, perceiving that this had paved the way to the enemy's success, thought they should equally serve both their king and their country by introducing a form of government upon the basis of a constitution, likely to promote and secure the true interests and liberties of both. The Junta accordingly applied themselves to the task, and having framed such a constitution as the nature of circumstances would allow, they solemnly bound themselves to observe its laws.

As the arms of the allies subsequently prevailed, the same was proclaimed in every part of Spain, and received by the people with the utmost demonstrations of loyalty and affection. On the day we entered Madrid in 1812, it was proclaimed there, with great pomp, under the immediate auspices of the two Spanish generals Don Miguel d'Alava and Don Carlos de Espana, and was then styled the fruits of the victory of Salamanca [1].

No sooner had the policy of Buonaparte against Spain become known in England than a British force was ordered to march from Lisbon (which had already been liberated from the French yoke), to aid the cause in Spain. Before they could reach the scene of action, however, all efficient resistance on the part of the Spaniards had ceased, so that Lieutenantenant-General Sir John Moore was under the painful necessity of ordering a retreat upon Corunna, which although conducted with the most judicious skill and courage, in face of a French army very superior in numbers, subjected our troops to the, most serious privations and losses, and terminated in a severe engagement on the plains of Corunna, in which General Moore was killed,

Buonaparte now returned in triumph to France, leaving with his brother a very large portion of the French army, under the Marshals Soult, Mortier, Jordan, Victor, and Bessieres, to keep the country in subjection, reduce Cadiz and other fortresses still occupied by the patriotic forces, and, finally, to consolidate and protect this new order

---

1. To the surprise of every reasonable man, Ferdinand the 7th, at his restoration in 1814, rejected the whole of the above named articles, abrogated the laws thereby enacted, and punished the parties concerned in framing them.

of things. The failure of the expedition under Sir John Moore caused a short suspension of operations; but this soon terminated in the commencement of those memorable campaigns, which in their progress so ennobled their hero, and led to results beyond all that the most sanguine hopes could have anticipated.

On the 22nd of April 1809, Lord Wellington (then Sir Arthur Wellesley,) landed at Lisbon, in command of a British force destined to defend Portugal against the designs of France, and moving with that dispatch and decision so peculiar to himself on the 12th of May he surprised Marshal Soult at Oporto, and after a sharp but partial engagement, obliged the French to fly into Spain. This dashing and propitious opening of the campaigns of Sir Arthur Wellesley was immediately followed by his rapid advance into Spain, as far as Talavera de la Reyna, where he was joined by a Spanish force under Don Cuesta, and on the 27th and 28th of July a very obstinate and bloody engagement was fought against the French army under Joseph Buonaparte and Marshal Jourdan, in which the enemy were repulsed in every direction and obliged to retire; but the British having borne the brunt of the battle, and lost the services of nearly five thousand of their best troops, were not in a state to follow up the victory; and as other French corps were marching from the south of Spain, with the view of interrupting the communication with Portugal, the British General determined upon a retreat to the frontiers, and established his head-quarters at Badajos.

The campaign in itself had been so glorious, and the victories so splendid, that Sir Arthur Wellesley was now created a peer, with the style and titles of Viscount Wellington of Talavera and Baron Douro of Oporto. From this period until the summer of the following year, no movement of importance appears to have been made: each party acting upon the defensive, were occupied in laying foundations for future struggles. The British General Beresford having been appointed marshal and commander-in-chief of the Portuguese army, in concert with Lord Wellington augmented its numbers, improved its discipline, and, in the sequel, brought into the field, in defence of the country, almost all the Portuguese nation.

British officers by special permission were appointed to commands therein, and an auxiliary force of 20,000 men entered into the pay of England. The barriers on our side were thus gaining strength, when early in the summer of 1810, a French army of 80,000 men. Under the command of Marshal Massena, and named by Buonaparte "The

Army of Portugal," began its march for the avowed purpose of planting the imperial French eagles upon the walls of Lisbon. Generals Wellington and Beresford now assembled their forces on the frontiers of Castile, near to Ciudad Rodrigo, which fortress had a Spanish garrison: this place was immediately besieged, and at the end of forty days fell. Massena then advanced, took Almeida also, and forcing his way into Portugal, carried murder and devastation in whatever direction his legions moved.

The allied forces retreating through the mountains by Celorico, Pinhances, Galizes, &c. on the 27th of September were posted upon the Sierras de Busaco, near Coimbra, where a severe action was fought, and the enemy repulsed in all his attacks with dreadful loss. Lord Wellington, however, pursuant to the plan of operations he had adopted, withdrew the army from Busaco, and continued his retreat, pursued by the French, to the fortified lines of Torres Vedras, near Lisbon, where the British army arrived in the month of October 1810; at which period the ensuing *Narrative* commences.

Journal

Falmouth, Nov. 1, 1810.

Having received from the Lords Commissioners of His Majesty's Treasury an appointment upon the Commissariat Staff of the Army serving in Portugal, with orders to proceed to that country, I left London on the evening of the 30th of October for Falmouth, and arrived there the following afternoon.

Nov. 3rd. At 10 o'clock in the morning I embarked for Lisbon in the *Prince of Wales* packet, just then weighing anchor; with a fair wind we soon cleared the roads, and at 5 p. m. lost sight of England. My fellow passengers were Portuguese merchants of Lisbon and Oporto,

4th. The wind continuing in our favour, we reached the mouth of the Bay of Biscay, and entertained hopes that we should have a quick passage.

5th. During the night the wind unfortunately changed, which, together with the extreme badness of the weather, drove us out of our course into the Bay. It was scarcely day before we discovered a strange vessel in chace of us, which induced the captain to crowd all the sail he could carry towards Corunna, hoping to fall in with some British ship of war cruising off that port. The strange vessel gaining upon us, signals were made to her, but none of them being answered satisfactorily, it became obvious that we were chased by an enemy, and as all efforts to escape appeared unavailing, we prepared to meet her in the best manner we were able.

The deck was accordingly cleared for, action, the boarding nets raised, each passenger furnished with a cutlass, and the mail got ready to be thrown overboard. At 6 o'clock in the evening, by moonlight, this unwelcome guest had approached so as to be able to hail us, and she fired one of her guns; the salute was soon returned by us, and as quickly answered by them; so that everything seemed: to portend the approach of a serious conflict. As far as we could observe, the vessel appeared to carry fourteen guns, and was probably one of those French privateers which at this period so infested the Bay.

Considering how much superior she was to us in strength, it was with astonishment we saw her slacken sail and suddenly give up the pursuit, by completely changing her course. Whether some accident had happened to her rigging (for it blew very hard), or whether from our vicinity to Corunna she expected that the firing might bring some vessel to our assistance, we could not determine; but we, saw no more of her.

6th. Shortly after daybreak we discovered another vessel, which we at first thought might be the same: she was in chace of us, and by 2 o'clock in the afternoon came up. She proved to be the English brig *Conflict* The usual question being put, (what news?) they told us that Marshal Massena and Lord Wellington, with their respective forces, were under the walls of Lisbon, where a battle had probably, ere this, been fought; and we, on our part, informed them of the death of her Royal Highness the Princess Amelia, the account of which event had reached Falmouth previous to our leaving that port.

We also told them what a disagreeable visitor we had been forced to entertain the preceding evening; and having described the course she took at leaving us, they bade us farewell and went in quest of her. From this time until the night of the 12th, we had a constant succession of heavy, contrary gales and bad weather, which kept us beating about the Bay, and produced in me a violent sea-sickness, so that I would gladly have exchanged my berth for the poorest hut on shore.

13th. This morning, early, we doubled Cape Finisterre, and got clear of the Bay of Biscay. We sailed at the rate of about four knots in an hour throughout the day, having the coast of Spain almost within sight. In the evening, two hours after dark, a sailor fell overboard from the jib boom: the boat was let down and two men leaped into her; by some accident, however, occasioned by the hurry, the boat unfortunately upset, and as the sea was rolling mountains high and the vessel in full sail, it was with the greatest difficulty that the two men were saved by ropes thrown out to them: in the meantime the other poor fellow was left to a watery grave. From this time until the 17th, we sailed quietly on our passage off the coasts of Spain and Portugal.

17th. Shortly after it had become dark, the weather being very thick and hazy, we were considerably alarmed by a vessel bearing down close upon us before she was discovered. She proved to be a Portuguese sloop just out from Lisbon, bound to Oporto. They informed us that we were not far from the Rock of Lisbon, and also that the great battle had not been fought, notwithstanding that the two armies had been in face of each other but a few leagues from Lisbon, upwards of six weeks.

18th. At break of day we discovered the Rock of Lisbon, which rises out of the water not far from the mouth of the river Tajo or Tagus: from this point may be seen on a clear day the palace of Mafra, which stands on the coast not far distant from the sea-side. A Lisbon pilot now came on board, bringing us all the news—how that the whole population of the kingdom of Portugal had fled into Lisbon, where they had created the greatest scarcity and distress;—how every man capable of bearing arms was forthwith enrolled in the *"ordinanza"* or militia, and sent up to the great English General, who some folks thought would yet beat the *Francezes,* though for his own part (shrugging up his shoulders), he dare say *"nada"* (nothing),—only that being an old man he had escaped the levy, and being very poor, he hoped that whatever party proved conqueror, he should not be molested in his useful occupation of pilot.

19th. During the night, in a storm of thunder and lightning, we were again forced out to sea, and losing sight of land, our poor pilot was quite out of his element, and afforded us some diversion.

20th. We continued during the whole of the day and night beating about at the mouth of the Tagus, not daring to attempt to pass the bar.

21st, The weather having cleared up, we passed the bar in the morning, and anchored not far from Belem Castle, about noon.

22nd. At 10 o'clock in the morning I landed at Lisbon, and put up at Banwell's Hotel at Buenos Ayres.

Thus safely landed, I come now to play the part of Mr. Newcome, a character which I shall not be ashamed to make it appear might be well applied to me; for, like a young soldier, at the very commencement I set out by losing the passage which had been provided for me in the *Eagle* transport, and the consequences were, not only that I had been obliged to come out entirely at my own expense by the packet from Falmouth, but my baggage, which had been put on board the said transport, and which I fully expected to find on my arrival in the Tagus, instead of being conveyed hither as I anticipated, had been left at Portsmouth previous to the sailing of the convoy from thence; depending so fully upon finding these things on my arrival, I had provided no second stock, and what was not the least material, my "portfolio, containing my letters of introduction to some few Peninsular officers, &c. and even my treasury appointment, had been left—nay, what perhaps was still more so than all the rest, my purse of dollars and Portugal coin, which from the high rate of exchange was, of course, considered a necessary appendage to every "*Newcome's*" outfit, had also been left in one of those unfortunate boxes.

Oh the day after my arrival, however, I reported myself to the principal officer of the Commissariat in Lisbon, and with an advance of pay and credit, I began to weather my difficulties.—A few days afterwards I obtained a very good billet upon the house of Señhor Lopez, in the Rua Sacramento la Lapa, at Buenos Ayres, agreeably situated upon the rising ground, near Alcantara, and opposite to the fort of Almada. From my room there was a pleasant view over the Tagus; and I was treated with much civility by my "*Patron*" and his family, during the whole of the month that I remained quartered upon them.

POSITION OF THE ARMIES

Early in the month of October, after the battle of Busaco, the British army under Lord Wellington having arrived in the lines of Torres-Vedras, which had been fortified in a wonderful manner for its reception, and being most judiciously posted in the several strong positions which there presented themselves, occupying the numerous redoubts and field-works which had been constructed, so as to block up or cover every road or pass through the mountains leading to Lisbon, was prepared to meet the enemy. Gunboats were also sent from the fleet up the river as high as Villa Franca, to aid the operations of the army; and many transports as well as ships of war were assembled in the Tagus to carry home the troops in case of a reverse.

On the other hand, the French army, named the army of Portugal, under the command of Marshal Massena, (having closely pursued the British in their retreat) arrived, and formed its line from the river Tagus to the sea, in face of Lord Wellington's position:—Villa Franca was in the enemy's possession, and his piquets came as far as Alhandra. Massena's head-quarters were established at Alenquer, a village near Cartaxo, only eight leagues from Lisbon, Ciudad Rodrigo, Almeida, and all the country from the Douro to the Tagus being still in the enemy's possession, Coimbra only excepted, which had been taken possession of by a party of militia from Oporto under Colonel Trant Thus did the two armies face each other in a threatening attitude the whole of the month of October, and the two first weeks in November, during which period, demonstrations were repeatedly made by the enemy upon different points of our position.

Several skirmishes or affairs of outposts and piquets were fought, and the French Marshal was one day observed with a large force of cavalry reconnoitring the whole extent of our fine. The French army it was fairly supposed amounted to at least sixty thousand combatants, while the English and Portuguese together scarcely numbered fifty thousand.

However, on the 14th November, the French Marshal considering his position in the plain unsafe, withdrew his army during the night from its advanced situation in face of Torres Vedras, &c. to one which he had chosen as more secure, near Santarem, where he fixed his head-quarters. Lord Wellington now moving out of the lines, descended into the plain, and cantoned his troops in the villages about the country in as connected a line as possible, in face of the French position, establishing his head-quarters at the town of Cartaxo, and the periodical rains having commenced, the two armies remained in a state of inactivity during the winter: the British, Portuguese and Spanish forces being posted nearly as follows; *viz.*

HEAD QUARTERS, CARTAXO.

INFANTRY.

1st Division - - - - - - Lieut.-Gen. Sir Brent Spencer, K. B.	5000	Cartaxo.
2nd Division - - - - - - Major-General Hill	6000	Chamusca, &c.[2]
3rd Division - - - - - - Major-General Picton	4000	Torres Vedras.
4th Division - - - - - - Major-General Cole	4000	Azambuja.
5th Division - - - - - - Major-General Leith	4000	

2. On the left banks of the Tagus, opposite to the French position at Santerem, keeping open our communication with Abrantes, Elvas and Badajos, which towns were all still in our possession.

15

6th Division - - - - - -	4000	Cantoned in the Plains of Alenquer, &c.
Major-General Campbell		
7th Division - - - -: -; -	2000	
Major-General Houston		
Light Division - - - - -	3000	Outposts in front of Cartaxo.
Major-General Crawford		
Spanish Army - - - -: - -	8000	Villa Franca.
Capt.-Gen. the Marquis de la Romana		

CAVALRY.

Major-General Cotton - - - - - 2000

Dec. 25th, I received orders to proceed up to head-quarters, which was extremely inconvenient to me, my baggage not having yet arrived from England.

27th. I purchased a pony, hired a Portuguese servant, and made such other arrangements as were necessary to enable me to leave Lisbon; and here I beg leave to introduce a few remarks upon this celebrated city, for the information or amusement, of such, of my friends who have not been there, Lisbon and its environs (seated on the north bank of the river Tagus, about ten miles from its mouth), present to the eye a most brilliant spectacle. The houses, churches, convents and other public buildings are generally very lofty, built of white stone, and occupy several hills inclining to the waterside: the ancient castle of Belem near which we anchored, is a Gothic building of some magnificence.

Belem is joined to Lisbon by a long street or paved road running parallel with, and by the side of the river; within its limits stand Buenos Ayres, and the little village of Alcantara, which might be supposed to form a part of Lisbon, as it is difficult to define their boundaries; in short, though Lisbon itself is ten miles up the river, yet from the city to Fort St. Julian's, near the Bar, there is almost one uninterrupted mass of buildings. The Tagus is here at least four times as wide as the Thames at London, and forms a remarkable fine harbour near the town, where at the time we entered, were no less than six hundred vessels lying at anchor: the day being fine, many of their sails were spread to dry after the storm, which, together with the rays of the sun shining upon the white and cloudless town, produced a very pretty effect, excited my admiration, and raised expectations which were ultimately disappointed.

When I landed I was astonished at the extreme filthiness of the streets, rendered more conspicuous by the light colour of the houses,

16

which themselves on a nearer view were but a sorry aspect from the general disuse of glass windows and the dark appearance of the ground floor, the whole front of the shops being laid open by large folding doors: this part of the house is much neglected by private families—sometimes converted into a stable or coach house, over which you occasionally find an elegant drawing-room or suite of apartments. The houses of the gentry are so large, that you often pass through eight or ten spacious and lofty rooms to a small retreat where the family live.

The streets of Lisbon are for the most part built with much irregularity, owing possibly to the extreme inequality of the ground. Some of the most public streets are too steep to admit of carriages or persons on horseback passing, and the ground so uneven that in many instances the foundations of one street are above the housetops of the next: very high flights of stone steps are consequently necessary to lead from one street into another.

The only part of the town where the ground is at all level consists of two large squares in a very forlorn and unfurnished state, which serve for market places: in the space between these two squares are "*Os ruas dos Mercadores,*" the streets of the merchants: these streets are superior to any other in Lisbon, being flagged for foot passengers, and an uniformity and regularity observed in the buildings nowhere else to be seen: they have no windows to their shops, but the goods are exposed for sale at the doors as elsewhere.—What adds not a little to the uniformity of these streets is, that each branch of trade is confined to its particular street, from which it derives its name—as for example, "the street of the Goldsmiths, the street of the Drapers, the street of the Silversmiths," &c.

There are balconies to almost every house in Lisbon, which in fine weather are filled with people: it is generally such bad walking in the streets, that few persons walk in them for pleasure, Ruins of the dreadful earthquake which happened here in the year 1755 are yet to be seen in many parts of the town, and especially on the hill at Buenos Ayres. The climate of Lisbon, I need scarcely observe is remarkably fine and salubrious, in general some degrees warmer than we experience it in England. At my arrival in Portugal, I was sensibly struck with the superstitious nature of their religious ceremonies: the religion of the country is Roman Catholic, and no people can adhere more closely to its forms and rites than they do.

Their churches are superbly ornamented, and their processions of the Hoste or Holy Incense are so frequent, that it is scarcely possible to pass down any public street without encountering one: the inhabitants all fall upon their knees as it passes; and by a late order of Lord Wellington, the officers of the British army were required to show their respect by taking off their hats or caps. The next thing calculated to attract the notice of a stranger in Lisbon is, the singularity of the Portuguese dress, so little adapted to so warm a climate. They wear a large heavy cloak both winter and summer, buttoned under the chin, with sleeves hanging useless, and a kind of high Opera hat without any ornaments.

Almost the only carriage in use here is a chariot, the body of which resembles an English post-chaise: it moves upon two high wheels, and is drawn by two mules, upon one of which rides the postilion in his cloak and high cocked hat. These vehicles may be hired for the day: they will carry two or three persons. *Sedans* are also in use. I have already noticed the extreme filthiness of the streets of Lisbon, and this remark may be well applied to its inhabitants, particularly to the lower class, who in their persons and houses exhibit a picture of wretchedness inconceivable. They live chiefly upon salt fish, *fisaos* (a kind of pulse), and roasted chesnuts. Many of the houses are seven or eight stories high, on each of which may be found several families.

The peculiar situation of Lisbon at that period, her population so suddenly augmented by thousands of refugees from the country, and two great armies at her gates on the eve of combating for her fate, may account in some degree for the distress which prevailed. The Portuguese ascribed all their grievances to the French, and if you required anything which could not be had, the want of it was attributed to the war and the "*Franceses.*" I now take leave of my Lisbon friends, wishing them health and better times.

Dec. 28. I left Lisbon in the morning, and passing through Sacaveen, Alverca, Alhandra, Villa Franca and Azambuja, arrived in the evening at Cartaxo: here I found myself more a *"Newcome"* than ever, for little imagining the scene of desolation which this country presented, and confiding in the imperfect information which I had obtained from persons who had either never been up the country or, who were, disposed to put a trick upon me, I had most improvidently left Lisbon without even a blanket or a boat-cloak, and unprovided with any comforts, arrived on a cold winter's night in a crowded camp where I knew nobody.

The inhabitants of the country who fled at the approach of the enemy, had but very few returned to their homes, which were in general so completely stript of their furniture that an old oak chair or deal table was considered a prize. A great part of the town had been wantonly destroyed, particularly such houses as were constructed of wood, which had been used for fuel.

No sort of comforts therefore could be obtained beyond what each individual had provided for himself, and these, from the limited means of transport allowed on account of the scarcity of forage, admitted of no superfluities. Besides Lord Wellington and his head quarters, there were upwards of six thousand troops quartered in Cartaxo; every hut, nay the very stables were in some instances officers' quarters, while the soldiers were in a kind of half-bivouac amongst the ruins, and. the face of the country for many miles round was studded with fires of troops in camp or bivouac.

Under such circumstances, I really know not what I should have done had it not been for the kindness of Mr. M. of the Commissariat Department, who offered me a share of his quarters, such as they were. This gentleman occupied a small tenement not far from Marshal Beresford's quarters in Cartaxo, the greater part of which was in ruins. His room had not so much as a chair or table, the door was gone, and the window had no casement, even the floor had in part been torn up for fuel: here he slept on the floor in his blanket, and I laid myself down in another corner of this forlorn apartment in my great coat and worsted gloves, with my portmanteau for my pillow, and my saddle laid over my feet; as for my pony, it fared no better, there being neither hay nor straw to be obtained at any price.

29th. No morning had ever been more welcome to me than this, after passing the night in so comfortless a situation.

30th. This night a soldier of the Guards lent me his blanket for a few hours, but I had scarcely got to steep before he called upon me to give it up; the regiment having orders to fall under arms, and the baggage to be packed with as little delay as possible, in consequence of some movements made by the French. At daylight I found my servant had decamped.

31st Assistant Commissary General D—— arrived at head quarters, and I received orders to return with him to Alverca, one of the villages which I had passed on my way from Lisbon.

1811

January 1st. After hiring an Irish boy as my servant, I left Cartaxo, and in the evening arrived at Alverca.

2nd. In the morning I took possession of an uninhabited house which had no doubt been the residence of a fisherman, as I found two old chairs, a kind of bureau, a barrel of salt and some fishing nets. Expecting to remain here some weeks, I got a straw bed and a blanket to make myself more comfortable. In the course of the month I had the pleasure of receiving my long-lost baggage and went down to Lisbon for a few days, during which time the remains of the Marquis de la Romana were conveyed there from Cartaxo where he had died. This noble Spaniard (it will be remembered) was one of the most distinguished of the Spanish Patriots, and the same who adhered so faithfully to the interests of the British army under Sir John Moore in its critical retreat upon Corunna. He was succeeded in the command of the Spanish troops by General Mendizabel.

February 3rd. A few minutes after 11 at night, as I was reading at a table formed by a door placed upon the salt-barrel in the fisherman's house, I was alarmed by the shock of an earthquake: it was sensibly felt in Lisbon and other places in its vicinity, but I heard of no serious injury occasioned by it.

Early in the month, a skirmish took place at the outposts, in which it was reported that the French general, Junot, was slightly wounded. About the same time; Marshals Soult and Mortier, holding commands in the southern and interior districts of Spain, concentrated their forces in the neighbourhood of Seville, and moved down against Badajos, the frontier fortress of Spain on the Alentejo side of Portugal, then garrisoned by Spanish troops enlisted in the cause of Ferdinand 7th.

This was a masterly movement of the French marshals, being calculated to prove a formidable diversion in favour of Massena, whose difficulties at Santarem increased daily from the extreme want his army was suffering of provisions, forage and equipment; the whole face of the country from the Douro to the Tagus being laid waste and deserted by its inhabitants, whilst their foraging parties which attempted to pass the Douro or the Tagus, were repulsed, and their convoys from Spain often intercepted and cut off by the activity and gallantry of the Portuguese Militia on this, and the Spanish guerrillas on the other side of the Spanish frontiers.

The Spanish army at Villa Franca now received orders to march for Badajos to succour their countrymen in garrison there. They passed through Alverca, crossed the Tagus in boats, and marching up to the frontiers, on the 19th of the month, met the French army under Soult and Mortier in the plains of Badajos; where, after a sharp but short contest, they sustained a complete defeat, were routed, and as a military force, totally destroyed; upon which the two French Marshals commenced the siege of Badajos without further molestation.

All the movements of Marshal Massena at Santarem indicated the arrangement he was making to retrace his steps to the frontiers of Castile:—the forces here under Lord Wellington (the Portuguese of which under the auspices of Marshal Sir W. C. Beresford had, during the winter, been wonderfully improved in discipline), now began to concentrate, and to prepare in their turn for offensive operations. On the 26th we moved up to Villa Franca.

RETREAT OF MARSHAL MASSENA

March 5th. Marshal Massena commenced his famous retreat from Santarem by the road of Thomar and Pombal to Coimbra; upon which orders were given for the reserves to move up. Cavalry, artillery and ammunition were passing through from Lisbon and the lines towards Cartaxo; and the army was to move forward on the morrow.

It was on this day that the British forces under Major General Graham were engaged with and obtained a glorious victory over the French army under Marshal Victor at Barrosa, near Cadiz.

6th. The army advancing this morning, followed the route of the enemy, and our head-quarters moved from Cartaxo to Santarem. The communication with Abrantes on this side of the river was now thrown open, and the whole army joined in the pursuit. The route which the French Marshal had chosen, was (as above stated) by Thomar and

Pombal upon Coimbra, at or near which place he would probably attempt to pass the river Mondego, with the view of taking up the stores and field equipage which we understood he had left in *depôt* at Viseu, and so by the mountainous route of Celorico and Guarda, ultimately reach the frontiers near Almeida and Ciudad Rodrigo.

It was calculated, that with whatever facility the French army continued its retreat, under such circumstances it could not possibly reach Almeida before the last day of March or the beginning of April, which would give time for the execution of a grand plan of operations said to be in agitation, to effect which one part of our forces was to continue in close pursuit of the enemy, while another, by a circuitous march, should act in his rear, and the 2nd Division with some cavalry under the command of Marshal Beresford, in the absence of General Hill, which had been stationed on the left bank of the Tagus, had received orders accordingly.

In the meantime the Portuguese Militia were to keep possession of Coimbra and blow up the bridge over the Mondego: fleets with supplies of provisions and ammunition sailed from the Tagus for that river and the Douro, to meet our army as it passed. Marshal Beresford's corps was preparing to act, and Lord Wellington had nearly reached the Mondego, when, tidings came that Badajos had been surrendered to the French army, through the treachery or imbecility of its governor, on the 11th, and that Marshal Soult (thus relieved from the siege) was preparing to advance upon Lisbon by the open and level country of Alentejo.

The 4th Division which had advanced with us as far as Condexa, and two regiments of cavalry now marched to join the 2nd Division, and the whole under the command of Sir William Carr Beresford, advanced towards Elvas, to meet Marshal Soult, who upon their approach retired towards Seville, leaving a French garrison in Badajos, under the command of a general named Phillippon. This was (no doubt) a severe check to the views of Lord Wellington. The bridge, however, at Coimbra, was destroyed, and the French (shut out from that town) were obliged to cross the river higher up—from this circumstance, our troops came up with them, and a severe skirmish took place on the 12th near Condexa, where they concealed one of their eagles, which was afterwards found and sent to England.

Marshal Massena himself was near falling a prisoner at the passage of a little river. Continuing their retreat, however, by Pinhances, and Celorico, and availing themselves of the numerous strong positions which every day's march presented, they passed the mountains of Guarda, and their advanced guard reached the Coa on the 1st day of April.

March 10th. Sunday. It was not until this morning that we left Villa Franca, under directions to proceed as far as Thomar, and there wait for further orders. We passed through Cartaxo early in the afternoon, then traversed a very extensive heath, and just as it was getting dark came to the causeway leading up to Santarem, near which spot were several dead men lying in the road, and a small village completely in ruins. We reached Santarem about 7 o'clock at night, where a large building was still burning.

I understood it to have been the French hospital, and therefore might possibly have been destroyed to prevent infection. Santarem is divided into two parts, *viz.* the high and low town: having to descend into the latter, it was 10 o'clock before we could get our horses into a stable where a party of drivers or muleteers had kindled a fire: unable to obtain billets we were obliged to remain there ourselves in a very comfortless condition, our baggage not having arrived.

11th. The servants coming up with the baggage, we got a cup of chocolate and some biscuit, drew our rations, and leaving Santarem, put up this night in a stable at Golegoa, where we lighted a fire to dry our clothes, which had got wet from the rivers we had to ford in our route.

12th. We moved from Golegoa soon after daybreak, and early in the day reached Thomar, where we got possession of a house, and finding two sofas in one of the rooms, they served us for beds. We remained at Thomar three days, during which I suffered very severely from rheumatism, insomuch that I was afraid I should be obliged to give up and go to the rear. It is totally impossible to describe the picture of desolation and distress which this unhappy country exhibited.

In Thomar, a town of considerable magnitude, whole streets appeared deserted, and we found scarcely any inhabitants, saving a few poor people, who unable to escape to Lisbon at the general desertion on the approach of the enemy, had concealed themselves in the mountains off the road, and even these had in many instances (during this sorrowful winter) been subject to the incursions of foraging parties from the enemy's camps and cantonments in the plain, who never failed to treat them with the greatest brutality and cruelty, often maiming and not unfrequently wantonly killing even women and children: so enraged were they at the failure of their enterprise; to which the general desertion of their homes by the inhabitants had so much contributed.

Indeed the Portuguese might well compare the French troops to so many famished wolves, for such was their distress, that during the last two months they had in some, positions been reduced to a scanty allowance of horse-flesh and Indian cornflour, and sustained privations under which an English army would have been completely disorganized, if not destroyed.

When the inhabitants of this part of the country quitted their homes and fled, to Lisbon or the mountains, they naturally carried with them such part of their property and furniture as they were able to remove, and that remaining, which might serve for food to either men or horses or in any way facilitate the operations of the enemy (at the suggestion of Lord Wellington), they destroyed, so that the French in the first instance had to march as it were through a desert, and then subsist in it in face of a bold and formidable enemy: thus subjected to daily sufferings and privations, they were exasperated to the very last degree against the English general who had suggested and the inhabitants who had executed what they termed so barbarous and unnatural a measure, proposed and urged on the part of Lord Wellington as a choice of evils, being the only means of saving the country, and carried into effect by the inhabitants, was on their part a noble sacrifice in defence of their nation, which has ever since redounded to its glory and prosperity.

Exasperated by these circumstances, and baffled in their hopes of finding all in Lisbon—the French determined upon revenging themselves in the best way they could, by destroying such little furniture as remained, and doing all the injury they were capable of to the tenements and buildings of every description they found in their way, so that what with the havoc first made by the inhabitants and afterwards by the French, the country presented a scene of ruin and devastation truly designative of the seat of war, and which no other occasions I should imagine would produce. It will naturally be supposed that our army, in the pursuit of an enemy through such a country, would be subjected to distresses and privations which no measures of the commander in chief nor exertions of the Commissariat could fully remedy.

From the extreme badness of the roads, the transport of the country could seldom follow and never keep pace with the march of the army;

and in consequence of the exhausted state of the country through which we were compelled to march, our chief dependence for the support of our troops rested on magazines formed upon the rivers, which were supplied by means of water carriage, subject of course to unavoidable delays and disappointments. On leaving the Tagus, therefore, our object was to gain the Mondego.

16th. Leaving Thomar in the afternoon we marched through a large forest of cork trees, of which there are many in this country, and were overtaken by a dark and wet night while passing through some high and rocky mountains, which obliged us to halt and bivouac under a large tree, where I slept in my blanket, being the first night I had slept in the field. The 3rd Dragoon Guards were at bivouac at the foot of a high mountain not far from us. This regiment was one of the two on the march to join Marshal Beresford in the Alentejo.

17th. We came to Pombal, and the town being very much crowded by troops of the 7th Division, we were forced to sleep in the stable where we had put our horses.

20th; We left Pombal in the morning and were obliged to take up our nightly quarters at Condexa, in a house so much injured and abused that the floor was not fit to sleep upon, so I lifted a door from its hinges for the purpose of a bedstead, and in the morning restored it to its proper station.

21st. From Condexa we proceeded to Coimbra, a small city seated on the right bank of the river Mondego, where we remained three days, during which time several detachments of French prisoners were brought in from the army.

24th. We repassed the Mondego and proceeded to Espinhal, which we found to be in the same state as the rest of the country: very few of the inhabitants had returned from the mountains.

27th. Left Espinhal, passed through Fosse de Arroz, and in the afternoon came to the river Alva, a branch of the Mondego, about thirty English miles above Coimbra: slept under an apple tree in an orchard not far from the village of Ponte Murcella, where we found a French soldier in a stable severely wounded. Colonel Jackson of the Foot Guards and Mr. Dumaresq, behaved with great humanity to him. We here sent our servants and muleteers down to Raiva for rations, as nothing could be purchased on the road but fruit—the few inhabitants left subsisting chiefly on herbs and Indian-corn bread, which were very scarce.

28th. We arrived in the evening at Galizes and slept in a room without any furniture.

29th. At Pinhances, about six leagues from Celorico, we took up our quarters in a room which as usual had neither furniture or ceiling.

30th. We came up with Lord Wellington's head-quarters at Celorico, a town seated upon a rock near the banks of the Mondego. It was here that Marshal Massena wrote his dispatches to Buonaparte a few days before explaining the causes of, and detailing the progress made in his retreat

31st. Being ordered to proceed to Lamego on the Douro, I left Celorico in the afternoon, and slept at Trancoza.

April 1st After passing through Moimento de Beira and several inhabited villages we were quartered at a large convent, where we slept upon beds with sheets and pillows, a luxury I had not enjoyed since I left Lisbon.

2nd. Arrived in Lamego, and got quarters in the Bishop's Palace. Meanwhile the army had passed over the mountains of Guarda, following the enemy as far as the river Coa; and Lord Wellington had moved his head quarters from Celorico to Marmeliero, a few miles from Sabugal.

AFFAIR OF SABUGAL.

April 3rd. Two divisions of the enemy having taken a position on the rising ground above the town of Sabugal, the Light Division and part of the 3rd attacked them in the morning, and obliged them to fall back upon Alfaiates, Colonel Beckwith of the 95th regiment was much distinguished, and received a wound on this occasion. After the affair the enemy passed the Coa, and not only crossed the frontiers into Spain, but retired beyond the Agueda, leaving garrisons in Almeida and Ciudad Rodrigo, and our army went into cantonments upon the frontiers, with the head quarters in Villa Formosa.

5th. In proceeding from Lamego to the army, late in the night, I for some time lost my way on the mountains, but at length I reached Sabugal, where for want of a better lodging, I slept in the church.

9th. I returned to my duties at Lamego. This town is seated on the declivity of a hill, at the foot of which runs the little river Balcamao, its distance from the river Douro being only six miles: it had been subject to the protection of the militia: this circumstance, together with its remote situation from the route pursued by the French army (nearly twenty leagues), occasioned it to escape with comparatively little injury.

The French foraging parties, however, did occasionally visit this part of the country, and levied contributions. The Douro is navigable for large boats as high as the vale of Lucaia near this place, where its banks are beautifully romantic, and the current very rapid.

On the opposite side stands the town of Peco de Regoa. We continued at Lamego until the 22nd, when we moved to St João de Pesqueira, a station higher up the Douro. The army having passed the Coa, had gone into cantonments (as I have already mentioned) on the frontiers, its right wing occupying the villages in the plains of Almadillo to the little river Azava, and its left extending towards Fort Conception, investing or blockading Almeida, so that on the 16th, Lord Wellington leaving the command to Sir Brent Spencer, set out for the Alentejo to inspect the operations carrying on under Marshal Beresford, who had moved up to Badajos, which he was preparing to besiege. About the same time the town of Olivenza in that vicinity was captured by the 4th Division, under Major General Cole.

27th. Lord Wellington returned to Villa Formosa.

May 1st. Marshal Massena having recruited his army, held a council of war at Ciudad Rodrigo, when it was resolved to attack the English army for the relief of Almeida, the garrison of which was reduced to distress from the want of provisions. Lord Wellington therefore prepared for battle in the position of Fuentes d'Onor, and formed his line on the river Duas Casas, which divides Portugal from Spain. Within a few days several spies had been detected carrying communications between the garrison of Almeida and the French army: one had a letter from Marshal Massena to the governor of Almeida, concealed in a walking-stick, stating his intention to attack the English near Fuentes, and requiring the governor, by a sortie, to aid the operation, and by that means to obtain relief.

3rd. Early in the morning the French army crossed the Agueda in great force: the Light Division, posted near Espeja, retired upon Fuentes d'Onor: and the army then fell under arms.

BATTLE OF FUENTES D'ONOR,
3rd to 5th May 1811

The village of Fuentes d'Onor stands on the banks of the little river Duas Casas, which divides Portugal from Spain, at an equal distance between the two frontier towns of Almeida and Ciudad Rodrigo. In front of the village is a beautiful plain, skirted by the wood of Carvalhos, and in the rear of it, a range of hills, behind which are the villages of Frenada, Castello Bom, and Villa Formosa, near a branch of the river Coa. The British army occupying this position was posted nearly as follows, with its advanced posts in front of the village, and amongst the rocks about Fuentes:

Right Wing.

7th Division	Major-General Houston.
Light Division	Major-General Crawford.

Near Poco Velha, and in the wood of Fuentes.

Left Wing

5th Division	Major-General Leith.
6th Division	Major-General Campbell.

Investing Almeida, and supporting the centre.

Centre Column.

1st Division	Lieut.-General Sir B. Spencer
3rd Division	Major-General Picton.

Occupying the village of Fuentes d'Onor, &c.

Cavalry, reserve artillery, and Don Carlos d'Espana's Spanish division.

May 3rd. In the afternoon; the French Marshals Massena and Ney, with eight divisions of infantry, and a considerable force of cavalry, advancing by the roads of Gallegos and Espeja, Attacked the right and centre of our army, which gave them possession of a part of the village of Fuentes, against which post their principal efforts were directed.

4th. A severe action was expected, but the French not choosing to attack, and Lord Wellington's operations being merely of a defensive nature, nothing important occurred. Several movements took place, by which both armies strengthened their left. Our Light Division marched from the right to the left of Fuentes; and at night, our armies and those of the enemy bivouacked in face of each other.

6th. Sunday morning. Soon after daybreak, three divisions of the

French, with some cavalry, were discovered advancing upon the village of Fuentes d'Onor, occupied by the light troops of the 1st and 3rd Division, under the command of Lieutenantenant-Colonel Williams, of the 60th regiment. This officer was wounded early in the contest, and the command then devolved on Colonel Cameron, of the 79th, who was soon after so severely wounded that he died on the 13th, at Villa Formosa.

Our right and centre columns being warmly engaged, fresh troops were sent, into Fuentes, under the command of Lieutenant-Colonel Cadogan, of the 71st regiment; and so severe was the contest at this point, that the village was, at the point of the bayonet, repeatedly lost and won during the day. A very superior force attacked the 7th Division on our right, which withdrew (as Lord Wellington himself said) in admirable order from the advanced post they occupied. Our cavalry charged, and while our right wing fell back, our left advanced, threatening the enemy's communication with the Agueda, which obliged Massena to relinquish the view of turning our right

His efforts to force our centre about Fuentes, too, being unsuccessful, he at length returned to the ground he had left in the morning; and the French troops were called off from the attack at the close of the day, all their attempts against our position having proved fruitless. It was calculated that they left nearly three, thousand men on the field of battle, besides one thousand prisoners. Such a contest as this had been could not be sustained without a considerable and painful loss also on our side.

Our sufferers amounted to about one thousand two hundred men, a number which must have been considerably augmented but for the great skill displayed by Lord Wellington and the general officers in their disposition of the troops. Major-General Nightingale was wounded, but not dangerously. The 71st, 79th and 88th regiments were particularly distinguished on the occasion; and the Portuguese received great praise for their gallantry. The Spaniards were not engaged. At night Lord Wellington returned to Villa Formosa, and the two armies bivouacked in view of each other.

6th. Was spent in removing the wounded and burying the dead. The two armies continued in sight of each other.

7th. The French commenced their retreat, and crossed the Agueda. The British army returned to its cantonments, as before the action; the 6th Division continuing to invest Almeida.

11th. The governor of Almeida (disappointed of the relief which the battle of Fuentes was intended to afford), had formed a plan for dismantling the fortress, and the escape of his troops; in pursuance of which the garrison (by three separate detachments) left the town in the night, and conducted their march so quietly, that before their flight was discovered, they had nearly joined the French army beyond the Agueda.

About this time, Marshals Massena and Ney (probably tired of serving in a campaign redounding so little to their honour), left the army, and repaired to France, upon which the command devolved upon Marshal Marmont, Duke of Ragusa. Lord Wellington having learnt that Marshal Soult, in the south, was preparing to attack Marshal Beresford, ordered the 3rd and 7th Divisions, under Generals Picton and Houston, to march for the Alentejo, and he himself set out for the same destination on the 16th; the very day on which the sanguinary engagement was fought at Albuera.

BATTLE OF ALBUERA
16th May, 1811.

Albuera is a village, about five Spanish leagues in front of Badajos, and derives its name from a little river or stream which runs through the plain. The ground is generally levels and the country open and uncultivated, which rendered it admirably adapted for the operations of cavalry. Marshal Soult having received a reinforcement from the interior provinces of Spain, augmented his army to thirty thousand fighting men, and having reached the vicinity of Albuera, obliged Sir William Beresford to convert the siege of Badajos into a blockade when it was judged expedient to meet the enemy and prevent his farther advance. Sir William Beresford, therefore, assembled his little army on the field of Albuera; and a most sanguinary conflict ensued.

Army of Albuera.

2nd Division	Major-General Stewart.
4th Division	Major-General Cole.
Cavalry	Major-General Lumley.
Spanish Divisions.	

The Spanish General Blake, though senior officer, waved the command in favour of Marshal Beresford; and the army having taken its ground about nine o'clock in the morning, the Spaniards, occupying what was deemed one of the strongest points, were attacked, and lost the important post committed to their charge. The brunt of the engagement then fell upon the British troops, who sustained the shock with the greatest firmness and valour. For several hours successively the carnage was terrific: almost every regiment charged with the bayonet, and some companies, it was said, perished to the last man.

Generals Stewart and Cole were both severely wounded, and Major-General Hoghton, commanding a brigade in the 2nd Division, was killed at the head of his troops; as were also Colonels Sir William Myers, of the 7th Fusiliers, and Duckworth, of the 48th regiment. The action continued with great violence until about three o'clock in the afternoon, when the enemy (repulsed at all points) began to retire, and passed the river Albuera, leaving almost all their wounded in our hands. They retreated by Zafra upon Seville the next day, pursued by our cavalry. Our loss in this sanguinary contest was calculated to exceed in killed and wounded four thousand men, owing, in some, degree, to the.superiority the enemy had over us in cavalry, of which their Polish lancers were particularly active, causing us great loss. Major Arbuthnot, of the Guards, was the officer selected to carry the dispatches to England.

18th. Lord Wellington arrived at Elvas, and, there met Marshal Beresford. The 3rd and 7th Divisions, under the command of Generals Picton and Houston, arriving at the same time, the siege of Badajos was resumed with increased means and activity, under the auspices of Lord Wellington. At this period Major General Hill arrived from England, and relieved Marshal Beresford in the command of the corps which had followed the French army on the road to Seville.

June. Marshal Soult was not so crippled but that he determined upon making another effort to relieve Badajos. The army of Marshal Marmont having moved to the south by Placentia and the bridge, of Almaraz, induced Sir Brent Spencer (upon whom the command of the army on the frontiers of Castile had devolved), to put his troops in motion, and marching by Castello Branco and Villa Velha, they joined Lord Wellington in the Alentejo about the time that Marshal Marmont arrived at Merida.

The junction of, the two French armies being thus effected, they advanced again upon Albuera, where it was expected that another battle would have been fought; but Lord Wellington (probably not deeming the object worth so great a sacrifice) withdrew the army over the Guadiana, and posted it in a strong position near Elvas. Badajos was in consequence left in communication with the French army; and the two marshals made a pompous entry into the town.

Having recruited and provisioned the garrison, they again left general Phillipon in command, and the French army, after reconnoitring our position, without daring to attack it, fell back again upon Seville and Merida, and, as Lord Wellington had foreseen, began to separate and disperse for the want of subsistence, which together with the increasing activity of the Spanish guerrillas, rendered it impossible for so large a force to remain assembled for any length of time in one province,

July 13th. We joined the camp near Elvas, having marched by Guarda, Belmonte, Castello Branco, Niza and Portalegre from Celorico, where we had been on duty more than five weeks. Here we bivouacked in a little meadow by the side of a rivulet near the Quenta de St Joze, and not far from the 1st Division camp. We slept out four nights, and then got into a small convent.

22nd. Head-quarters (to which I was now attached) set out for Portalegre. At night we halted at a house by the road side in a wood, and requested admittance, which was infused under the plea of there being a *doente* or sick person in the house with an infectious fever; but we were too much accustomed to hear this excuse to be alarmed, and after a little altercation with the old woman we were admitted, and four of us slept upon the floor in the kitchen, in our blankets or boat-cloaks.

23rd. Soon after sunrise we passed through Assumar, a little town pleasantly situated in a fine fruitful country, and arrived at Portalegre early in the day: here I obtained neat quarters. The people were extremely civil, and placed beds for us upon the floor, but we were obliged to move out on the following day, when the 1st Division marched in, and a change of quarters took place.—About this time Lieutenant-General Sir Brent Spencer left the army, and General Graham (the hero of Barrosa) arrived as second in command. His Serene Highness the hereditary Prince of Orange joined Lord Wellington as extra *aide-de-camp.*

20th. Late in the afternoon, after the heat of the day had subsided, the 1st Division and head-quarters marched out of Portalegre. I slept in a field near Alpalhão, and passed the night very miserably.

31st Passing through Niza, we crossed the river Tagus this afternoon in boats, and slept under a tree near Villa Velha. The Light Division had hutted themselves with the boughs of trees on the banks of the river.

August 1st We moved on to Castello Branco, and remained there seven days, during which time the troops crossed the Tagus, excepting the 2nd Division and four regiments of cavalry, which were to remain in the Alentejo, under the command of General Hill, whose headquarters were fixed at Estremoz. Marshal Soult had withdrawn his troops entirely from Spanish Estremadura, and Marmont re-crossed the Tagus at Almaraz, leaving a French corps of observation on the frontiers near a village called Arroyos dos Molinos.

The celebrated Heroine of Saragosa was at Castello Branco at this time, and called one morning at the Commissary General's office. In the memorable siege of Saragosa, sustained by the patriot Palafox, where the inhabitants and women of the place assisted in bringing balls and ammunition to the batteries; the husband of this extraordinary woman, holding an important command, was killed in her presence. The fall of this officer was about to be followed by the loss of the battery, when in an animated tone she addressed the troops, and by her personal intrepidity and address so rallied them, that they not only repulsed the enemy, but in a successful sortie beat them back from the walls. For this extraordinary act she was at her own request rewarded with a commission in the Spanish army, in which she ranks as a field officer.

4th. Head-quarters left Castello Branco, and were fixed at the village of Fuentes de Guinaldo, a few miles on the Spanish side of the frontiers, and about five leagues from Ciudad Rodrigo. The troops were in cantonments or at bivouac about the villages of Alburgaria, Almadilla, Ituera, El Bodon, Aldea de Bispo, &c. and we were stationed at Casillas de Flores, a little village in the woods near Fuentes de Guinaldo, and remained there a month, during which period the weather was extremely warm, but the mornings and evenings were delightfully fine.

September. We passed the three first weeks of this month chiefly at Fuentes de Guinaldo, nothing of moment occurring until the 24th, when it was found that the French army under Marshal Marmont, very considerably reinforced, was again approaching the Agueda with a large convoy of provisions designed for the garrison of Cuidad Rodrigo. Orders were in consequence given for the divisions to leave their cantonments and assemble on the Azava. Some field works were thrown up this afternoon on the rising ground in front of Guinaldo, where the 3rd, 4th and 7th Divisions were posted.

Affair of El Bodon,
25th September, 1811.

Early this morning our advanced guard, .consisting of the 5th, 77th and 83rd regiments of Foot of the 3rd Division, under the command of Major-General the Honourable Charles Colville, with the 11th Light Dragoons and 1st Hussars of the King's German Legion, commanded by Major-General Victor Baron Alton, posted in the plains of Cuidad Rodrigo in front of the village of El Bodon, were attacked by a very large force of cavalry, supported by artillery. These troops had a very arduous task, and behaved themselves with so much spirit that their gallant conduct was specially noticed by Lord Wellington in the general orders of this date.

Three squadrons of our Light Horse were repeatedly charged by fourteen squadrons of the enemy, and maintained their superiority, retiring in excellent order upon our infantry. The little 2nd battalion of the 5th Foot, commanded by Major Ridge, sustained a charge from the enemy's cavalry, and recaptured the Portuguese guns which had fallen into the enemy's hands after the artillerymen had been cut down at their stations.

The 77th and 83rd regiments also had their share in the engagement, and conducted themselves to the satisfaction of Lord Wellington, who had been in the front with them all the morning. His Serene Highness the hereditary Prince of Orange was on this day; for the first time, under fire. In the afternoon the enemy brought into the plain forty-two squadrons of cavalry, and his infantry beginning to cross the Agueda near Cuidad Rodrigo, Generals Colville and Alten were ordered to retire upon the position of Fuentes de Guinaldo, where they joined the rest of the army in the evening, and our troops lay out all night without their baggage, which had been packed and sent to the rear.

26th. During the night and all this day the French forces were passing the Agueda, and assembling in front of our position on the river Azava and at Fuentes de Guinaldo, so that it was fully expected that an engagement would have ensued. The day closed, however, without any movement of importance on either side, and the two armies bivouacked in face of each other, covering the country with their fires.

Two hours after dark I was on the field: at this time everything was quiet, and no movement appeared in agitation, until about 10 o'clock, when, as the baggage assembled at Casillas de Flores was unloading for the night, and we were going to rest, an orderly came express from Guinaldo, with directions for us to retreat with all possible expedition through the woods, by Forcalhos, into Portugal, and before we could get clear of the village the troops were filing through, and all the roads thronged.

The face of the country here is covered with extensive woods of stunted oaks and underwood, through which the roads and avenues are very narrow and intricate, and there being no moon much confusion occurred, until we reached the high road near Aldea de Ponte. We reached the village of Nave about daybreak, and Lord Wellington arrived shortly after. The enemy's army being seventy thousand strong, was considered, too powerful to be attacked with any prospect of success in a country so open and level as that we had just left. Marshal Marmont also, conscious of his superiority, had dispatched a large force of cavalry and artillery, under cover of the night, to march round our left by Alburgaria, and cut off our retreat before daylight; but Lord, Wellington's penetration enabled him, by a precipitate retreat, completely to frustrate his views.

The French army, however, continued to follow us on the 27th, but was repulsed in an attack upon General Cole's division and our outposts of cavalry at Aldea de Ponte. The head-quarters moved during the day as far back as Sabugal, where we arrived in the evening. The troops were assembling on the hills round the town all night; and it was expected that Lord, Wellington would here have given battle to the enemy.

28th. We were ordered off to Marmeleiro, where we hutted ourselves with the boughs of trees, which however the wind blew down in the night. From thence we proceeded to Celorico, and there waited for further orders.

October 1st, Instead of advancing to Sabugal, Marshal Marmont contented himself with having relieved Ciudad Rodrigo, and fell back again towards Salamanca, upon which the British divisions went into cantonments on the frontiers, nearly as before, with the head-quarters in Frenada.

Everything being quiet on these frontiers, the army in cantonments, and Lord Wellington in Frenada, I proceed to notice the movements of General Hill's corps which was left in the Alentejo, and which had been ordered upon an expedition against the French corps of observation stationed at Arroyos dos Mollinos.

Affair of Arroyos dos Mollinos
28th October, 1811 .

General Hill, with a part of his corps, on this occasion conducted his movements with such promptitude and secrecy, that on the evening of the 27th, the British forces had arrived within gunshot of the town of Arroyos before the enemy knew that they had left Portalegre. No fires were allowed that night in the camp, and so judicious were the arrangements made by General Hill, that at break of day on the 28th the village was surrounded, and the French so completely taken by surprise, feat after a slight distance, nearly the whole of their troops were made prisoners. General Hill having completed this important service in so brilliant a manner, returned to his cantonments.

Great difficulties occurred about this time in supplying the army, owing to the non-arrival of boats up the Douro from Oporto, the violence of the weather having rendered the navigation of the river for some days impracticable.

It is here worthy of notice, that about this time the artificers of the army were employed. Under the directions of Lieutenant-Colonel Sturgeon of the Royal Staff Corps, in a work which afterwards proved of great utility. It had been found, from experience, that the transport of the country was inadequate to the purpose of supplying the wants of the army, or affording that aid to the mule transport attached to each division which circumstances required, and that the country carts, in some instances, had proved of little or no use; so that a plan was suggested and put in execution for constructing a certain number, upon a model which had been approved by Lord Wellington, to be given over to the Commissary-General, and to be called the Commissariat Wagon Train.

These carts or wagons were each to be drawn by four oxen purchased for the purpose, and were made capable of bearing eight hundred pounds weight each. Upwards of six hundred carts were thus constructed during the winter at Lisbon, Oporto and Almeida, and were formed into divisions and sub-divisions, under the superintendence of commissariat officers, with conductors, artificers and other subordinate persons attached to each:—and thus the army became possessed of an independent wheel transport of its own, by which the requisitions upon the inhabitants of the country became less oppressive and obnoxious. These carts were employed in conveying ammunition at the subsequent sieges of Ciudad Rodrigo and Badajos; and in the Spanish campaigns they were the means of forming many of the *depôts* in the interior.

14th. About this time I was sent into the mountains near Sabugal, to a little village called Val de Espina, where the country abounds with chesnuts. I remained there two days.

23rd. Head-quarters advanced this day to Fuentes de Guinaldo, and the army, moving up to the river Agueda, was posted in the road by which Marshal Marmont was again coming with a convoy of supplies for Cuidad Rodrigo. He was, however, on this occasion, forced to retire upon Tamames without effecting his object, and the army then returned to its cantonments on the frontiers, with the head-quarters at Freneda as before.

December. Marshal Marmont having marched his troops into the interior of Spain, probably with a view to repress the rising spirit of the guerrillas, and possibly supposing that all operations of the English had ceased for the winter. Lord Wellington gave orders for the battering train to be brought to the frontiers; and during the latter part of the month the soldiers in the villages nearest to Ciudad Rodrigo were employed in making facines and gabions, for which they received a small gratuity; and the whole of the arrangements necessary for the commencement of the siege were nearly completed by the last day of the year.

1812

SIEGE OF CIUDAD RODRIGO

January. The new year commenced with the siege of Ciudad Rodrigo, by the following divisions:

1st Division	Lieut.-General Graham.
3rd Division	Major-General Picton
4th Division	Major-General Colville.
Light Division	Major-General Crawford.
Royal Artillery	Major-General Bothwick,
Royal Engineers	Lieut.-Colonel Fletcher.
Acting Adjutant General	Lieut.-Colonel Waters.
Acting Q. Master General	Lieut.-Colonel de Lancey.

January 6th. Head-quarters advanced this afternoon from Freneda to the village of Gallegos, where we arrived late at night, and got very bad quarters in a Spanish cottage.

8th. Shortly after dark, parties from the 3rd, 4th and Light Divisions broke ground before Ciudad Rodrigo, under a heavy cannonade from the besieged. An outwork or fortified convent, called the Convento de San Francisco, was most gallantly stormed by detachments from the light division. The immediate directions of the siege were vested in Lieutenant-General Graham, in whose skill Lord Wellington placed the highest confidence. The weather continued dry and very cold, and the country around wore a wintery aspect, the "*Sierras de Gata*" being covered with snow.

15th. The batteries being fit to receive the guns, which had arrived during the night, they were drawn into the trenches, and a heavy fire was opened upon the walls this morning, and was continued without intermission day and night Marshal Marmont being informed of this unlooked-for attack upon Ciudad Rodrigo, reassembled his army near Salamanca, and proceeded by forced marches to the relief of the place.

STORMING OF CIUDAD RODRIGO,
Sunday Evening, 19th January

At 8 o'clock Ciudad Rodrigo was carried by storm by the following divisions of the army, which were formed into five columns.

3rd Division   Major General Picton.
Light Division   Major General Crawford
Portuguese Division   Brigadier General Pack.

The troops moved from the camp as the sun went down, and concealed themselves in the trenches until the signal for the attack was given. The 1st, 2nd and 3rd columns, led by Lieutenant-Colonel O'Toole, Major Ridge and Major-General Mackinnon, and consisting of troops of the 3rd Division, all under the command of General Picton, were ordered to storm the breaches made on one side of the town, while the 4th column, consisting of the 43rd, 52nd and 95th regiments, under Major-Generals Crawford and Vandeleur, the forlorn hope or advance of which was led by Major Napier of the 52nd, should assault the town on the other side; and Brigadier-General Pack with the Portuguese troops was to draw the attention of the enemy by a feint or false attack at a third point.

These several attacks were crowned with complete success, although the 4th column, composed of the 45th, 74th and 88th regiments, sustained a momentary check by the explosion of a mine, by which Major-General Mackinnon was blown into the air, and the column suffered severely. In about half an hour from the commencement of the assault the town was in possession of the British, and the garrison (about one thousand seven hundred men, with the governor, General Banier) made prisoners.

As I passed by the convent de San Francisco about 10 o'clock, some parties were removing the poor wounded out of the ditch. Lord Wellington soon afterwards returned to his head-quarters at Gallegos, where he arrived about midnight. Our loss by the storm was not so severe as might have been expected. Valuable as the services were of those whom we had lost, it was a subject for congratulation, that in killed and wounded they did not exceed five hundred men. Major-General Mackinnon was killed, and Major-Generals Crawford and Vandeleur were wounded.

January 21st. The prisoners marched from Gallegos for Lisbon.

24th. Major-General Crawford, who had commanded the light division, died at Ciudad Rodrigo of the wounds he received in the storm, and was buried with military honours according to his rank. Lord Wellington and other general officers attended the funeral. The Hon. Major Gordon, *aide-de-camp* to Lord Wellington, set out for London with the dispatches; and the Spanish General, Don Miguel Alava, for Cadiz, where the news of this conquest was so joyfully received, that Lord Wellington was created Duke of Ciudad Rodrigo, and a *grandee* of Spain of the first class,

February. Marshal Marmont assembled his army, and commenced his march from Salamanca about the time of the capture of Ciudad Rodrigo, but finding himself too late to save the place, he resumed his former cantonments between the Tormes and the Douro.

The British army was again withdrawn over the frontiers, the 5th Division, occupying Ciudad Rodrigo, the walls and outworks of which place were ordered to be repaired and improved. Lord Wellington returned to Freneda, and the battering train was moved to Almeida. Four divisions of the army now commenced their march for the south, by the circuitous route of Abrantes, by which the troops obtained their new clothes and other articles of equipment which had come up the Tagus.

The ulterior object of their march, if not their march itself, was thus concealed; while the 5th Division, the cavalry, and head-quarters remained as usual on the frontiers of Beira. The five divisions above-named having joined the corps of General Hill in the Alentejo, they moved up to Elvas, while a battering train was conveyed up the Guadiana, and magazines formed upon that river and the Tagus to aid the future operations of the army, which it now became obvious were to be directed against Badajos.

Everything was conducted with the greatest caution and secrecy, in order that the enemy's troops in that quarter might not be assembled in sufficient time to succour the place.

March 6th. Everything being prepared in the south for the commencement of operations, Lord Wellington left Freneda this morning, and on the 11th reached Elvas. We marched this day to Rendo.

7th. To Pena Macor.

8th. To St. Miguel.

9th. To Castello Branco.

10th. To Villa Velha, where we bivouacked under the same tree as in July last year.

11th. We crossed the Tagus, and we put up at Alpalhao.

12th. Put up near Assumar.

13th. Reached Elvas. This, is the frontier town of Alentejo in Portugal, and is a fortress of great strength, built upon a very high hill skirted with woods, through which are causeways or paved roads leading up to the town, which stands about one league from the shores of the Guadiana, and three from the bridge of Badajos.

15th. The several divisions of the army having assembled round Elvas, were encamped this night at the foot of the hill, and formed a most brilliant and interesting spectacle from the ramparts. The 4th division only were in the town. On the march a mail reached us from England, by which we learnt that Lord Wellington had (in consideration of his eminent services) been advanced to the dignity of an Earl, under the title of Earl of Wellington, and that Generals Hill and Graham had been nominated Knights of the most honourable Order of the Bath.

16th. This morning at break of day, the 4th Division marched out of Elvas, and the several divisions encamped at the foot of the hill, falling under arms, began to move in grand procession towards Badajos, the baggage, ammunition, facines, gabions, entrenching-tools, and all the apparatus for a siege following the troops through the plain. The scene was so interesting that hundreds of spectators had assembled at this early hour on the ramparts of Elvas, from whence not only the movements of the army, but the town of Badajos also could be distinctly seen, situated in the extensive plain below, through which the river Guidiana winds its course, and passes close under the walls of Badajos, between the town and Fort San Christoval.

The army was passing the river all day by a pontoon bridge, laid down about six miles below the bridge of Badajos.

SIEGE OF BADAJOS

Disposition of the Forces.
Corps employed in the Siege, under Lord Wellington.

3rd Division	Lieutenant-General Picton.
4th Division	Major-General Colville.

Light Division	Lieutenant-Col. Barnard, 95th Regt

Corps on the road to Seville, under Sir Thos. Graham, K. B.

1st Division	Major-General Stopford.
6th Division	Major-General Burne.
7th Division	Major-General Hope.

Cavalry and Artillery.

Corps near Merida, under Sir Rowland Hill, K. B.

2nd Division	Lieutenant-General Stewart.

Cavalry and Artillery.

Corps left on the frontiers, near Ciudad Rodrigo.

6th Division	Lieutenant-General Leith.

Two regiments of Cavalry.

March 17th. The army having passed the river, marched over the plain round the town, and bivouacked in face of the eastern and southern fronts of the fortress, the 3rd Division camp spreading nearly to the banks of the river in front of the castle. The weather had hitherto been remarkably fine, but it now became stormy and wet; the rain fell in torrents this afternoon and throughout the night. Ground was broken before the town during a violent storm of wind and rain, so that for some time our operations were not discovered by the enemy.

18th. The day opened with the same distressing weather; notwithstanding which the troops persevered at their arduous task in the trenches, although exposed to the fine of the enemy and the fury of the elements, a heavy cannonade being kept up from the town all day.

19th. The rain continued with increased violence. The troops had not even a tree to shelter them in the camp, and generally were destitute of tents. Never had the duties of any siege been known to be so severe. Lord Wellington, with Marshal Beresford and the head-quarters staff, now quitted Elvas, where head-quarters had hitherto been kept, and ordered his tent to be pitched in the field with the troops. They were accordingly posted under shelter of a little hill, near the 4th Division camps.

While this was going on, early in the afternoon the enemy made a very spirited sortie, in which Colonel Fletcher, our chief engineer, was wounded. They were charged back into the town, however, with the bayonet, and our troops resumed their arduous task, in which they continued to persevere, in spite of every obstacle, for several days and nights, under the same unfavourable weather.

20th. The difficulties and distress in the camp and trenches before Badajos were at this period so great, that it was thought the siege would be raised.

21st. During the night the pontoon bridge over the Guadiana gave way, owing to the violence of the rain and swell of the river, Which rendered it impossible to withdraw the troops, with whom communications were now kept up only by means of a very indifferent fly-bridge or ferry, by which not more than fifteen animals could pass at a time, and which sometimes occupied half an hour in passing from shore to shore. By this channel only could the troops receive their supplies of ammunition and provision, and that in quantities so disproportionate to the demand, that the most serious consequences were apprehended. The reports from our two corps of observation in front, under Generals Graham and Hill, stated, that Marshal Soult was advancing by forced marches with a large army to the relief of Badajos.

24th. The violence of the rain still continuing, the river overflowed its banks, insomuch that it was still impossible to lay down the pontoons. Double working parties were employed in the trenches with buckets, some throwing out the water, while others proceeded with the works, so that by the force of great exertions, several of the batteries were at length rendered fit to receive the guns. The zeal and devotedness of the army had seldom been more severely tried or conspicuously shown.

25th. This morning we were all enlivened by a change in the weather: the rain ceased, and the blue horizon again appeared. In the afternoon twenty-eight guns were drawn into the trenches and opened their fire, At the close of day a very important outwork called Fort Pieurini, was stormed in the most gallant manner by detachments from the regiments of the 3rd Division, under the command of Major-General Kempt. The enemy made a very stout resistance, and could not be prevailed upon to surrender until, of the two hundred and fifty men with which this work was garrisoned, one hundred and seventy had suffered. All the leading officers of the British were killed or wounded; and this attack presented a true specimen of what the grand assault was likely to be.

26th, The cannonading was very brisk this morning. To a flag of truce sent into the town demanding its surrender, the governor (General Phillipon) replied, that he was resolved to defend it to the last extremity.

30th. Lieutenant-General Leith, With the 5th Division, which it had been deemed necessary to withdraw from the frontiers of Beira, arrived at Elvas, and joined the camp before Badajos.

April. All reports now agreed in stating, that the army of Marshal Soult was advancing, and that Generals Graham and Hill, unable to check his march, were retreating upon Albuera. Marshal Marmont having assembled his forces, was endeavouring to create a diversion and draw off at least a part of our forces from the siege, and with this object in view, he once more passed the frontiers, and masking Ciudad Rodrigo and Almeida, marched by Sabugal upon Guarda and Castello Branco, plundering the country as far as Covilhão, in the Sierras des Estrellas. The Portuguese militia succeeded in keeping them out of Celorico, but the alarm there was so great, that it was deemed advisable to destroy our magazines at that place.

From these circumstances, and the great exertions which were making to collect ladders for escalading, and to complete the preparations for the storm, it was inferred that the assault would be made as soon as possible. Two breaches had already been effected by the batteries in front of the 4th and Light Division camps, but they were not at present deemed practicable.

4th. It was confidently said this afternoon that the storm would take place at the rising of the moon, a little before midnight; but the difficulties of the enterprise were so manifest, that his Lordship directed the attack to be postponed another day, to give time for a third breach to be made; and that the others, by an incessant fire, might be rendered as easy of access as possible.

Early in the day, about two thousand Portuguese troops marched from Elvas to assist in the storm. Returning from the camp, I met these poor fellows, many of whom had quitted their homes to visit them no more, They were well appointed soldiers, and seemed in tolerable spirits.

6th. It was no longer a secret that Generals Graham and Hill were retiring upon Albuera, before the army of Marshal Soult, who it was reported had halted at Zafra last night. While on the other hand, the breaches being pronounced practicable, the troops were mustered, the ladders distributed, and all preparations made for this terrific assault.

Monday Night, 6th April, 1812.

ORDER OF ATTACK.

3rd Division   Lieutenant-General Picton.
To escalade the Castle.

4th Division   Major-General Hon. C. Colville.
Light Division   Lieutenant-Colonel Barnard, 95th Regt.
To storm the breaches in the bastions of La Trinidad and Santa
Maria, and in the curtain connected therewith between Fort
Pardeleros and the Castle.

5th Division   Lieutenant-General Leith.
To attack Fort Pardeleros, and to escalade the walls of Badajos
near the western gate.

Portuguese Division Brigadier-General Power.
To storm the bridge over the Guardiana, and attack the works
on the right banks of the river.

About two hours after dark the divisions marched from the camp,
and advanced to the several points of attack a few minutes before
ten o'clock, conducted by engineer officers. The 3rd Division, led
by Major-General Kempt, and commanded by General Picton began
the assault by an escalade near the castle. Much difficulty occurred in
passing the river Rivellas, and afterwards in placing the ladders, some
of which were too short, and others broke, Major-General Kempt and
General Picton were carried back into the trenches wounded, and
many brave officers and men were killed or drowned.

The troops, however, advanced under a heavy fire from all the batteries of the town. Major-General Colville and Lieutenant-Colonel
Barnard, with the 4th and Light Divisions, moved out of the trenches,
and began their arduous task of storming the breaches; led by their
officers, these brave troops (after a dreadful carnage) gained the top
of the breaches, and cheered by the divisions escalading on their right
and left, looked for conquest; but such were the obstacles prepared
by the enemy, and so obstinate was their defence, that almost all our
foremost band shared a forlorn hope and perished.

The mouths of the breaches had not only been blocked up with
sand-bags and *chevaux de frise,* but behind the ramparts broad and deep
trenches had been dug, along the beds of which were planted iron
spikes and old swords, every house or building near being loop-holed,

and occupied by the enemy's Light Infantry. The obstacles altogether were of such a nature that our troops, notwithstanding all their heroism and devotedness, were obliged to give way. They renewed the attack, however, and were a second time forced to withdraw.

Major-General Colville was carried off most dreadfully wounded; and nearly all the commanding officers had fallen. Meanwhile, on the left of these, Major-General Walker, with his brigade of the 5th Division, was seen assaulting the town by escalade, under a most tremendous fire, which caused them great loss.—Many of their ladders, unfortunately, broke, and Major-General Walker was carried away badly wounded.

The troops, however, continuing to persevere, and to resist every obstacle, fought with a courage well suited to the occasion, which acquired for them the approbation of Lord Wellington, who viewed this terrific scene from a little eminence near the trenches, from whence he directed the several movements and attacks. For the space of one hour and more, the troops had been engaged in this trying assault without making any sensible progress or impression, an Lord Wellington was in a state of the greater anxiety as to its result, when an *aide-de-camp* galloping up from the trenches, announced the surrender of the castle to the 3rd Division. This distinguished corps (which now acquired the name of the "fighting division," from its having been so often and so success fully engaged), after Generals Picton and Kempt were wounded, fell under the command of Lieutenant-Colonel Campbell of the 94th regiment, a most distinguished officer, who, in the absence of Major-General Colville in command of the 4th Division, commanded the left brigade.

Destined (as mentioned in the order of attack) to assault the castle, they had to escalade the walls where they are highest and most difficult of access, and doubts were, entertained of the possibility of these troops effecting their object. The attention, however, of the enemy being in some degree drawn to the breaches by the formidable attacks made at those points, the 3rd Division, by a gallant promptitude and perseverance which covered them with glory, seized the favourable moment, and after a severe struggle, completely established themselves in the Castle of Badajos before the clock struck twelve.

The conduct of the officers and troops in general was such, that it was difficult to say who most distinguished themselves. Major Carr of the 83rd regiment was the first field-officer in the castle, and held the proud command until Colonel Campbell appeared. I heard also that the French colours which were flying on the citadel were pulled down by the hand of Lieutenant Macpherson of the 45th Foot. Lieutenant-Colonel Ridge of the 5th regiment, who had acquired so much fame at the head of his battalion in the recent storm at Ciudad Rodrigo, and in the affair at El Bodon, after again shewing his soldiers the way to victory, fell near the castle gate.

The 3rd Division having thus conquered the castle, orders were given for the 4th and Light Divisions to renew their attacks upon the breaches; and the 5th Division, as well as the Portuguese troops on the other side of the place, persevering in their assaults, the town was at length taken. General Phillipon and his Lieutenant-Governor, whose name I understood to be La Valette, with about 400 of their men, escaped across the river to Fort San Christoval; but that being also invested by our troops, they all surrendered before two o'clock, which completed the conquest.

The moon arose about midnight on a scene of slaughter too dreadful to contemplate.—Humanity shudders and recoils from a sight so melancholy and terrific as that which here presented itself. Thousands of brave men lay weltering in their gore, many of whom were breathing their last farewell to this sublunary world.

I would not check the tender sigh,
Nor chide the pious tear,
That heaves the heart and dims the eye
For friend or kinsman dear,
E'en though their honoured relicks lie
On victory's proudest bier.—
But I would say, for those who die
In honour's high career—
For those in glory's grave who sleep—
Weep fondly, but exulting weep.—Croker.

In detailing the operations of this important night, Lord Wellington expressed himself highly satisfied with the conduct of the 4th Division, under Major-General Colville, and of the Light Division under Lieutenant-Colonel Barnard, in their attacks at the breaches, where the obstacles opposed to them were acknowledged to be of such a nature as to render it necessary to call off the troops for a time from the assault. The 5th Division also received great praise for their gallant perseverance; and in speaking of the 3rd Division, Lord Wellington paid them the high encomium of saying, that they, as usual, maintained the distinguished reputation which they had acquired, and by their success against the castle very essentially contributed to the reduction of the place.

The Royal Artillery and corps of engineers, also, whose services were so essential on this occasion, were respectively noticed. The services of Marshal Sir Wm. Carr Beresford, of the adjutant-general, the quarter-master general, of Don Miguel Alava, of Lord Wellington's own personal staff, and of the staff in general, were acknowledged, and, with the exception of some excesses which were committed by the troops in the town after the storm, Lord Wellington seemed highly satisfied with the conduct of the army altogether, acknowledging that he never saw troops victorious over greater difficulties.

Captain Canning, of the Guards, the *aide-de-camp* appointed to carry the dispatches to England, set out for Lisbon, and Brigadier-General O'Lawlor, of the Spanish service, left the camp for Cadiz. The town and fortifications of Badajos having thus surrendered, the troops of the several divisions were reassembled as soon as circumstances would permit, and marched out to their respective camps; Brigadier-General Power, with a Portuguese garrison, being left in command of the town.

RETURN OF KILLED, WOUNDED AND MISSING OF THE ARMY IN THE STORMING OF BADAJOS, 6TH APRIL, 1812.

General Officers Wounded.

Lieutenant-General Picton	3rd Division	slightly.
Major-General Kempt	ditto	slightly.
Major-General Colville	4th Division	severely.
Major-General Bowes	ditto	severely.
Major-General Walker	5th Division	severely.
Brigadier-General Harvey	Portuguese Service	severely.

Total Loss in the Storm.

	Killed.	Wounded.	Missing.
British	641	2110	22
Portuguese	155	561	30
Total	803	2671	52

7th. When the news of the fall of Badajos arrived in Elvas this morning, a feeling of sorrow and regret as well as of exultation spread itself among the Portuguese inhabitants, many of them having to lament the fall of some dear friend or acquaintance. In the afternoon the French prisoners, in number about four thousand, with General Phillipon at their head, under an escort, were marched in on their route to Lisbon. The people were so exasperated at the severe losses our army had sustained in this trying siege, and at the sufferings to which their country had been so recently subjected, that they could not refrain from insulting them, but they endured all with that air of unconcern so common to the French soldier.

8th. The prisoners marched for Lisbon. Head-quarters were still in camp before Badajos, but as it was expected they would be removed to Elvas in a few days, preparations were consequently making to receive Lord Wellington and Marshal Beresford in the most distinguished manner. By directions of the Portuguese Governor, General Victoria, triumphal arches, festooned with laurels were erected at the Badajos Gate of the city, and in the "*grande placa*," and the guns on the ramparts were to fire a salute on the occasion.

12th. Head-quarters moved into Badajos today, and the divisions were all again in motion. Marshal Soult having (like Marmont at Ciudad Rodrigo) arrived too late to succour the town, fell back upon Seville, pursued by a large force of cavalry and infantry, under the command of Sir Rowland Hill, while the rest of the army, which had been brought from the North of Portugal, marching by Campo Mayor, Arronches, Portalegre and Niza, repassed the Tagus at Villa Velha, and obliged Marshal Marmont (whose army had penetrated as far as Castello Branco, and plundered some towns and villages in the Sierras des Estrellas) to fall back, beyond the Agueda, by the road to Salamanca.

I had almost forgot to mention, that in walking round the ramparts of Elvas one evening, I came to the grave of Major-General Hoghton, who (it will be remembered) fell in the battle of Albuera. He is buried on one of the highest batteries of Elvas, which commands a most extensive view of the surrounding country, particularly over the plains of Badajos, extending even to the field of Albuera. A stone laid flat over the grave bears the following simple inscription:

Beneath this stone is deposited
The body
Of
Major-General Hoghton,
Of the English Army.
He was killed at the head of his Brigade

49

In the Battle of Albuera
16th, May, 1811

TRIUMPHANT ENTRY OF LORD WELLINGTON INTO ELVAS.

April 13th. Ever since the fall of Badajos, preparations had been making at Elvas to receive Lord Wellington in such a manner as should evince the estimation in which his transcendant services, especially in the recent conquest, were held by the inhabitants. At the gates leading into the city from Badajos, at which the procession was to enter, triumphal arches, supported by beautiful columns enwreathed with laurels and evergreens, had been erected. General Victoria, the governor in full dress, with his staff, mounted, had been nearly all the morning waiting there to receive him.

The streets through which the procession was to pass made a gay appearance, the balconies being full of ladies waving white handkerchiefs and showering garlands of roses and laurel-wreaths from the windows. Leading into the *Praça* or great square, the procession had to pass under a kind of arch, something similar to Temple Bar in London: this was richly hung with crimson velvet, and tastefully ornamented with laurels, and being supported by two very beautiful columns festooned, formed a triumphal arch, on the pinnacle of which was placed the figure of Fame sounding a trumpet, and bearing the following motto in the Portuguese language:

A os Hieros,.
Wellington e Beresford.

In the square a fine band of music was posted to play martial airs, English and Portuguese. About one o'clock Lord Wellington's arrival was announced by a discharge of artillery from the ramparts. His Lordship wore a blue frock coat, extremely plain and neat, a white waistcoat, white cravat, and a staff cocked-hat, feathered according to the then prevailing mode. He rode first in the procession, followed by about thirty officers, amongst whom it was said Marshal Beresford was *incog.* His Lordship appeared highly pleased with the attention shown him, bowing to the people as he passed under the triumphal arches. At night there was a general illumination; and orders were circulated for head-quarters to march from Elvas in the morning.

April 14th. We left Elvas as the gun was rising, and in the afternoon got into a deserted house between Assumar and Portalegre.

15th. Passed through Portalegre, and halted at a little village on the road to Niza,

16th. Arrived at Niza, and encamped near the town. We suffered much inconvenience from a heavy rain which fell in the night.

17th. Lord Wellington left Niza this morning, and passing the Tagus at Villa Velha, in the evening arrived at Castello Branco. About 3 o'clock in the afternoon we reached the river side, where we were detained two hours in a heavy rain. The road was completely thronged with troops, so much time being occupied in crossing the river by the bridge of boats. The brigade of German Heavy Dragoons, a remarkable fine body of men, just arrived from England, passed at the same time, and bivouacked in a wood at the foot of the hill of Villa Velha.

By the time we had crossed the river, night was approaching, and in a very wet and comfortless plight we sought shelter about the country. The village of Villa Velha was one entire mass of ruins and plundered huts, and even these were crowded with sick soldiers. Accompanied by a guide we climbed the rocky heights of Villa Velha, which were enveloped in clouds: here we discovered, a cluster of huts, which I should imagine could scarcely have been visited by any part of the army before.

Exposed to the inclemency of a most dreary night, any shelter was better than none, even in these miserable huts, the inhabitants and furniture of which were in the most wretched condition. Having our baggage with us we felt ourselves somewhat independent, and managed to light a fire, cook our rations and dry our clothes, which were comforts by no means to be despised.

18th. We arrived at Castello Branco this afternoon, and being unable to obtain quarters encamped near the town, and slept put four nights. The weather was dry, but rather cold for the field. The brigade of German cavalry, under the command of Major-General Baron Bock, was reviewed in the square of Castello Branco the day after our arrival.

22nd. The army having marched towards the frontiers, in the direction of Ciudad Rodrigo, head-quarters left Castello Branco this morning, and put up for the night at Pedrogão.

23rd. We marched from Pedrogão to Sabugal. At this place I invariably experienced the most indifferent accommodation and on the present occasion, an empty room only could be obtained.

24th. This afternoon our troops came up with the rear-guard of the enemy, near Fuentes de Guinaldo. We halted at Alfaiates.

25th. Head-quarters moved forward this morning, and were fixed at Fuentes de Guinaldo. The enemy having retreated upon Salamanca, the army was sent into cantonments.

May. Orders were now given for the formation of large magazines of provisions and forage at Ciudad Rodrigo, Almeida, and upon the Douro, which had been rendered navigable for small boats as high as Barca d'Alva, a few leagues only from the river Coa.

16th. Lord Wellington gave a dinner in Fuentes de Guinaldo to Marshal Beresford and the general officers, in commemoration of the battle of Albuera.

Marshal Soult having retired into the province of Andalusia, to assist Marshal Suchet in the siege of Cadiz (which from the magnitude of the means used they seemed now fully resolved to reduce), Lieutenant-General Sir R, Hill was ordered, with a part of his corps, to attack the enemy's pontoon bridge and works at Almaraz on the Tagus.

STORMING OF THE FORTS, &C. AT ALMARAZ

May 19th. The line of communication between the French forces in the south under Marshal Soult, and those in the north under Marmont, extending across the Tagus, a bridge of boats had been laid down upon that river near Almaraz, which was protected by works, on each side of the water, and was further defended by the castle and redoubt of Mirabeto, about a league distant. Upon the south bank of the river a strong field-work had been constructed, called Fort Napoleon, and opposite to it, one called Fort Ragusa, probably erected by order of Marmont, whose title is Duke of Ragusa.

These works were garrisoned by about one thousand men, with eighteen guns. On the 12th Sir Rowland Hill moved from Almendralejo with his little army, consisting of the 28th, 34th, 50th, 71st and 92nd regiments of Infantry, a proportionate artillery, the 13th Light Dragoons, and three Portuguese regiments, provided with ladders for escalade, and arrived in the vicinity of Almaraz on the 18th. From the difficulties which the ground presented, it was found impossible to use the artillery with any effect.

The brave infantry had consequently no other support than what their own skill and gallantry afforded them. The troops (formed into three columns) advanced in the night, and early on the morning of the 19th the attack commenced. Fort Napoleon was most gallantly carried by assault by the 50th and part of the 71st regiments, under the command of Major-General Howard.

Fort Ragusa surrendered. All the works, together with the bridge, magazines and stores of every description were taken, and destroyed, and most of the garrison either killed, drowned or made prisoners of war. General Hill having performed this service according to his instructions, returned to his cantonments; and Lord Wellington expressed himself highly satisfied with the conduct of Sir Rowland Hill and of the troops on this occasion.

The arrival of an English mail about this time informed us of the disturbances and riots in England, and of the assassination of the Right Honourable Spencer Perceval, Chancellor of the Exchequer. The fate of this distinguished statesman was severely felt and lamented in the army, where his character was highly esteemed.

About this period war broke out between Russia and France, and Buonaparte commenced his memorable campaigns in the north of Europe, which in their progress led to the capture and burning of Moscow, and closed in the downfall of Paris.

June 12th. The formation of magazines at Almeida, Ciudad Rodrigo and upon the Douro, and other preparations for opening the campaign having been completed, the divisions moved out of their cantonments, and the whole army (formed into three grand columns) encamped this afternoon in the plains of Ciudad Rodrigo, with its advanced posts beyond the Agueda.

ADVANCE OF THE ARMY INTO SPAIN

Return of the forces under the command of General the Earl of Wellington in the advance into Spain in June, 1812; shewing also the means of transport attached to the commissariat of each division or corps, for the conveyance of supplies.

	Infantry Men.	Mules
1st Division	7,500	700
3rd Division	6,000	553
4th Division	6,600	590
5th Division	6,000	590
6th Division	6,800	530

		Horses	
7th Division	6,000	540	
Light Division	4,000	514	

Cavalry

		Horses	
3rd Dragoon Guards	450	470	270
5th Dragon Guards	380	390	280
4th Dragoons	460	490	240
11th Light Dragoons	500	510	280
11th Light Dragoons	450	440	272
14th Light Dragoons	430	420	272
16th Light Dragoons	350	340	275
1st Hussars, K. G, L.	500	500	250
1st Dragoons, ditto	480	485	280
2nd Dragoons, ditto	490	500	281
Horse Artillery (unattached)	580	520	270
	47,470	5,060	6,917

If to these we add the public mules employed in transporting ammunition (about 800), and those appropriated to the conveyance of intrenching tools, regimental books, medicines, forges for the shoeing of cavalry horses, &c. it will be found that scarcely less than 10,000 public mules were perpetually following the army, besides the crowd of baggage animals belonging to officers, which, at a very moderate computation, would swell the list to 12,000 beasts of burden, independent of wheel transport, which was restricted as much as possible. In this calculation, too, it should be observed, that the corps under Sir Rowland Hill, which at this period was separated from the grand army, and formed of itself a very respectable force, has not been included. The train which followed them could not fall far short of 3000 animals.

June 13th. At break of day the several divisions of the army began to pass the river Agueda at the fords below Ciudad Rodrigo, and advanced by the roads leading to Salamanca. We left Fuentes de Guinaldo at 5 o'clock, and passing through El Bodon and La Encina, came to the ford of the river about two miles distant from the walls of Ciudad Rodrigo. Lord Wellington was attended by the Spanish General Don Miguel Alava, Lord Fitzroy Somerset, &c. The morning was remarkably fine, and the country being beautifully picturesque and romantic, Lord Wellington frequently paused to admire the scenery. We reached the village of Guadapero early in the afternoon, and encamped in a meadow by the side of a rivulet, near the right column of the army.

14th. Leaving Guadapero at sunrise we marched over a beautiful country of rich soil intersected with rivulets, until we came to a village called Cabrilhas, situated upon the little river Yeltes, where we encamped under some trees at a short distance from the village. The Spanish peasantry here are very cleanly, their cottages being whitewashed, and kept very free from vermin, which if more than could be said for our poor friends the Portuguese.

15th. We struck our tents at 1 o'clock this morning by starlight, but did not leave Cabrilhas until 3. The day now began to dawn, and all the roads were lined with marching troops. The left column of the army passing by Cabrilhas with their bands playing, moved by the great road leading to Salamanca, by Castro: following their march, about 11 o'clock we came to Aldea Guella de Boveda, and pitched our teats in a field adjoining that village, about seven leagues or twenty English miles from Salamanca.

16th. We continued moving forward towards Salamanca through a fine open country covered with corn and watered by some beautiful little streams. At 9 o'clock we were ordered to halt at Canero, a small village by the road side, and we encamped upon a little grass-*plat* close by a field of corn, under shade of some very lofty trees, to which we tied our horses.

17th. At 3 o'clock, (under a very heavy dew) we were all again on the march, and soon after sunrise pitched our tents in the wood of Fragoas, about five miles from the bridge of Salamanca: here we breakfasted, being ordered to remain until further orders. Since daylight we had at intervals heard discharges of artillery in front, from which we supposed our advanced guard to have fallen in with the enemy. This firing was found to proceed from some forts which the French had constructed upon the ruins of some convents at Salamanca, and which had been garrisoned with about eight hundred men.

On reconnoitring these works it was discovered that they commanded the bridge over the Tormes, and the fords of the river under the town—that from their strength they were capable of making a serious resistance, being assailable only from the other side of the city, and altogether gave Salamanca so much the character of a fortified place, that until they were reduced, the further advance of the army must necessarily he suspended.

A ford having been found at the village of Santa Martha, about two miles higher up, the army passed the river, and was posted on the heights above the town. Marshal Marmont with the rear guard of his army having left Salamanca last night and retreated towards Valladolid, the 6th division, under Major-General Clinton, moved round and invested the forts, and head quarters; marched into the town.

SALAMANCA.

The ancient and celebrated city of Salamanca in old Castile, is seated on the banks of the river Tormes, in an open and very fruitful country, about, fifty English miles from Ciudad Rodrigo, and an equal distance from Valladolid. It has a free communication by good roads with all parts of Spain. Prior to the late invasion by the French, Salamanca, is said to have had no less than twenty-five monasteries, and two or three most valuable public libraries:—of these some have been completely destroyed—others converted into barracks, and one from the natural strength of its position outside the town near the river, had been fortified and connected with a redoubt garrisoned by light infantry.

The cathedral of Salamanca, about the centre of the town, is a beautiful structure adorned in the richest style of architecture, but has not the appearance of antiquity. Like the Roman Catholic chapels and churches in general in this country, it has a profusion of gold and silver ornaments about the altar-piece: the steeple, though not very lofty,. rises above the other buildings of Salamanca, and has an imposing appearance: several minor turrets are visible, and the houses in general as well as the monasteries and other public edifices are high and well built The *Plaça* or square though rather small, is built uniformly of white stone: all the houses of it being equal in height and having balconies with very neat casements and window frames painted green.

A fine *piazza* runs entirely round the square supported by pillars ornamented with busts of distinguished personages who have lived in Spain. These *piazzas* are well paved with flags and are full of neat shops. The bridge over the Tormes is a work of antiquity, having been built in the time of the Romans; but its gates and watch-towers are fallen into decay. It was at Salamanca that we now expected first to see the disposition of the Spaniards towards the great cause, from which we might be able in some degree to form an estimate of the assistance or at least good will to be looked for from the country in our future operations against the common enemy; and such was the character of our reception, that nothing could be more flattering or agreeable. It would be difficult to describe the cordial (not to say enthusiastic) burst of feeling which showed itself on this occasion.

No sooner had the troops passed the river and pitched their tents, than thousands of the inhabitants of Salamanca flocked to the field to welcome "*los mas amigos de Espana,*"—(the best friends of Spain) as they termed us.

The head-quarters and that part of the army which marched into the town were everywhere greeted with the cry, of "*Viva Ingleterra,*" "*Viva los Inglezes,*" &c. (Long live England, Long live the English). Indeed no demonstration of joy and satisfaction was omitted; even the very nuns at the grating of their cells waved their handkerchiefs as the troops marched by. It was about one o'clock when we left the wood of Fragoas, and crossing a hill grown over with wild thyme, which perfumed the air, we passed near to the little village of Tejares, about a mile from the bridge, and had then to cross a deep ravine, which being commanded by the guns of the enemy in one of the forts, they fired at us, but I do not think any person was hurt

We forded the river at Santa Martha, marched: through the camp of the light division; and reached Salamanca about 3 o'clock. At our billets we were treated with the greatest kindness and attention. The master of the house as well as the servants seemed to think that they could not do too much for us. Such civilities were very gratifying; and the agreeable novelty which surrounded us, together with the extreme loveliness of the weather, made it very pleasant.

Yet it must not be forgotten that our friends the Portuguese were very generally glad to see us, and (considering the nuisance we must often have been to them) used us very well; but here there was such an air of comfort and cleanliness wherever we turned—the country around us so much richer than the barren and rocky banks of the Coa, and the language and manners of the Spaniards so superior to those of the Portuguese, at least that portion of them whose guests we had lately been, that but few, if any, of us felt any wish to return to the mountains of Lusitania.

The three forts outside the town were called St Vincente, St. Cayetano, and La Mercia. From the natural strength of the ground upon which these works stood, and the pains which had been taken in their construction, they were considered capable of sustaining a regular siege; and the 6th division, under the command of Major-General

Clinton, being appointed to this duty, commenced operations this afternoon in the usual way, by digging trenches for heavy artillery, and making other preparations for assault

June 18th. Operations against the forts continued. The army being posted on the heights outside the town.

19th. Some heavy guns were this morning drawn into the trenches, from which a fire immediately commenced upon the walls and palisades of the works; but the enemy, not content with firing at the troops in the trenches, was perpetually throwing shells into the town, which caused the death of several persons. The streets near to the forts being within range of their artillery, were necessarily deserted, and it required great caution to avoid these and such other openings in the direction where the enemy was lodged. In the evening it was reported by many who came in from the army in the field, that Marshal Marmont had assembled his forces on the Douro and was advancing to the relief of Salamanca.

20th. Confirmation of this report being received this morning, orders were given for everything belonging to the army to be ready to move out at the shortest notice. The baggage was accordingly packed and loaded upon the mules, the sick and wounded removed, and the stores sent away. The baggage of the army in the field was ordered to cross the river. These arrangements completed, at 5 o'clock, in the afternoon orders were brought for the town to be cleared, and directing the head-quarters to pass the Tormes at Santa Martha, there to wait for further orders. The troops of the 4th Division, however, still, continued to invest the forts. The sun went down as we reached the ford of Santa Martha, where there was a great crowd of baggage, women and children passing in confusion. Some of us however, having obtained leave to return and sleep in Salamanca, I repaired again to my old quarters.

21st. As it was expected that an engagement must take place this day, we were all up at daybreak: walking through the *Plaça* about sunrise, I heard the nuns as they were passing to mass conversing about the "grand combat" pending between the "*Inglezees*" and "*Francezes.*" The men of Salamanca too assembled early on the hills to see the expected fight; but the day passed without any movement of importance on either side, and each army kept its ground. About noon I joined the baggage camp, which had during the night fallen back to the wood of Fragoas. The weather was extremely warm; but we found good shelter in the wood, and the ground was delightfully scented with wild thyme.

22nd. The right wing of our army under General Graham, was engaged this morning in dislodging the enemy from a position which was considered of importance; but this did not bring on a general action.

23rd. It was discovered this morning that Marshal Marmont had, during the night, withdrawn his army from the field in front of our position, in consequence of which the baggage was again ordered over the river, and head-quarters returned to Salamanca. Anxious to get into the town as soon as possible, and to avoid the circuitous march by Santa Martha, some of us forded the river near the bridge, hoping to escape the vigilance of the enemy on the works: discovering us, however, they opened a battery, and fired also with their muskets from the walls.

Nevertheless we had the good fortune to get safe into the town, principally by the friendly guidance of a Spaniard in one of the houses on the banks of the river. The movement made by Marshal Marmont last evening was not a retreat but a change of position, as the French army now showed itself on the heights of Huerta, and passed a small force over the river. Orders were therefore given for the 6th Division to attack the forts.

STORMING OF THE FORTS

The troops of the 6th Division having assembled as the sun went down, and the signal for attack being given, the light companies advanced with ladders to escalade, led by Major-General Bowes. The whole were soon enveloped in fire and smoke, and we caught a view of them only at intervals by the flash of the firing, which was exceedingly vivid. General Bowes was presently brought off wounded, and shortly after a pause ensued, our troops having unfortunately failed. The attack however was renewed, and General Bowes, having had his wound dressed, returned to his command.

The contest continued until it was quite dark, when (after the severest efforts to carry the works) the troops were necessarily withdrawn, having found the obstacles opposed to them insurmountable. General Bowes was left dead under the walls of La Mercia, and about one hundred of our men had been killed or badly wounded, The troops returned to their trenches, and I went home to my quarters about 10 o'clock.

24th. Early this morning we were all hurried again out of the town, and ordered to pass the Tormes at the ford of Elcanton, about a mile below Salamanca. The French army having passed a large force over the river above Santa Martha, obviously with a view of bringing off or opening a communication with their troops in the forts. We encamped on the banks of the river.

25th. We were ordered to move again into Salamanca this morning, and some heavier artillery than had hitherto been used against the forts, coming up, the fire against them was renewed, and in the evening of the following day the convent was set on fire.

FALL OF THE FORTS

27th. The convent having continued burning all night, about ten o'clock this morning Lord Wellington summoned the garrison to surrender. The French commanding officer requested until twelve o'clock to consider the proposals, probably with the hopes of being relieved by that time, as the French army were at so short a distance that it was easy for them by signals to inform them of their situation; but Lord Wellington refused all parley, and ordered the troops forthwith to storm the works.

Surprised at so bold a decision, the enemy surrendered after a very slight resistance, in which I believe we had only two men killed. Marshal Marmont having thus failed in his object of bringing off these troops or even communicating with them, repassed the Tormes in great haste, and retreated with his army towards the Douro.

28th. Salamanca was illuminated this evening for the fall of the forts, and a ball given by its inhabitants to Lord Wellington and the army. The orders were for head-quarters to leave Salamanca tomorrow.

29th. We left Salamanca at 5 o'clock this morning, and marched four leagues to La Orbado, a poor little village with very few inhabitants. We encamped near to the military chest in a little meadow: the country presented a rich prospect of ripening corn. We were on the line of march of our right corps commanded by General Graham.

30th. Marching at 6 o'clock, before the heat of the day, we came to Fuente la Pena, a small town having an *alcalde* or magistrate. The country around presented one of the richest prospects I ever beheld. The Spanish farmers were busily occupied in cutting their barley, which (and even rye sometimes) from the scarcity of oats, being used, by us as forage corn, they thrash out immediately, by a process totally different to the mode of thrashing in England.

The grain being thinly spread ever a stone thrashing floor, of which there are several round a Spanish village, a sledge drawn by two oxen is passed over it, which not only beats out the corn but also cuts the straw. This is the common method of thrashing in all parts of Spain that I have seen, excepting in Navarre, where they use horses instead of oxen, and manage them with so much dexterity, that the man rides upon the sledge while they trot or canter over the floor. The first flail that I recollect having seen in the country was in the Pyrenees.

July 1st. Order for marching. "Head Quarters to move from Fuente la Pena at 4 o'clock, and to follow the centre column on the Alaejos road." We arrived at Alaejos about eleven o'clock, where the troops in marching through the town were cheered by the inhabitants. The enemy's rear-guard had quitted this place at 3 o'clock in the morning. The heat was so excessive that we were glad at being allowed quarters; and nothing could exceed the civility with which we were treated by the people: everything they possessed they seemed to hold at our disposal.

2nd. We marched from Alaejos at half past four. In this serene and charming climate the mornings are lovely beyond all description at this season of the year. Two leagues from Alaejos we passed a considerable town called Nave del Rey. The soil here is very sandy, but the same luxuriant prospect of cornfields and vineyards surrounded us. About five miles beyond this place we came to Villa Verde, where being ordered to halt, we encamped in a field of stubble, the best farmhouse being marked for Lord Wellington, and the scarcity of quarters such as to exclude us from any chance of shelter. The French Marshal having thus continued his retreat from the vicinity of Salamanca, passed the Douro, and posted his army on the rising ground on the other side of that river, in the neighbourhood of Valladolid.

3rd. We remained in camp at Villa Verde while the divisions moving up by Rueda spread themselves along the banks of the river to observe the enemy on the other side.

4th. Head-quarters advanced this morning to Rueda, a small town about three miles from the river, where the 1st Hussars, K. G. L. and the 14th Light Dragoons were in quarters, and the light division in camp. Here we obtained, as usual, very poor quarters, three of us sleeping in our blankets upon the floor in one small room.

The enemy having chosen a very strong position, and the bridges and fords of the river being all in his possession, our further advance was for the present suspended, though several skirmishes and slight affairs of outposts occurred between the piquets in taking their ground for observation. The heat of the weather was excessive; and though the regiments were generally healthy, some of our most distinguished officers were obliged to quit the army on sick leave, amongst whom were Generals Graham and Picton, by which the command of the 1st Division devolved on Major-General Campbell, and that of the 3rd on Major-General Pakenham.

11th, While we were at dinner this afternoon in Rueda, the trumpets and bugles suddenly turned out the cavalry and light division, the enemy having passed the river in considerable force and drove in our piquets. in front of the town. The baggage was all loaded in the greatest haste, and the head-quarters hurried out of the town, while the troops marched forward to the tune of "the downfall of Paris," to meet the enemy. On perceiving our divisions ready, however, they retired to their former position across the river, and withdrew some of their piquets from this side, which together, with that of feeling our position, was probably their only object in this movement.

15th. The French General Bonnet having, joined Marshal Marmont with, such part of his division which could be safely withdrawn, from the province of Gallicia, where they had been employed in suppressing, the enterprising spirit of the guerrillas, and Marmont having rendered his cavalry as effective as possible, by reducing the forage allowances of his officers and purchasing their spare horses, he commenced offensive operations by marching the greater part of his army down the river from the vicinity of Valladolid to Toro, and passed the river there in great force this afternoon.

As soon as this movement was discovered, our divisions were all ordered under arms, and the baggage loaded and sent to the rear. About 4 o'clock in the afternoon we were ordered to retire upon Nave del Rey, where the right column of our army was encamped, and the town so crowded that much difficulty occurred, as usual, in providing quarters for those who, from their rank and situations, were entitled to them.

16th. We remained all this day at Nave del Rey, in readiness to march, and in momentary expectation of orders.—The heat was so excessive that the Portuguese troops under arms in the camp were allowed to enter the town and rest themselves on the shady sides of the streets. The enemy's army we supposed to be passing the Douro at Toro, in which direction the greater part of our forces were marching, as by this movement the enemy threatened to cut off our communication with Salamanca. Everyone looked most anxiously for Lord Wellington's return to his quarters, to learn the results or probable tendency of these important movements—he had gone out as usual about daybreak.

At half past 10 at night we were all hurried out of Nave del Rey with orders to retreat to Canizal (twenty miles distant): it was a line moonlight night, and the dusty roads were thronged with baggage and marching troops. We reached Canizal at daybreak and encamped. It now appeared that the French army assembled yesterday at Toro (a part of which had actually passed the river) had during the last twenty-four hours been marching back to Torredesillas, where the French cavalry crossed the river, and marching upon Rueda, took possession of Nave del Rey, a few hours after our head-quarters and the army baggage had left it

The whole French army having how passed the Douro moved forward, and their advanced. guard this afternoon pushed on as far as Torrecilla del' Orden, a small village we had passed about midnight, and where some Spanish peasantry were dancing to their favourite airs on the *castenettes;* This extraordinary contre-movement of the enemy rendering it necessary to recall our troops again from the some of the divisions were marching all night. The great force which the enemy displayed at different points, and the boldness of his movements shewing that he had confidence: in his own strength, everything seemed to portend the approach of a bloody engagement.

A report also was very current that Joseph Buonaparte was coming down upon our rear with an army from Madrid, but Lord Wellington knowing what degree of credit was due to these reports, and his object being not so much to avoid an action as to find a favourable opportunity of engaging, some time too being required to clear Salamanca of the sick and wounded, and for the removal of the military stores there, the retreat of the army was now suspended, and the divisions were posted on the rising ground in front of the village of Canizal.

AFFAIR OF CANIZAL

18th. The enemy finding our retreat suspended proceeded to reconnoitre our position, which brought on a very sharp skirmish between the outposts of the two armies. The brunt of the action on this occasion fell upon our cavalry, particularly the heavy dragoons, who distinguished themselves, and in a charge on our left early in the morning made more than 200 prisoners, amongst whom was a French General. Lord Wellington was in front with the troops engaged until late in the day, when he entered Canizal to get some refreshment. The affair was then nearly over, as the enemy finding that his attacks made no impression whatever upon our troops, declined a general engagement in this position, by moving his whole army by our right, towards the Tormes.

As soon as this movement became known to Lord Wellington, a corresponding one was ordered on our part, and the two armies continued manoeuvring and marching in a parallel line, in sight of each other along the banks of the little river Guerrena during the whole of this night and the following day. Shortly after dark we received orders to leave the wood of Canizal, where we had been waiting all day with our horses saddled, and soon after midnight pitched our tents in the field of La Orbada, where we remained all the next day.

20th. At 5 o'clock this morning we moved to Espina de Orbada, and encamped on the road side: at noon we were ordered to retreat with all possible haste to Villa Verde, a small village about seven miles from Salamanca: here we encamped and were permitted to cook, but before even a steak could be got ready, or many of the camp fires lighted, we were ordered to strike our tents, load the baggage, and hasten away to Salamanca, where we arrived in the night excessively harassed, fatigued and hungry. The civil authorities of the town and the inhabitants in general having retired to rest, no billets could be had, and we encamped in the *prado* or public walk not far from the forts.

21st The town of Salamanca was in a state of great agitation and alarm all this morning, the head-quarters' baggage being loaded in the streets and ready to move. The two contending armies, ever since the affair at Canizal on the 18th, had been bending their course towards the Tormes, and were now manoeuvring on that river between Santa

64

Martha and Alba. Since our first entering Spain early in last month until now, we had scarcely seen a drop of rain, and the weather had latterly been so extremely hot that it was sometimes impossible to march in the heat of the day. This afternoon, however, the horizon became darkened, and a thunder-storm gathering over Salamanca, attracted general notice.

About 5 o'clock in the afternoon an order was issued for the town to be cleared forthwith, in doing which an alarm spread itself, created by an idea that a division of the enemy were at the gates of the town, and the confusion which it produced was terrible. The head-quarters being ordered to pass the river at the ford of Elcanton, and assemble at Doninos, we marched until near midnight, when we reached the camp of Doninos, and were obliged to encamp upon ploughed ground. The storm burst over Salamanca soon after our departure, and while crossing the river we beheld her lofty turrets encircled with lightning. A more awful thunder storm I never before remember to have witnessed.

22nd. The day had scarcely dawned when we were roused by a sharp firing of musketry on the banks of the Tormes, in the direction of Santa Martha. During the night the enemy had passed the whole of his force (excepting one division) over to this side of the river, and was now disputing with our troops the possession of two very high hills, called, the Sisters-Arapiles, from their exact likeness to each other, situated on the right of a position which they had taken in front of a large wood.

The enemy succeeded in occupying one of these hills, but the other was held by a brigade of Portuguese troops under Brigadier-General Pack, and formed the extreme left of the position, which our divisions were ordered to occupy.

The two hostile armies having thus at length posted themselves within cannon-shot of each other, an engagement seemed inevitable, and at ten o'clock the headquarters and army-baggage were ordered to fall back into the woods near Aldea Guella de Boveda, as the enemy's intention seemed to be, by an extension of his left, to cut off our retreat upon Ciudad Rodrigo. It was one of the hottest days I can remember, and at noon not a breath of air was found to move a leaf of the trees. The troops being all under arms in an open position, were anxious to engage the bold and enterprising enemy.

Battle of Salamanca
Wednesday, July 22nd, 1812.

The twenty-second was the day,
And be that day revered,
When ranged near fifty thousand strong,
The hostile force appeared!

His numbers far beneath the foe
Our Hero sought to cheer;
Th' unequal force brave Wellington
Disdained to feel or fear.

Fierce was the fight of that dread day,
And long continued so;
Till Martnont wounded fled the field—
Then terror struck the foe.

The two armies had faced each other all the morning, neither of them seeming willing to commence the attack; but about 3 o'clock in the afternoon the enemy was observed to be strengthening and extending his left, and information was brought that the division which he had left at Babila Fuente, on the other side of the Tormes, was passing the river. In anticipation of these movements, the 3rd division, under the command of Major-General Pakenham (which when the army passed the river last night, remained to observe the French division at Babila Fuente), had received orders to withdraw quietly from its position on that side of the river, assemble on the bridge of Salamanca, and instead of joining the, left, or centre of our army, as might have been expected, from being nearest, to march away to our extreme right, where the enemy anticipated no such opposition, and were actually moving with the apparent view of turning our right, when the division (which but a few hours before they knew to be several leagues distant, and on the opposite side of the river), met them with its usual spirit, and drove them back at the point of the bayonet.

Thus began the famous battle of Salamanca; and the action soon became general: for Lord Wellington observing how they had by this movement weakened their centre and right, and what efforts they were leaking to retrieve their error, ordered a general attack; along the whole line. The battle now raged with great fury: the enemy so far from shrinking from the contest met it with unusual ardour, and conscious of their superiority in numbers, seemed to anticipate our total overthrow. The 3rd Division, in its advance, fell in with fresh columns of the enemy, and was very severely engaged.

The brave General Pakenham, as he passed the several regiments, encouraged the men by bidding them to remember Assaye, Egypt, Fuentes and Badajos, and was several times observed in the hottest fire, with his hat off, cheering and encouraging the troops, who drove the enemy before them, with so much spirit, that in some instances the very colours of our regiments waved over the flying battalions of the enemy, and almost unassisted by cavalry they made many prisoners. In the centre the 4th Division became opposed to so very superior a force, that the Portuguese troops thereof were compelled to give way; but Marshal Beresford being on the spot ordered up the 6th division, under Major-General Clinton, which became so severely engaged, that it lost near two thousand men.

Our cavalry was here brought into action, and in a charge made by the brigade of Major-General Le Marchant, that gallant officer fell. The battle continued with unremitting severity until sunset. The enemy having fallen into an error from which he was not allowed time to redeem himself, and finding all his plans frustrated, fought with a spirit bordering on desperation: but such were the admirable dispositions and movements directed by Lord Wellington, and seconded by the unyielding gallantry of the army, that all his efforts proved unavailing. His left having been driven in with great loss, and his centre assailed at every point, he at length yielded the palm, and fled towards Alba de Tormes, leaving in our hands seven thousand prisoners, two eagles, three standards, and eleven guns.

Marshal Marmont, the French general-in-chief, and General Bonnet, his second in command, having both been carried off the field severely wounded, the command devolved upon General Clausel, whose chief object now was to reach the Douro with the shattered remains of the French army.

This was indeed a glorious change in the state of affairs: those very guns which for, the last week had been driving us down to. the Tormes, were now dragged in triumph into Salamanca; and not a soldier of the French army entered that town but such as were marched in as prisoners of war. The 1st and Light Divisions, which had been in reserve, and consequently but partially engaged, were sent in pursuit of the enemy, and the rest of the army encamped on the field of battle.

Commander-in-Chief,
General the Earl of Wellington, K. B.

Second in Command,
Lieutenant-General Sir Stapleton Cotton, Bart.

Portuguese Troops,
Marshal Sir W. C. Beresford, K. B.

Spanish Troops,
Don Carlos D'Espana.

1st Division:
Major-General Campbell   In reserve.

3rd Division:
Major-Gen Hon. E. Pakenham   Attacked the enemy's left.

4th Division:
Lieutenant-General Cole
5th Division:
Lieutenant-General Leith
6th Division:
Major-General Clinton
7th Division:
Major-General Hope
These four divisions; attacked the enemy in front of the wood.

Light Division:
Major-General Charles Baron Alten   In reserve.

Return of the Killed, Wounded and Missing:

	Killed.	Wounded.	Missing
British	388	2,714	74
Portuguese	304	1,552	182
Spanish	2	4	—
	——	——	——
	694	4,270	256

Killed.
Major-General Le Marchant—Heavy Dragoons.
Wounded.

Lieutenant-Gen. Sir Stapleton Cotton; Cavalry	severely.
Lieutenant-Gen. Leith	5th division	ditto.

Lieutenant-Gen. Cole	4th division	ditto.
Marshal Beresford	Portuguese	ditto.
Major-Gen. Baron Alten	Light Cavalry	ditto.

July 23rd. Early this morning we were ordered to march into Salamanca. It had been a moonlight night, and four of us slept upon straw under the porch of a chapel, by the side of our horses. In Salamanca, the female inhabitants had prepared a great quantity of lint and rags for the use of the wounded, and displayed a feeling of humanity which was no less creditable to them than pleasing to us. Numbers also repaired to the field of battle, carrying with them tea, coffee, and such other refreshments as they thought would be most acceptable: and here might be seen the interesting spectacle of Spanish girls supporting from the field such of our wounded as were able to walk, carrying for them their knapsacks and muskets.

The army moved forward this morning in pursuit of the enemy, crossing the river at Alba de Tormes and moving upon Penaranda. Our advanced guard, however, consisting of the brigade of German Dragoons under Major-General Baron Bock, and some troops of the light division, had proceeded but a few leagues, when they fell in with a division of the enemy very strongly posted in rear of the village of La Serna. An attack was immediately made upon them, and the position carried with such spirit that the whole of the French infantry were made prisoners; their cavalry fled, and the march of the army was continued without further interruption.

24th. At 4 o'clock this morning we left Salamanca, and following the march of the army passed over the field of battle, and near to the village of Calvaraxa de Abaxo. A great portion of the field about the hills of Arapiles, was grown over by a kind of shrub, and the ravines were full of corn nearly ripe. On the slope of a little hill at one corner of the field, about two hundred wounded men had crept or been collected together, and were waiting very patiently to be removed: each man was wrapped in his blanket, by which they might be distinguished from the dead tying about. Some wagons of the royal waggon train and some country wagons and mules supplied by the Commissariat, were moving over the field taking up the wounded: but it is to be feared many poor fellows concealed amongst the corn must have perished before they were found.

In passing through the wood our ears were assailed by the cries of the distressed; (chiefly Portuguese). We passed the river by the bridge at Alba de Tormes, where there was a great crowd of prisoners marching under a strong escort for Salamanca. In the afternoon we reached Penaranda. The 1st Division was quartered upon that town, and the army camp spread along the banks of a little river at the foot of the hill

25th. Early this morning we joined head-quarters at Flores de Avila, and pitched our tents by the side of a little rivulet near the camp of the Light Division. Captain Lord Clinton set out for England with the dispatched, eagles and colours. Joseph Buonaparte very narrowly escaped being made prisoner this evening by one of the patrols of the 14th Light Dragoons, at a little village called Blasco Sancho, a few leagues in front of this place. It appears that the king had left Madrid on the 21st with about twelve thousand men, to come to the support of Marmont: before he could join, however, the marshal had not only been defeated, but so closely pursued, that the road by which the king was advancing was cut off, and the approach of our army was the first information he received of the events which had occurred. His Majesty had quitted Blasco Sancho only a few hours before our cavalry arrived: twenty-seven men of his body guard were made prisoners.

26th. Head-quarters moved from Flores de Avila this morning, and in the afternoon occupied the villages of Aldea Seca and Villa Nueva. Soon after our arrival at the latter place (where we were quartered for the night) the right wing of the army marched through and encamped near Villa Seca.

27th. Lord Wellington made a kind of triumphal entry this morning into Arevalo, a very considerable town pleasantly seated on an eminence encircled by the little River Adaja, the banks of which being very steep and rising almost perpendicularly to the walls of the place, give it the appearance of a strong fortification. At a very early hour a large assemblage of the inhabitants, headed by the chief magistrate and civil authorities of the town, repaired to the Penaranda gate to welcome "*Los heroes de Salamanca:*" the bells were all ringing, and about fifteen thousand of our troops had encamped on the banks of the river. About 10 o'clock Lord Wellington made his appearance, followed by about twenty officers of his staff.

The anxiety manifested by all ranks and descriptions of the people to get a sight of him exceeded anything of the kind I had before seen. The procession moved slowly up the street towards the "*Grande Plaça,*" preceded by the crowd, shouting "*Viva Ingletierra*" (Long live

England, &c.). On reaching the square the people pressed so much round Lord Wellington, that the procession for several, minutes could not proceed. Hats, gloves and handkerchiefs were now tossed into the air which rang with shouts of "*Viva* Wellington and Victoria." Lord Wellington proceeded across the square to his quarters, which were marked, "*Duque de Ciudad Rodrigo*" and the people returned then to their occupations.

28th. Leaving Arevalo this morning at 5 o'clock, we passed through the villages of Elmanera, Boçigas, and Elcalçaren, near to which place we crossed the river Adaja and were put up at Olmedo, the same as mentioned in the celebrated adventures of Gil Blas. Lord Wellington was received here with the same attentions as at Arevalo, and in the evening his Lordship gave a ball to the principal inhabitants, in commemoration of the battle of Talavera.

29th. We moved forward this morning to the village of Mojados, where I encamped on the banks of a small river (the Cega.) On the day following, the French army having crossed the Douro, and two of our divisions having passed the river and entered Valladolid, we advanced to Boeçilla, and encamped on the hill near that village.

31st We expected to move forward again this morning and pass the Douro, but about ten o'clock we were ordered to march back to Mojados. Joseph Buonaparte, after his escape from Blasco Sancho, was returning to Madrid; but finding Lord Wellington still following Clausel, he repassed the Sierras de Guardarama, and advanced as far as Segovia, threatening to interrupt our communication with Salamanca and Portugal (a circumstance of the highest importance). Having seen Clausel safe across the Douro, and taken Valladolid, Lord Wellington therefore now determined upon leaving General Clinton with the 6th division and a brigade of cavalry to watch the army of Portugal (as the French still called it), while he should at once march upon Madrid, to engage the king or drive him from his throne.

August 1st The head-quarters advanced this morning along the banks of the little River Cega, through a fruitful and beautiful country, where the scenery was sometimes quite enchanting, especially near two little villages, the one called Mohethes and the other Cohethes, seated within a mile of each other on the river Cega, over which there are two little bridges grown over with ivy. At night we were put up at Cuellar, a very old town, with a kind of Moorish tower and some ancient fortifications; here we halted five days, for the left column, artillery and military chest to come up, during which period several English mails arrived, having been detained at Ciudad Rodrigo ever since out retreat from Rueda, previous to the battle of Salamanca. Several mules arrived one morning laden with letters.

6th. Leaving Cuellar this morning, we marched over a large sandy plain, passed through Villarejos, and were put up at Monzoncilla, a village about twenty miles from Cuellar, and an equal distance from Segovia.

7th. At a very early hour, the divisions were all again in motion, and marching upon the famous town of Segovia, where we were destined to meet with a most flattering reception. Lord Wellington made his "*entre.*" much in the same way as at Areyalo.—Joseph Buonaparte, on learning our march in this direction, hastened back to Madrid, leaving in Segovia a small portion of his forces to observe our movements, and to cover the retreat of his army over the Sierras de Guadarama. These troops however left the town at the approach of a division of Spaniards under Don Carlos de Espana, whom Lord Wellington had on this occasion sent forward as our advanced guard.

The Spanish citizen is so extremely tenacious of his national honour, that he is never so well pleased as when he sees his own countrymen at the post of distinction; and Lord Wellington aware of this feeling amongst them, availed himself of it to win their approbation, by ordering the Spanish troops to take the lead whenever they were most likely to prove victorious; and this was a very judicious measure, for while it pleased the Spanish citizen, it encouraged and emboldened the soldier. About 10 o'clock we reached the summit of a hill, at the foot of which runs the river Adaja, encircling the ancient and famous tower of Segovia, so celebrated in the adventures of Gil Blas.

The rocky banks of the river and all that side of the hill where the tower stands, were thronged with beautiful females dressed in black (the Spanish costume); indeed I may venture to say that nearly the whole population of the town was here assembled to meet us. About one o'clock Lord Wellington arrived, and his "*entree*" was a complete march of triumph from the gates of the city to his quarters, led by the magistrates of the town under a sound of trumpets, which could scarcely be heard for the shouts of exultation which rent the air. We had good quarters in Segovia, and were willing to hope that we should halt here two or three days; but at night orders were given to move at the usual hour in the morning.

8th. At break of day the 3rd and 7th Divisions of British Infantry and Don Carlos de Espana's army commenced their march through the town, with their bands playing and colours flying, and the balconies and streets were soon thronged with people cheering the troops and wishing them glory and success; the scene was very exhilarating indeed. We left Segovia about 6 o'clock and head-quarters being ordered as far only as the palace of St Ildefonso, a summer residence of the King of Spain, we there pitched our tents in the park.

The beauty of this palace arises chiefly from its romantic situation at the foot of the Sierras de Guardarama: its western view towards Segovia commands an extensive prospect over a fertile plain, with the town and tower of Segovia in the distance; while in the eastern front (which is by far the most superb) are beautiful gardens and shrubberies with royal baths and fountains, one of which casts up the water as high as the palace. These gardens also are ornamented with a great number of marble statues upon pedestals: each window of the palace pointing to some fresh object through the beautiful avenues of the plantations.

Close upon the edge of the gardens, and forming a kind of crescent round the palace itself, passes that chain of woody mountains called the Sierras de Guardarama, the sides of which, are here almost perpendicular, and so lofty that the top of them is generally obscured in a cloud. The interior of the palace is remarkable for the smallness of the rooms: in one range there are fourteen of an equal size, elegantly furnished and hung with the richest velvet. Marble busts and paintings kept in the nicest order were disposed so as to have their proper effect: the sofas, chairs and curtains were all of the finest velvet, generally crimson, with deep gold lace and fringe; but there were, I think, two of the rooms entirely sky-blue, and another straw colour. Adjoining the palace is a very neat chapel, where high mass was performed about the time Lord Wellington arrived. Here are the sepulchres of Charles 5th and Ferdinand 6th. In the evening there was a fine display of water-works in the gardens.

9th. We halted this day at St Ildefonso while our advanced guard passed the Guardarama Mountains.

10th. We quitted St Ildefonso at sunrise, and were all the morning ascending the Guardaramas by a paved road winding up the mountain, and in the afternoon pitched our tents in a field near a little village called Nave Cerrada, where there were but few trees, which from the heat of the weather were considered of that consequence that they were all allotted to the cavalry for shade to their horses, and we suffered very much from the intense heat, which made it quite impossible for us to continue in our tents; though in the night they were a comfort to us, by sheltering us from the dew,

11th. At 3 o'clock this morning the army began moving, the heavy cavalry leading the march, followed by the 3rd and 7th Divisions of Infantry and the head-quarters. About 9 o'clock (where the road passed over a small eminence) we caught a view of Madrid, at the distance of about fifteen English miles; and a little on our right we had a full view of the Escurial. The army halted about 10 o'clock, and we were ordered to encamp in a field near Torres les Dones. At 5 in the afternoon, while at dinner in our tents, we heard the sound of cannon, apparently at no great distance, and which soon approached so as to create some alarm and, bustle in packing the baggage, while the two divisions of infantry encamped in the adjoining fields assembling under arms, soon joined the cavalry, who were descending into the plain, where there was by this time a brisk cannonade, and some heavy clouds of dust discernible in the road between us and Madrid.

AFFAIR OF LAS ROSAS

The brigade of Portuguese cavalry under the command of Brigadier-General D'Urban forming our advanced guard, had been very suddenly attacked by a large force of French cavalry, which obliged them to fell back rather precipitately upon Major-General Bock's brigade of German Dragoons posted at the village of Las Rosas, upon whom the enemy then advanced.—These troops, however, behaved with so much spirit and gallantry that they had beaten the enemy and drove him from the field before any other part of the army arrived to their support. This movement of the French had for its object the concealment of Joseph Buonaparte's retreat from Madrid.

12th; Lord Wellington went out this morning to reconnoitre Madrid with the 3rd and 7th Divisions of Infantry, and a large force of cavalry. The enemy had abandoned the place, leaving a garrison of about two thousand men in some field-works called El Retiro, where we understood there were considerable magazines of ammunition and other ordnance stores. The 3rd and 7th Divisions, commanded by Generals Pakenham and Hope, were ordered to invest these works,

and the army was to take military possession of Madrid on the morrow.

TRIUMPHANT ENTRY INTO MADRID.
13th August, 1812.

Madrid, the celebrated metropolis of Spain, and seat of the Spanish
Government, is seated in an open country upon the banks of the little
river Manzanares. The palaces and other public buildings are superb
beyond anything I remember having seen; and the parks, and beautiful
avenues of trees which encircle the court end of the town conspire to
make it a very agreeable residence. The king's palace is built of white
stone, upon a little eminence near the river, along the banks of which
spread the royal gardens bounded by meadows, and the view termi-
nates in the lofty mountains of Guardarama at a distance.

The arrival of Lord Wellington and his victorious army at the gates
of Madrid was marked with all those demonstrations of public joy
which such an event was calculated to produce, and although it would
be difficult if not impossible to describe the enthusiastic animation
which prevailed, it is with pleasure one recalls to mind the honours
and caresses which were so lavishly heaped upon us. All business was
suspended, the shops closed, and people of all ranks quitting their
occupations assembled in the public streets or the parks, and even in
the fields for some miles distant from the town; bearing branches of
laurels and oak-boughs to meet the army, exhibiting a scene at once
so flattering and pleasing that it was difficult to suppress the feelings of
honest pride and exultation which it. created.

Having marched from Torres les Dones as soon as it was light, We
reached the gates of Madrid about 7 o'clock. Upwards of fourteen
thousand troops encamped in the meadows under the palace, were
just then falling under arms, an order having come down to throw
open the royal gardens, where many thousands of people now assembled with laurel boughs and banners bearing the words "Wellington,"
"Victory," "Salamanca," and "England and Portugal forever," and other
mottoes of a similar description. The children's hats and caps were
decorated with the words "Wellington and Salamanca;" and where a
general officer was recognized, or the shattered colours appeared, the
air rang with acclamations.

Wherever an English woman passed, she had her full share of notice; and on one occasion I was greatly amused at the embarrassment
of an officer's lady, who on alighting from her horse at one of the

75

gates of the garden, was for several minutes exposed to the most immoderate caresses and unreserved embraces of at least twenty Spanish girls. Leaving the 5th Division marching through cheering crowds, accompanied by my friend T——, I forded the river not far from the palace, and entering the town by the gate near the Inquisition, went in search of a coffee-house to breakfast, by which we avoided much of the bustle; but we were everywhere saluted with the cry of "*Viva Espana, viva Ingletierra.*"

The bells were ringing, and the "*Calle Mayor*" or High Street, exhibited throughout the day a scene of public rejoicing impossible to describe. Lord Wellington was conducted to the king's palace, where he and his personal staff were lodged. Colonel Gordon, quarter-master general of the army, occupied the palace of the Prince of Peace. At night there was a general and brilliant illumination, and the weather being remarkably fine, the "Calle Mayor" and the other principal streets were thronged with people. There were but few transparencies; but illuminations in Spain are rendered peculiarly striking by an immense display of rich tapestry suspended from the balconies and windows, in such a manner as to hide the whole front of the buildings, and which with the reflection of the variegated lamps produces a very pretty effect. These illuminations were repeated for three nights successively.

14th. This morning the works of El Retiro were surrendered to the 3rd and 7th divisions, and the garrison marched out prisoners of war. I obtained a billet this morning upon No. 9, Calle Sarten. Senhor Juan Inclan, my landlord, was a great politician: he asked me what was become of the famous Sir Arthur Wellesley, who commanded the English at Talaviera, and why he was not in the battle of Salamanca, when I surprised him very agreeably, by saying that Lord Wellington and Sir Arthur Wellesley were one and the same person.

On the 23rd of this month I obtained promotion, in consequence of the recommendations of Commissary-General Bisset, dated from the camp of Flores de Avila, 25th July last.

25th. The siege of Cadiz, in the prosecution of which so much blood had been spilt and such extraordinary exertion used, was this day raised, and Marshal Soult withdrew into Catalonia. This event was one of the most advantageous effects resulting from the victory of Salamanca. When we advanced into Spain, the corps of Sir Rowland Hill in the south broke up from its cantonments at Almendralejo, and advanced to Zafra, in the Spanish province of Estramadura, where they sustained a series of partial conflicts with the enemy, until they received the news of our triumph at Salamanca. The journal of an officer with that army (after detailing the operations of that corps) relates the receipt of the dispatches from Salamanca in the following terms.

The news of the battle of Salamanca has been brought to us by a Spaniard, who states himself to be an eye witness to the event, and has travelled all the way hither on the same mule that he might be the first to communicate such glorious news to our gallant General and the loyal Spaniards in the South. As we had been prepared, by letters from the northern army, to hear of its retreat upon Ciudad Rodrigo, the account of the battle thus given was almost entirely discredited: and it having been intimated to the Spaniard that he was suspected of being a spy, he made a voluntary offer of himself to be incarcerated in the common gaol of Zafra until such time as the official account of the battle should be received by Sir Rowland Hill, when, should his information prove false, the British general might order him to be punished as a traitor.

After making such an offer no one could doubt the truth of what he had related, and the same evening Sir Rowland Hill received an account of the battle from Lord Wellington. On the morning following as the troops were on the march, Sir Rowland in passing them took an opportunity of communicating the substance of the accounts he had received, which was answered by loud and long continued cheering, and when we went into bivouac a copy of the dispatch was given to each regiment, to be inserted in the regimental and companies' orderly books, and ordered to be read at the head of every regiment at the evening parade. A double allowance of grog also was issued to every individual to drink the health of Lord Wellington and his incomparable warriors.

The victory of Salamanca and our subsequent advance and entry into Madrid, having forced Marshal Soult to retire to Catalonia, Sir Rowland Hill, thus released from his opponent, prepared to advance to Madrid, and to unite his corps with the army there assembled.

28th. The French army of Portugal, under General Clausel, having been considerably reinforced, advanced and obliged General Clinton to evacuate Valladolid and to repass the Douro, in consequence of which the 1st, 5th and 7th Divisions were ordered to march from Madrid to join the 6th Division at Arevalo; and all the cavalry excepting the 1st Hussars, K. G. L. and 14th Light Dragoons followed the same route, so that it was fairly presumed our holiday at Madrid was nearly over. Indeed it now appeared certain that head-quarters would march in a few days.

31st. This afternoon there was a famous bullfight at Madrid, exhibited in honour of Lord Wellington and the army, at which many thousands of individuals were present. This is a very ancient and favourite amusement of the Spaniards, being a sort of tournament, at which a fierce bull bred for the impose is turned loose into a ring fenced round, to contend with an armed man on horseback, whose skill and dexterity in conquering the animal is highly applauded by the audience. Sometimes the fight will continue a long time and several horses fall a sacrifice to the bull's horns. All this, however, seems to augment the entertainment; and the poor animal is pronounced a brave beast and to have died nobly. It is a pity that these barbarous games are not exploded as irrational, at least in Christian countries. In the evening marching orders for the morning were issued.

September 1st. Head-quarters left Madrid this morning. We could not without some reluctance quit this place, where we had been very comfortable, and had received marks of great kindness and attention. At night we were put up at the Escurial, a celebrated palace of the kings of Spain, with a chapel dedicated to St. Laurence: here are the sepulchres of the ancient Spanish monarchs and many curiosities of great antiquity, which I had no opportunity of seeing. The Escurial is seated at the foot of the Sierras de Guardarama, about twenty-one miles from Madrid.

2nd. We crossed the mountains this morning, from the summit of which we had a fine view of Madrid. At night we were put up at Villar Castin, in wretched quarters as usual.

3rd. Arrived at Arevalo. General Clinton having been joined by three divisions of infantry and the cavalry from Madrid, moved again towards the Douro, and Lord Wellington resumed the command.

4th. We moved forward this morning from Arevalo to Olmeda, and halted there one day. Here a mail arrived from England with the news that Lord Wellington had been created Marquis of Wellington on account of the Battle of Salamanca.

6th. Advancing through Mojados, and by the same route as in July, we encamped this night at Boecilla.

7th. This morning, after passing the Douro, the army took possession of Valladolid. We experienced some little difficulty in fording the river, which was here very deep and rapid. I obtained a good billet in the suburbs of the city.

Valladolid is a city of considerable importance, possessing many privileges, and in some respects is but little inferior to Madrid. It is seated in a fine fruitful plain on the banks of the river Pisuerga, about five miles distant from the Douro: being a manufacturing town, it is both populous and wealthy. It has been remarked, that its inhabitants are attached to the French interests: this may arise from its situation upon, the right bank of the Douro, and in the great military road from France, which circumstance must subject it, in times of hostility with that country, to serious inconveniences and losses: however, be this as it may, the people received the British with much cheerfulness and apparent goodwill. We halted at Valladolid two days to repair the bridges which the French had destroyed in their retreat The Spanish army of Gallicia joined us about this time.

10th. Head-quarters moved forward this morning to Cigales, a village twelve miles from Valladolid, on the road to Burgos.

11th. We advanced to Duenas, the same as mentioned in the adventures of Gil Blas. It is a poor village, and our quarters were very bad..

12th. Continuing to advance; we encamped this evening near Megas. A wet and stormy night.

13th. We encamped this evening upon the banks of the Pisuerga, near Cordovilla, where Lord Wellington was quartered, on a poor farmhouse, and the Prince of Orange in a cottage.

14th. We advanced only a few miles and pitched our tents in a field under some willow trees.

15th, Encamped near Pampleja. Some skirmishing between our advanced and the enemy's rear-guard kept us in a state of preparation all night,

16th. This morning the enemy having retired, upon Burgos, we advanced to Frandovinez, where we encamped in a meadow, and slept upon newly-mown hay. The army fires made a very brilliant show, and covered all the mountains.

17th. Head-quarters remained this day at Frandovinez.

18th. We marched early this morning, and moving over the mountains about 11 o'clock came in view of Burgos. The French army had retired from before the town and was retreating towards the river Ebro, leaving a strong garrison in the old castle of Burgos and in several very formidable field-works, which they had constructed upon the declivity of the hill on which the castle stands.

About 12 o'clock we were ordered to halt upon the mountain: Lord Wellington soon alter passed by with a very full staff and proceeded to reconnoitre the approaches to the town. The enemy occasionally fired from the works. Whenever they thought any of our party within range of their shot. In the afternoon we were ordered to turn off the road and encamp in a meadow near Villal Villa.

19th. Head-quarters moved across the country to Villa Toro, where I encamped in an orchard.

SIEGE OF BURGOS CASTLE

The siege of Burgos being allotted to the 1st and 6th divisions, under Major-Generals Campbell and Clinton, these two corps began to invest the works by taking the posts allotted to them respectively: *viz.* the 6th Division possessing itself of the suburbs of the town, and occupying the passes on that side of the castle-hill, planted its batteries in the plain; while the 1st Division (moving round the western front of the castle by Villa Toro) encamped in the woods between that village and the forts. In addition to the works already mentioned on the declivity of the hill on which the castle stands, there was found on our side the deep ravine which intervenes, a very formidable horn-work capable of containing a large garrison, and held by a strong detachment of the enemy.

Against this work the light companies of Colonel Stirling's brigade in the 1st Division, and the whole of the 42nd regiment (Highlanders) commanded by Lieutenant-Colonel Dick, all under the direction of Major-General Pack, were ordered to move this evening by moonlight; accordingly the assault began about 8 o'clock, and lasted until 9, during which time our brave troops suffered severely; but having at length by escalade forced their way, the work was carried, and on the following day three heavy guns were drawn up and planted there, with a view to aid the ulterior operations of the army; but the enemy kept up so hot a fire from the castle upon the horn-work, that two of our guns were after a few days dismantled.

22nd. This evening an attack was made by detachments from several regiments, led by a Major Laurie, upon the first or exterior line of works upon the castle-hill, which unfortunately failed. Major Laurie was killed, and a young acquaintance of mine, (Ensign Cullen of the 42nd regiment) also fell. On this occasion an affecting circumstance occurred. Captain Williamson of the 42nd having escaped unhurt, at the close of the assault attempted to bring off the body of poor young Cullen, in hopes that his wound might not prove mortal, but fell a sacrifice to his generous friendship, being struck with three shots, which almost instantly deprived him of life. He had previously lost his brother in the storming of Ciudad Rodrigo in January.

29th. Another attack made at 4 o'clock this afternoon failed. The guards and all the 1st Division suffered very severely.

October 4th. This afternoon at 4 o'clock the exterior line of the enemy's works was attacked and carried. The 24th regiment was particularly distinguished on this occasion.

5th. The enemy made a very spirited sortie this afternoon from the castle with a large force, and at the point of the bayonet drove our troops out of the works they had taken on the preceding day, forcing them back into their own trenches. The French then gave three cheers, and the castle batteries ceased firing. Lord Wellington was soon seen galloping across the plain from Villa Toro. The pause (which lasted only a few minutes) was then interrupted by a loud British huzza, and we could perceive our men returning to the assault. The tremendous and destructive fire from the castle batteries again opened, and a desperate struggle ensued. Before dark, however, our brave fellows had retaken the works, and forced back the enemy into the castle.

8th. Before daybreak another sortie was made from the castle, in which a very distinguished officer, Major Cocks, commanding the 79th (Highland) regiment, was killed. He was buried with military honours in the camp.

11th. The second or interior line of works was attacked this day and carried.

12th. This evening the weather being very cold and wet, we struck our tents, and obtained leave to occupy a room over a blacksmith's shop, having been under canvas every night since the 11th of September, For the last three weeks scarcely a night had passed without rain; and as we had no beds, our situation was rendered very uncomfortable; yet thousands were faring much worse, enduring greater privations, without even a tent to shelter them, and having much harder duty to perform.

About this time Lieutenant-General Sir Rowland Hill with his corps, and Colonel Skerrett with the British garrison of Cadiz, joined the divisions we had left at Madrid. Marshal Soult (as before stated) having retired to Valencia in Catalonia, joined his forces to those under Joseph Buonaparte; and the British expedition in that quarter, under the directions of Sir John Murray, Bart having unfortunately failed, the French Marshals Soult and Jourdan assembled their troops, and began to move once more upon Madrid, with the view of replacing King Joseph upon the Spanish throne.

While this was going on in the east, the French army of Portugal, now under the command of Count Souham, reinforced from France, crossed the Ebro, fend began to act offensively for the relief of Burgos. I have omitted to, mention that at the commencement of the siege in September, the 5th and 7th Divisions of Infantry, all the cavalry, and the Spanish forces were posted in the front of Burgos as a corps of observation, the outposts of which were attacked on the 13th by the French army, but the enemy afterwards retired.

18th. The necessary preparations for the assault of the castle having been completed, at 4 o'clock this afternoon (Sunday) the Guards and German legion in the 1st Division, to whose lot this unfortunate and perilous service fell, commenced the attack, and in a short time were forced to withdraw. Success is not always to be acquired, even by the bravest troops or the ablest commanders; and on this occasion they were doomed to experience a reverse. The moment too, was rendered peculiarly critical, by the advance of the French army, which had again attacked our corps of observation and drove in the Spanish outposts; so that it became necessary to reinforce our army in the field with the whole of the 1st Division. The siege was consequently converted into an investment or blockade, while the sick and wounded were ordered to be removed as fast as possible to the rear, and the army baggage sent into the high road leading to Valladolid.

20th. Lieutenant-General Sir Edward Paget, K.,B. arrived as second in command. The armies were throughout the day assembling in face of each other.

21st. This morning all the troops of the 6th Division that could be spared from the trenches joined the army in the field. At 4 o'clock in the afternoon the baggage was all ordered to fall back to Frandovinez, and immediately afterwards the army commenced its retreat. In our way to the high road we passed near an angle of the castle, at which time our troops were just leaving the works. The French flag was flying on the castle, and the garrison fired, a kind of *"feu de joye,"* no doubt wishing us a safe return to Portugal. After so many signal triumphs, the present failure was very mortifying; but the army consoled itself with the persuasion that either in the environs of Valladolid or the plains of Salamanca, they should be allowed to face the enemy, or, that if we were, doomed to pass our winter again in Portugal, it would only be a kind of second retreat to the lines. We reached Frandovinez about midnight, and rested a few hours.

22nd. We were all off early in the morning, and at night were put up at Torrequemada. The troops were assembling all night in the fields round that village under a heavy rain, and after resting a few hours continued their retreat upon Duenas.

In the early part of this month at reinforcement from England, chiefly of the guards with Lieutenant-General the Earl of Dalhousie, landed at Corunna, and were now upon their march to join us. An express had been forwarded to them to direct their march with all possible speed upon Palencia, and hopes were entertained that they would join us as we passed Duenas: but the French pursued us with so much spirit, that it was doubtful whether this could be effected without a battle: however by forced marches and changing their route they did effect a junction with us before we passed the Douro.

23rd. The army encamped in the plains of Duenas.

24th. Our divisions crossed the river Pisuerga, and were posted on the rising ground about the village of Cabeçon. I was ordered to proceed to Valladolid, where I arrived at 11 o'clock at night. The civil authorities of the town were at their posts answering the numerous requisitions making upon them for billets, means of transport, guides, &c. Our retreat had been so sudden and rapid that it was not without the greatest difficulty that we were able to bring off our numerous sick and wounded men: and the magistrates of Valladolid naturally giving the preference to the demands made upon them by the commissaries of the Spanish army, a great portion of them had not yet been able to pass the Douro. Lord Wellington therefore, to afford time for this service to be effected, placed the army in position at Cabeçon, and resolved for the present to resist the further advance of the enemy.

AFFAIR AT CABEÇON
25th October, 1812.

The French marching across the plain and passing their right wing near Cigales, moved upon the angle or turn of the river below Cabeçon, where finding a ford they drove back the Spaniards and attacked our 5th Division. The Spaniards having thus unexpectedly given ground, the engagement for a time was very serious: but the Spanish General Don Miguel Alava, being near to Lord Wellington when his countrymen gave way, galloped into the plain, and rallying them in a most devoted and spirited manner led them back to the charge, and the enemy being also repulsed in their attack upon the British division, were now beaten back over the river with considerable loss. In this affair Colonel Robe, commanding officer of the artillery, was severely wounded, and the noble Alava, in rallying the Spanish troops, received a severe wound in the thigh. Lord Wellington's own carriage was brought up to the field for this distinguished Spaniard, in which he was conveyed to Salamanca.

26th. During yesterday and the night nearly all the sick and wounded had been removed over the river—and it was well; for about 11 o'clock this morning orders were given for the town to be immediately cleared, the enemy having marched down the Pisuerga towards the Douro, and planted a battery which in some places commanded the road by which we were to retreat, so that they were actually at this moment cannonading the suburbs of the town, and the hospital waggons which were running down the road with the sick were exposed to their fire: this, with the noise of the artillery and cavalry galloping through the streets, and the trumpets sounding the retreat, produced a scene of bustle and alarm not easily described.

We had not proceeded far on the road before we saw Lord Wellington pass the town, and the infantry columns were in full retreat over the hills. We all knew that the Douro was now too high to be fordable here in any part, and that we had but one bridge over it at Puente del Douro. The rain fell in torrents, and some of the poor wounded, from their infirm state and want of conveyance, fell on the road side, Everyone seemed to act upon the principle of self-preservation. We slept this night at Valdesillas, a village about five miles beyond the river; on the following day we proceeded to Olmedo, and from thence on the morning of the 28th to Arevalo.

In the meantime, the whole of our divisions having passed the Douro, the bridge at Puente del Douro was destroyed, and those at Torredesillas and Toro having been previously demolished, our army was stationed along the banks of the river to observe the enemy on the other side, nearly the same as in July before the battle of Salamanca, with the head-quarters at Rueda, to which place I proceeded on the 30th. His Serene Highness the hereditary Prince of Orange, the Marquis of Worcester, the Honourable Lieutenant-Colonel Gordon and Major Canning formed part of Lord Wellington's staff at this time. Having thus got safe over the Douro with, the army from Burgos, it is now time that we paused to notice the occurrences at Madrid, where we left General Hill assembling his forces, and preparing for the approach of the enemy.

Army at Madrid

	Supposed strength,
2nd Division	7,000
3rd Division	4,000
5th Division	4,500
Light Division	3,000
Cavalry (six regiments)	2,000
Portuguese Division	4,000
Spanish Army	7,000

About the time that Count Souham commenced his operations against us at Burgos, the French Marshals Soult and Jourdan, with King Joseph, began their march from Valencia to Madrid, and arrived at Aranjuez on or about the 23rd instant. Sir Rowland Hill at their approach drew out his forces so as to cover Madrid, and preparations were made to give the enemy battle, when in the night of the 27th an express from Lord Wellington arrived, ordering them to retreat with all convenient dispatch upon Salamanca, unless an opportunity should offer of fighting the enemy under great advantages. Madrid was accordingly evacuated, the powder magazines of El Retiro blown up, the guns spiked, and the troops with reluctance began this unwelcome retreat.

All accounts from officers in that army agree in stating that the position which Sir Rowland Hill had chosen was excellent, and every arrangement that he had adopted highly judicious; but the army of Marshal Soult acting in concert with that of Souham, avoided a general engagement by marching from Aranjuez down to Toledo, where they threw a bridge over the Tagus, and thus endeavoured to pass to the rear of General Hill's position, which circumstance, together with the enemy's great superiority in point of numbers, independent of the orders received from Lord Wellington, rendered a retreat unavoidable.

November. On the morning of the 6th we left the banks of the Douro, and at night were put up at Torrecilla del Orden. On the 7th we fell back to Villa Verde, and on the 8th arrived in Salamanca. The forces from Madrid under (General Hill having crossed the Tormes, were posted at Arapiles, on the old field of battle, a part of which had, not been ploughed since, and many of the graves were yet to be seen. The divisions from Burgos rested on the heights of Sant Christoval above Salamanca, and a brigade of the 2nd Division occupied the town of Alba de Tormes. In the meantime the two French armies having formed a junction, Marshal Soult, as King's Lieutenant, took the chief command, and a grand review of the divisions forming their rearguard was said to have taken place on the 10th, in the plains of Medina del Campo.

14th. This afternoon orders were given for Salamanca to be cleared, and the baggage to assemble in the road to Ciudad Rodrigo. Marshal Soult having passed a portion of his forces over the river above the town of Alba de Tormes, Lord Wellington concentrated the army, and posted it about the old field of action, occupying both the hills of Arapiles. It was a wet night, and we slept in the little village of Tejares, about two miles from the bridge of Salamanca.

15th. A general expectation prevailed in the camp this morning that another battle of Salamanca would, before night, be enrolled in the annals of these campaigns. Everything seemed to justify this opinion: the hills were literally covered with troops; Salamanca was left open as in July; and all our forces withdrawn from that side of the river were assembled upon the hills around us. Lord Wellington was upon the Arapiles with the 3rd Division, observing the movements of the enemy. Things continued in this state until about 3 o'clock in the afternoon, when orders were given to retreat with all possible haste towards Ciudad Rodrigo.

Our columns descending from the Arapiles were seen retreating over the vast plain before us. We thought at first that they might only be retiring to the heights above Tejares; but we were soon undeceived. It was reported that our right was turned, and that the enemy's left was already in the road between us and Ciudad Rodrigo. Just at this time a very heavy rain commenced, with cold piercing winds, which rendered the roads in some places almost impassable, and obliged the men to wade, for a considerable distance, through water above their knees. As we were hastening through the wood of Fragoas about 6 o'clock, Lord Wellington passed by, attended by about fifteen staff-officers and a few orderly dragoons: he wore an oil-skin cloak, and looked extremely ill, which was not to be wondered at considering the anxiety of mind and fatigue of body which he was enduring.

Shortly after it had become dark we came to the little village of Canero, where Lord Wellington took shelter in a cottage, and many officers of rank were obliged to lie down in their cloaks under hovels near their horses. We pitched our tent in the wood near to the village. The night was dark, cold and wet; and I had a severe attack of rheumatism, which added much to my distress. We had but little to eat, and nothing to drink; and it was impossible to light a fire, owing to the violence of the rain.

16th. At daybreak we began to move. It rained incessantly all the day. At night we encamped on a little green near Aldea de Bovida, and I passed the night very miserably. Lord Wellington was in the village. In the morning Lieutenant-General Sir E. Paget had been taken prisoner by the enemy.

17th. We were all in motion again at daybreak. Having received permission to proceed direct to Ciudad Rodrigo, I made the best of my way thither, and arriving there soon after dark, was so fortunate as to get into a kitchen where there was a good fire, at which several officers were drying their boots, &c. and getting something to eat.— The town and even the fields around were so crowded with the baggage and sick of the army, that it was almost an impossibility to obtain shelter of any sort; so that mine was an enviable lot; and to add to my consolation, at midnight I received my baggage: this was cheering indeed, for independent of the comforts it afforded me, I had given it up as lost.

18th. Part of the army arrived this evening in the plains of Ciudad Rodrigo, glad enough to view once more the friendly mountains of

Portugal, and in the course of the two following days all our divisions reached the Agueda in safety; so that all Marshal Soult's attempts to surround us had been rendered fruitless; and as he felt no disposition to follow us beyond the frontiers, he contented himself by seeing us to the Agueda, and then returned to Salamanca. From Ciudad Rodrigo we moved today to Espeja.

19th. We passed the Duas Casas at Fuentes d' Onor, and at Villa Formosa, our old acquaintance the Portuguese, although alarmed at our unexpected return, greeted us with the usual salutation of, "*Viva,*" "*Pasa muito bem,*" and "*Onde são os Franceses Senhor.*" Having thus come to the close of this perilous and trying retreat, and the troops being about to enter their cantonments for the winter, I shall briefly notice the station allotted the several divisions in the friendly mountains of Lusitania, leaving the French to enjoy their triumph for a season, and for a season only, for they may assure themselves that in a few months they will see the British lion sally from his rocky den refreshed and more formidable than ever.

Distribution of the Forces under Lord Wellington at the close of the Campaign, 1812.

Out-posts on the frontiers near Ciudad Rodrigo:
Light Division
4th Division
Spanish Army

2nd Division	As a Corps of Observation at Coria, &c near Placentia.
1st Division	Vizeu and adjacents.
3rd Division	Moimenta de Beira and adjacents.
5th Division	Lamego and adjacents.
6th Division	Coa and adjacents.
7th Division	Meno, near Celorico.
Cavalry	Banks of the Douro, near Oporto, &c.

Head-Quarters, Freneda.

November 30th. In consequence of my promotion, I was ordered to join the 3rd Division of the army under the command of Major-General the Hon. E. M. Pakenham, now on the march to Moimenta de Beira.

December 2nd. Reported myself to General Pakenham at Freixadas, and was attached to the right brigade under Colonel Keane.

On the 11th of this month I was ordered on duty with the left brigade at Fonte Arcada, and remained there until the 24th, when I again joined the right brigade at Liomil, a village about two miles from Moimenta.

Third Division of the Army.

Major-General the Hon. E. Pakenham.

Right Brigade.

Colonel Keane, 60th Regiment

1st Battalion, 45th Foot,	
Lieutenant-Colonel Forbes	Moimenta de Beira
5th Battalion, 60th Foot,	
Lieutenant-Colonel Fitzgerald	Paradosa.
———— 74th Foot,	
Lieutenant-Colonel Hon. R. L. Trench	Sarzeda.
1st Battalion, 88th Foot,	
Captain Nickle	Liomil

Left Brigade.

Lieutenant-Colonel Campbell, 94th Regiment,

1st Battalion; 5th Foot,	
Lieutenant-Colonel Pratt	Ferrarin
2nd Battalion, 83rd Foot,	
Lieutenant-Colonel Carr	Villars
2nd Battalion, 87th Foot,	
Lieutenant-Colonel Gough	Adabares
———— 94th Foot,	
Lieutenant-Colonel Lloyd	Fonte Arcada.

Portuguese Brigade.

Major-General Power	Granja Nova

1813

We commenced the new year in our cantonments with building fireplaces and chimneys in our quarters, and making them as habitable as we could, for the weather was now very cold, and the winter evenings long. At Liomil I had just finished building a kind of chimney, and had plastered my room, which before was nothing but the bare stone walls with crevices letting in the air, when I was ordered to take up my quarters at Moimenta de Beira, and had the mortification to see the humble comforts which at some expense and trouble I had prepared for myself, possessed by another; this so discouraged me, that I had not the spirit to furnish and put in repair the comfortless room which I now got at Moimenta, but contented myself with a little tin *brasero* of live-coal, instead of a fire, all the winter.

We heard that Lord Wellington was gone to Cadiz and Lisbon to consult with the Spanish and Portuguese Governments respecting future operations; and also that he had been nominated *Generalissimo* of the Spanish armies.

February, Early in this month, Major-General the Hon. Charles Colville arrived to command the division, and General Pakenham was removed to the command of the 6th Division at Cea. General Pakenham was a great favourite with the 3rd Division, and being brother-in-law to Lord Wellington, and a very able officer, he stood very high in his Lordship's estimation and confidence.

March. On the 17th of this month, the festival of St. Patrick, the officers of the 88th regiment gave a grand dinner to Colonel Keane and the brigade staff. Soon after five o'clock dinner was announced in the usual way by the tune of "Oh, the roast beef of old England." We sat down more than fifty in number, and the evening was spent very convivially. Among the numerous toasts were the following:

St. Patrick (three times three)	Tune: St. Patrick's Day in the Morning
Shelah, St. Patrick's wife	
The King	God save the King.
The Prince Regent of England	The Prince and Old England Forever.
The Duke of York and the Army	The Duke of York's March.
The Wooden Walls of Old England	Rule, Britannia.
The Marquis of Wellington, and success to the next Campaign	The Downfall of Paris
General Picton and the 3rd Division	Britons Strike Home
General Pakenham and the Battle of Salamanca	See the Conquering Hero Comes. Song. Battle of Salamanca.
Colonel Keane and the right brigade (3 times 3)	British Grenadier

St. Patrick, the Shamrock and the Land of Potatoes
St. George, the Rose and prosperity to England.
St. Andrew, the Thistle and the Land of Cakes.

April. It would be quite superfluous here to notice the amusements and recreations with which we passed this dull winter away, or to mention the many romantic and often disagreeable rides I had over the mountains during the time. We had it once in contemplation to get up a play in imitation of the light division officers, who had performed several times before Lord Wellington. On the following page is a copy of one of their play-bills:

May 1st. Lieutenant-General Sir Thomas Picton arriving from England about this time, resumed his old post in command of the 3rd Division, in consequence of which General Colville joined the left brigade, which (from his seniority) now took the appellation of right; and Colonel Keane, also, having resigned his command to Brigadier-General Brisbane, lately from England, the Colonels Keane and Campbell both joined their regiments. It will naturally be supposed that, by the great destruction both of men and horses in the late active campaign, and the sickness and deaths which followed from the sufferings of the retreat, the army had been most lamentably reduced,

LIGHT DIVISION THEATRE,
GALLEGOS.

On Thursday Evening the 15th April, 1813, will be presented the Comedy of

SHE STOOPS TO CONQUER.

MEN.

Sir Charles Marlow - - Lieut. Edwards, 43d Reg.
Young Marlow - - - Capt. Beckwith, 95th Reg.
Hastings - - - - - Lieut. Pemberton, 95th Reg.
Hardcastle - - - - - Lieut. Pattinson, 43d Reg.
Tony Lumpkin - - - - Lieut. Hennel, 43d Reg.
Diggory - - - - - - Lieut. Hopewood, 95th Reg.

WOMEN.

Mrs. Hardcastle - - - Capt. Hobkirk, 43d Reg.
Miss Hardcastle - - - Lieut. Freer, 43d Reg.
Miss Neville - - - - Lieut. Havelock, 43d Reg.
Maid - - - - - - - Lieut. Lord C. Spencer, 95th.

Landlord, Servants, &c. &c.

To which will be added the Farce of

THE APPRENTICE.

MEN.

Wingate - - - - - Capt. Hobkirk, 43d Reg.
Dick (the Apprentice) - Lieut. Hennel, 43d Reg.
Gargle - - - - - - Lieut. Hopewood, 95th Reg.
Simon - - - - - - Lieut. Pattinson, 43d Reg.
Scotchman - - - - - Lieut. Gardiner, 95th Reg.
Irishman - - - - - Lieut. Cox, 95th Reg.
Catchpole - - - - - Lieut. Molloy, 95th Reg.

WOMEN.

Charlotte - - - - - Lieut. Lord C. Spencer, 95th.

Sporting Club, Watchmen, Porter, &c.

Vivat Wellington!

[Printed at Freneda.

and stood in need not only of rest and refreshment, but of considerable augmentation also, before it could be in a fit state again to take the field.

Reinforcements, however, of men and horses, and supplies of money and equipment having arrived from England during the winter, the army now made a most respectable appearance, many of the regiments having nearly their full complement of men, and others by their experience and soldier-like spirit making up for the deficiency. Several fresh regiments of cavalry had arrived, and others were almost completely remounted. The artillery, engineers, and in short every corps and department of the army had been brought into the best state possible.

In the late campaigns the health of the men had been found to suffer so severely from being exposed in their bivouacks to the inclemencies of the weather, that it was deemed advisable to provide against this for the future, by affording the men as well as the officers some shelter, and in consequence bell tents were provided and distributed to each regiment, in the proportion of five to each company, which, according to the strength of the army, must have taken about three thousand tents, besides those of officers.

From the very limited means of transport allowed throughout the service, hitherto I had been obliged (amongst other privations) to consent myself with no other bedding than a single blanket, which had constituted toy only covering, In deserted houses and in the field, both in winter and summer, very frequently for weeks and sometimes even months together. I had for the future, however, the prospect of being more comfortable in these respects, having row added to my equipment a small canteen, a hair mattress and an additional blanket: indeed the service had from experience been found of so trying a nature, and its termination appeared so uncertain, that everyone seemed now bent upon endeavours to provide themselves with as many comforts as their respective circumstances or rank would admit.

11th. Lord Wellington having returned from Cadiz and Lisbon, the army was ordered to hold itself in readiness to move, and some of the divisions were beginning already to concentrate for the march; so that it now became necessary for Senhor Don Joseph to prepare in earnest for our reception. Marshal Soult having been recalled from the army, in Spain, to take a command under Napoleon in the north of Europe, Joseph Buonaparte, with Marshal Jourdan as his major-general, commanded, in person against us We heard that he had quitted Madrid (expressing himself much dissatisfied with its inhabitants), and had joined his army, which was strongly posted on the right banks of the Douro, near Valladolid.

OPENING OF THE CAMPAIGN,
May 1813.

Preparation being completed for the commencement of operations, the troops began to move by the following routes.

1st Division from Vizeu,
4th Division from the frontiers,
6th Division from Cea,
7th Division from Meno; which four divisions were to pass the Douro at or near Torremoncorvo.
5th Division from Lamego, to pass the Douro in boats there.
3rd Division from Moimenta, to pass the Douro near St João de Pesqueira.

These six divisions of the army with a large force of cavalry, all under the command of Lieutenant-General Graham, who had by this time returned to the army as second in command, were to move along the right banks of the Douro, through the province of Tras os Montes, and; assemble about the last week in May upon the frontiers, near Braganza, while Lord Wellington with the light division, the Hussar brigade and Spanish army, and General Hill with his corps from Coria, should move upon the Tormes, drive the enemy's advanced guard from Salamanca, and meet General Graham; in the vicinity of Valladolid. By this grand movement, the position, of the enemy near Valladolid, as well as all the forces they might have had south of the Douro, was turned; and the whole was conducted with such promptitude and secrecy, that the French corps occupying Madrid, Cuellar, &c. had but just time to effect its escape over the river.

May 16th. (Sunday.) The 3rd Division left its cantonments this day; and after a most romantic mountain march halted at Trevão.

17th. The division marched to St João de Pesqueira, and encamped in a wood.

18th. At a very early hour this morning the troops began to pass the river Douro in boats: some little confusion unavoidably occurred, and a part of the baggage was not got over that night. We were all the afternoon climbing the rocky, heights beyond the river, which rendered it late at night before we encamped.

19th. Continuing our march we halted this afternoon at Villa Flor, the Portuguese brigade occupying the town. The two British brigades encamped.

20th. Halted at Villa Flor.

21st. Encamped this afternoon near Sardão.

22nd. Encamped at Limão.

23rd. And this morning in a wood near Bornos. All these are poor little villages. The extent of our march each day might be about fifteen English miles.

24th. We arrived this day at Vimiosa, a small town not far from Braganza, and only a few miles from the frontiers. Here we halted two days, for the 5th division and cavalry to come up.

27th. In our march this morning we traversed a very large heath, and soon afterwards entering Spain, we encamped upon a hill near Alcanizas,

28th. Our camp this afternoon spread along the banks of a little river near the village of Vegaletrabe.

29th. The troops began their march at sunrise, having their caps decorated with oak-boughs. After marching until near 10 o'clock we encamped near Losilla, a village about three miles from the river Eslau. Thus far had we advanced without seeing an enemy or hearing a shot fired; but the troops had scarcely grounded their arms in the field of Losilla, when the novel sound of the enemy's cannon on the other side of the river was heard, which was instantly hailed with a loud cheering from our brigade.

30th. We halted this day in the field of Losilla. The forces with Lord Wellington after having advanced upon the Tormes and beaten the enemy out of Salamanca, arrived this evening upon the Douro, and Lord Wellington crossing the river joined our camp. The fords of the river Eslau were afterwards reconnoitred, but being found too deep, the division returned to the camp of Losilla.

31st A bridge of pontoons was laid down upon the Eslau for the troops to pass.

June 1st The 3rd Division passed the Eslau this morning, and we encamped near Zamora.

2nd. The enemy retiring before our cavalry, which now took the lead, we advanced as far as Manocilla, and encamped in the vast plain near that town.

3rd. The division encamped this afternoon at Santiago. I obtained quarters in the village. The town of Toro was in view about five miles distant upon our right, and near it the encampment of the light division, which had just crossed the river. Lord Wellington's head-quarters were in Toro.

4th. The division made long and tedious march, being occasionally interrupted mid impeded by other divisions from the roads often crossing each other, which at length brought us all near together at La Mota, and the whole army encamped upon an extensive plain in view of that town, where Lord Wellington, in commemoration of the old King's birthday, gave a dinner to the General Officers of the army, to which the generals of the 3rd Division went from the camp.

5th. We marched at the usual hour this morning (4 o'clock), and encamped at night upon a hill in front of a little village, where General Picton was put up with the head-quarters of the army.

6th. Moving upon Palencia, I pitched my tent this evening upon a green at a village the name of which I could not learn. The Oxford Blues and Life Guards were in an adjoining field, exposed to a heavy rain which fell in the night.

7th. In consequence of the advance of the army in the order directed by Lord Wellington, the enemy's position near Valladolid became untenable. Evacuating that town and Palencia, he retreated upon Burgos, followed along the high road by Lieutenant-General Sir Rowland Hill. We moved down the hill this morning into the plains of Palencia, and encamped near the town.

8th. Expected to halt today; but the bugles were sounded at the usual hour in the morning, and we marched to the village of Monzoon, where we were obliged to encamp upon low marshy ground, which from the rain which fell in the night put us to much inconvenience.

9th. The division halted at Monzoon. I rode back to Palencia, but returned to the camp in the evening.

10th. It continued raining. We marched all the morning, and then encamped on the banks of a canal.

11th. The division made a long march again today, and we encamped near Perillo de Abaxo.

12th. The division was ordered to halt

13th. We resumed our march this morning, and encamped at Tapia. Here, to our most agreeable surprise, we learnt that the enemy had themselves destroyed the works at Burgos, and that they were retiring, beyond the river Ebro.

15th. We continued our march towards the Ebro, crossing the country through woods and bye-roads. The division of General Hill moving by the *Camino Real.*

16th. Passed the Ebro this morning by two little bridges near San Martinho, and encamped near the river.

17th. The division making a very long march this day, was obliged to rest several times. In the evening we came to a large plain, where meeting with the 6th and 7th Divisions, and General Hill's column, making altogether at least twenty thousand men, we formed a fine encampment. It rained almost all the night; but my tent was pitched upon one of the best spots in the field, and I had a tree for my horses. Two of our regiments were upon ploughed ground, the 7th Division occupied the wood, and Lord Dalhousie an old castle near the river.

18th. Passing through Medina we encamped on the side of a hill about five miles beyond that town.

19th. Marched through a beautiful vale well watered, and encamped near Kakoma.

20th. The troops did not move this morning until 10 o'clock: the baggage was ordered to halt until early in the afternoon, when the whole moved on. We passed through the village of Morillo, where Lord Wellington had fixed his headquarters, and at night encamped near a little village entirely deserted by its inhabitants. We were now within a few leagues of Vittoria, where, it was reported, the enemy intended to chastise us for our temerity.

Having thus, in the space of five weeks, marched from the mountains of Moimenta de Beira to the plains of Vittoria, and being now on the eve of a great battle, I shall, by way of preface thereto, give a list of the several corps or regiments composing the army at this time, observing, that each division of infantry generally consisted of two British and one Portuguese brigades, and each brigade of cavalry contained in general three regiments. The royal artillery of the army was so divided, that to each division of infantry was attached a brigade of six guns, and to each brigade of cavalry a troop of horse artillery, composed of the same number of field-pieces. Besides these there were the reserve artillery, the battering train and some light mountain guns.

A detachment of sappers and miners, under the directions of an officer of engineers, was generally attached to each division, and strengthened in the event of a siege or storm. It must be observed, that in the number of regiments enumerated, the 5th battalion of the 60th regiment (rifles) is omitted, having been apportioned in companies to the 3rd, 6th, and 2nd Divisions, in the proportion (I believe) of three companies to each; those attached to the 3rd Division being at this period commanded by Colonel Keane, Colonel Dickson was in command of the artillery; and Colonel Sir Richard Fletcher of the engineers.

CAVALRY.

Major-General Baron Bock.

1st Reg* of Life Guards	10th Light Dragoons (Hussars)
2d ditto - - ditto	12th ditto
Royal Horse Guards	13th ditto
3d Dragoon Guards	14th ditto
5th ditto	15th ditto - - - - - ditto
1st Dragoons (Royals)	16th ditto
3d Dragoons	18th ditto - - - - - ditto
4th ditto	1st Hussars, K. G. L.
1st Dragoons, K. G. L.	2d ditto - - ditto
2d ditto - - - ditto	

Portuguese Cavalry.

98

INFANTRY,

LIGHT DIVISION.

Major-General Charles Baron Alten

British.

43d (Monmouthshire) Regiment.
52d (Oxfordshire) Regiment.
95th (Rifle Corps.)

Portuguese.

17th Regiment of the Line.
1st Regiment of Caçadores.

FIRST DIVISION.

Four Battalions of Guards.   Four Battalions of the K. G. L.

SECOND DIVISION.

Major-General the Hon. W. Stewart.

British.

3d Reg. (East Kent or Old Buffs)	57th (West Middlesex)
	66th (Berkshire)
50th (West Kent)	39th (Dorsetshire)
28th (North Gloucestersh.)	71st (Highland Light Infantry)
31st (Huntingdonshire)	
34th (Cumberland)	92d (Highlanders)

Portuguese.

2d Regiment of the Line	10th Regiment of the Line
4th ditto - - ditto	14th ditto - - ditto
6th ditto - - ditto	18th ditto - - ditto

One Regiment of Caçadores.

THIRD DIVISION.

Lieut.-General Sir Thomas Picton, K. B.

British.

5th (Northumberland)
45th (Nottingham)
74th
83d

87th (Prince of Wales' own Irish)
88th (Connaught Rangers)
94th

Portuguese.

9th Regiment of the Line.   21st Regiment of the Line.
One Regiment of Caçadores.

FOURTH DIVISION.

Lieut-General Sir G. L. Cole, K. B.

British.

2d (or Queen's)
7th (Royal Fusileers)
20th (East Devonshire)
23d (Welch Fusileers)

27th (Inneskillens)
40th (Somertshire)
48th (Northamptonshire)
53d (Shropshire)

Portuguese.

11th Regiment of the Line.   23d Regiment of the Line.
One Regiment of Caçadores.

FIFTH DIVISION.

Major-General Oswald.

British.

1st (Royals)	38th (Staffordshire)
4th (King's own)	47th (Lancashire)
9th (East Norfolk)	59th (2d Nottingham)

Portuguese.

1st Regiment of the Line	15th Regiment of the Line
3d ditto - - - ditto	16th ditto - - - ditto

SIXTH DIVISION.

Major-General the Hon. E. M. Pakenham.

British.

11th (North Devon)	61st (South Gloucestershire)
32d (Cornwall)	79th (Cameron's Highland)
36th (Herefordshire)	91st (Highlanders)
42d (Royal Highlanders)	

Portuguese.

8th Regiment of the Line.   12th Regiment of the Line.
One Regiment of Caçadores.

SEVENTH DIVISION.

Lieut.-General the Earl of Dalhousie.

British.

6th (1st Warwickshire)	68th (Durham Light Infantry
24th (2d Warwickshire)	82d (Prince of Wales' Volun-
51st (2d York West Riding	teers)
Light Infantry)	Chasseurs Britanniques Reg^t
58th (Rutlandshire)	Brunswick-Oels Regiment

Portuguese.

7th and 19th Regiments of the Line, and one of Caçadores.

BATTLE OF VITTORIA,
Monday, 21st June 1813.

It was a night of lovely June,
High rode in cloudless blue the moon:
Ah! gentle planet, other sight
Shall greet thee next returning night.

Walter Scott.

Vittoria is a town of Biscay in Spain, delightfully situated at the end of a most beautiful and fruitful vale, a few leagues north of the River Ebro: it is a well-built town, and the capital of the province of Alava: the scenery around is charmingly diversified by gentle declivities of hill and dale, and encircled at a distance by romantic and towering heights, from which I remember counting upwards of twenty villages at one view, and was told, that on a clear day no less than forty may be seen with the naked eye. To these mountains the British army had advanced last evening, and, formed into columns for the attack, encamped within a few miles of the enemy's position.

Our advance from Portugal had been almost one uninterrupted march, in which we had scarcely met with any opposition, the French army retiring before us, having their right constantly threatened by our left and by the Spanish army of Gallicia, which had joined us as we passed the Ebro last week. Joseph Buonaparte and Marshal Jourdan, however, coming at length to Vittoria, all the French forces which could be brought together were ordered to assemble here:—pursuant to this the corps from Madrid, from Saragosa, from Navarre and the Gallicias, and in short from all parts of Spain, together with those Spaniards who had joined the standard of the usurper, farming one immense army nearly one hundred thousand strong, with one hundred and fifty-two pieces of cannon, were on the evening of the 19th inst. assembled and posted in the fine position of Vittoria, awaiting the arrival of the British army.

The advanced posts of the enemy's centre lined the banks of the River Zadora, the bridges over which were fortified, and wherever it was considered formidable fieldworks had been constructed. The left and left of his centre, supported by one hundred pieces of cannon, crowned the heights and rising aground above the village of Sabujana de Alava, while the right of his centre crossing the high road filled the plain, and kept open the communication with his right wing, which held a very strong position covered by formidable field-works on the other side of the town.

Almost the whole of the charming and beautiful vale of Vittoria was at this time covered with ripening corn, which served up conceal the light troops, and sometimes the movements even of whole corps during the action. Part of the ground upon which this memorable engagement was fought, had already a claim to the notice of history, from a victory gained there by the English under Edward the Black Prince, in the 14th century, and to this day there is a mount called the *"Altura de los Inglezes"* (the Hill of the English or English Hill.) This spot, which naturally excited some interest from its name, appears on the left of the great road leading to Vittoria, immediately after passing the Zadora.[1]

The enemy having thus chosen his ground for the conflict, and Lord Wellington having in the best manner he was able, made himself acquainted with their situation, orders were given for the divisions to number as strong as possible this morning, and to move up the mountains as soon as it was light

ARMY OF VITTORIA.

RIGHT COLUMN.

Lieut.-General Sir Rowland Hill, K. B.

2d Division - - - - -
Spanish Corps - - - } To commence the action by attacking the enemy's left in the mountains behind Sabujana de Alava.

LEFT COLUMN.

Lieut.-General Sir Thomas Graham, K. B.

1st Division - - - - -
6th Division - - - -
4 Regᵗ of Cavalry - -
Spanish Corps - - - } To endeavour to turn the enemy's right, and thus cut off his retreat to France by the high road from Vittoria to Bayonne.

---

1. The *Altura de los Inglezes* was very distinctly noticed in Barker's Panorama of the Battle, exhibited in Leicester Square, London; and I think that picture altogether represented the most perfect view of the scenery round Vittoria that could possibly be given.

3d Division - - - - - Lieut.-Gen. Sir Thomas Pictón, K. B.
4th Division - - - - Lieut.-Gen. Sir G. L. Cole, K. B.
7th Division - - - - Lieut.-Gen. the Earl of Dalhousie.
Light Division - - - Major-Gen. Charles Baron Alten.
Cavalry Columns - - Major-Gen. Baron Bock.

The 6th Division, under the command of Major-General the Hon. E. M. Pakenham, being one day's march in the rear, was not in the engagement.

At break of day the bugles sounded, and the troops of the 3rd Division began to ascend the mountains as the sun was rising, followed by the baggage. In about half an hour the sound of cannon was heard, and a native of the country whom we met informed us that the battle between the *Inglezes* and *Francezes* was beginnings Soon after 8 o'clock we reached the summit of the mountain above the village of Mendoza, from whence we had a fine view of the town across the vale, and of the enemy's positions.

The troops under Sir Rowland Hill were just commencing their attack upon the heights of Puebla and the position of the enemy above Sabujana, while the Light and 4th Divisions advancing immediately on their left so as to support this attack, were preparing to force the passage of the Zadora, when the 3rd Division being ordered to advance, headed by old General Picton, ran cheering down the hill, passed through Mendoza, and covered by their artillery under Captain Douglas, in concert with the light and 4th divisions, stormed the bridges and breastworks on the river, which they now passed, bearing everything before them, towards the Altura de los Inglezes.

The 7th Division also, under Lord Dalhousie, who had been anxious to take the lead on this occasion, coming up, passed the river, following and supporting the 3rd Division. Meanwhile in the mountains the action was well contested, and the enemy shewed a most determined resistance against the attacks of Sir Rowland Hill, the regiments of whose division consequently suffered severely, particularly that distinguished corps the 71st Highland Light Infantry, under the command of Colonel Cadogan, who had also the command of all the light troops in that quarter. (This is the same officer who so distinguished himself in the battle of Fuentes d'Onor, and commanded in that village after Colonel Cameron had fallen.)

In one of the earliest attacks made this morning upon the heights of Puebla he was mortally wounded, and lived only long enough to know that he was dying in the hour of victory. But our attention was now called from the mountains, for about noon while our right and centre corps were yet severely engaged in driving the enemy back upon Vittoria, a very heavy cloud of dust appeared in the plain at an immense distance upon our left, and almost at the other extreme verge of the vale, apparently moving down upon the town. This proved to be the column of Sir Thomas Graham, which had by a very long march succeeded in turning the enemy's right, and was now possessing itself of the high road to France, by storming Gomarha Mayor and the several little villages in that quarter.

The 5th Division was principally engaged in this duty, and Major-General Robinson was particularly distinguished on the occasion. Obviously unrepared for such an event, the baggage of the French army and even their military chest, from an unpardonable confidence of success, had been left in Vittoria until late in the morning, when seeing their positions both in the plain and in the mountains falling in succession, and the British army progressively advancing in triumph towards the town, directions were at length given for the baggage, heavy artillery, military chest and court equipages (amongst which were many carriages full of ladies) to retreat by the high road to Bayonne.

We may judge of their astonishment then when they found that Sir Thomas Graham had gained possession of that road, and was fighting his way to meet them. The whole cavalcade, as may be supposed, now ran back in the greatest consternation to Vittoria: by this time however all the positions of the enemy having been carried, and the fugitives overtaken, Vittoria fell, and with it one hundred and fifty-one pieces of cannon, all their ammunition-waggons, baggage, military chest, and several carriages with ladies, amongst whom was the Countess de Gazan. The Count, I understood, was Adjutant-General of the French army. King Joseph (whom we may in future with great safety call only Joseph Buonaparte) seeing that all was lost, fled towards Pampeluna.

One of his carriages was taken at the gates of the town and plundered, and such a complete route was perhaps never before seen in European wars. The French troops finding themselves so completely beaten, and their retreat by the high road to France cut off, fled by cross roads over the mountains towards Pampeluna, covered by their cavalry. Our cavalry, which had not hitherto been much engaged, now came up full speed along the high road, and the Life Guards took possession of Vittoria. The 15th Hussars made a gallant charge against the enemy, but the 18th Hussars not being up in time to their support they were obliged to retire, which created a momentary alarm.

This happened about 5 o'clock in the afternoon. Sir Thomas Picton was then on the road to Pampeluna, and the troops of Sir Rowland Hill were descending the mountains near Vittoria. Thus ended this memorable contest, which proved the final overthrow of the French power in Spain. Captain Freemantle of the Guards, *Aide-de-Camp* to the Marquis of Wellington, was sent home with the dispatches, carrying with him the colours of the 100th regiment and the baton of Marshal Jourdan, which had been taken' in the action, to be laid at the feet of His Royal Highness the Prince Regent The baggage having descended from the heights, was directed to rest for the night on the field of battle. I encamped near the Altura de los Inglezes.

RETURN OF THE KILLED, WOUNDED AND MISSING, IN THE BATTLE OF VITTORIA.

	Killed	Wounded	Missing
British	501	2,787	—
Portuguese	150	899	—
Spanish	89	464	—
	740	4,150	265

June 22nd. This morning the 6th Division marched over the field, and was ordered to halt in Vittoria, while the troops which had fought the battle were pursuing the enemy towards Pampeluna, A most shocking scene of carnage and distress presented itself, the French having suffered very much along the high road and near the town, but to what extent their loss amounted it was difficult to ascertain. It could not however be calculated at less than ours. Having been detained in Vittoria until late in the afternoon, it was dark before I reached the camp of Salvatierra, where at least forty thousand troops were lying in the open fields under a heavy rain without shelter, all the baggage and stores, from the darkness of the night and badness of the roads, being yet in the rear: scarcely a tent was standing in the field, and the men were lying about in their blankets, and the officers in their cloaks: for my own part I had neither cloak, great coat or blanket, and consequently passed the night very miserably. Lord Wellington, the Generals and head-quarters staff were in the town of Salvatierra, and our advanced guard some distance in front of that place.

23rd. We were all glad to see daylight, the rain having continued to fall without ceasing throughout the night. The bugles had sounded, and the troops were beginning to file off the ground, when a part of the baggage came in sight, and followed the divisions. We marched all this day through lanes and bye-roads almost impassable. In the evening the division turned off the road, and we encamped on the declivity of a hill by the roadside.

24th. We did not move off our ground so early this morning, because it was found necessary to repair some bridges which the enemy had broken in his retreat. At night we were put up in a village where we first heard the Biscayan language, which none of us could understand, not even the Spaniards who were with us, as it differs so much from the Castilian tongue. Our advanced guard, consisting of Major-General Victor Alten's brigade of cavalry and the 95th (Rifle corps), on this day captured the only gun which the enemy had carried off from Vittoria. A French corps under General Clausel which had not been able to join their army previous to the late action, advancing now from Logrono, threatened Vittoria, where all the trophies and wounded had been left; but finding there the 6th Division, which immediately advanced to meet them, they soon fell back towards the Pyrenees, about Jaca, near to which place there is a pass through the mountains into France.

25th. Passing through Irunzun we encamped by the road side about seven English miles from Pampeluna. Sir Thomas Graham with the column under his command took the road to Tolosa and St Sebastian.

26th. We arrived in the plains of Pampeluna, and were put up at Huarte, a small town pleasantly situated a few miles from the walls of Pampeluna, at the mouth of a pass into the Pyrenees. The enemy having left a garrison in Pampeluna, the place was now invested, and such of the inhabitants as chose to retire were allowed to quit the town and pass in safety through our camp. It was an interesting sight this afternoon to see such numbers of women and children availing themselves of this permission, leaving the town laden with their treasures.

27th. General Clausel with his corps, which it will be recollected was not in the action of Vittoria, having halted near Tafalla this afternoon, the light division and ours received orders to march against him, and we encamped in a beautiful wood near Tafalla.

28th. Clausel having received information of our approach decamped in the direction of Saragosa, pursued by the enterprising Spanish chieftain Mina: and we were ordered to march across the country to Casseda.

29th. We halted in the camp of Casseda.

30th. The two divisions marched to Sanguessa and encamped hear that town. This movement was intended to prevent General Clausel from joining the French army posted in the Pyrenees, and it succeeded, by obliging him to pass into France by a circuitous route pursued and harassed by the Spanish Guerrillas. The 3rd and Light Divisions therefore now returned to the camp before Pampeluna, and the corps of General Hill which had relieved us at Huarte was ordered to advance into the Pyrenees by Lantz and Barrueta: near the latter they found a division of the French army strongly posted, but after a series of skirmishes and attacks which lasted until the 7th July, they obliged them to pass the Bidassoa, into France, and took post themselves on the heights of Maya. Meanwhile the corps under Sir Thomas Graham, after a sharp affair with the enemy at Tolosa, succeeded in driving them from that quarter also into France, and prepared to besiege the important fortress of St Sebastian,

20th. A large force of Spaniards having arrived from the South to blockade Pampeluna, the British divisions advanced into the Pyrenees and were posted nearly as follows.

Position of the Army in the Pyrenees

4th Division	At the pass of Roncesvalles
2nd Division	At the pass of Maya.
3rd Division	Ulague.
6th Division	St. Estevan.
7th Division	Echalar.
Light Division	Echalar.
1st Division	At the pass of Irun.
5th Division	Besieging St. Sebastian.

Joseph Buonaparte and Marshal Jourdan after their inglorious campaign repaired to Paris, and the command of the French army of Spain and Portugal was now once more vested in Marshal Soult, Duke of Dalmatia; who was recalled from the north of Europe for that purpose, and honoured with the distinguished title of Lieutenant of the Emperor, which I imagine gave him the power of awarding honours and making promotion without any intermediate reference to the Emperor. Accordingly having arrived in the camp on or about the 20th instant, on the 23rd he issued a kind of proclamation to his troops, wherein he attributes their late disasters to a want of skill in those who had commanded them, and bade them drive "*the proud cotton-weavers of England*" from those heights from whence they proudly viewed the fertile valleys of the "Great Nation!!"

BATTLES OF THE PYRENEES
From 25th July to 1st August, 1813.

For several days past the movements observable in the French camp as well as the information obtained therefrom, induced a belief that Marshal Soult meditated a serious attack for the relief of Pampeluna, and Sant Sebastian; but at what point of our line it would be made was extremely uncertain, though his movements seemed to indicate that our left at Irun would be the post first assailed. The position which we occupied, although extremely formidable in itself, possessed its disadvantages.

The extent of our line from Roncesvalles to the seaside near Sant Sebastian was such, and the positions of the different corps of our army so isolated and distant from each other, that notwithstanding the necessity of a perfect co-operation, each division was in fact like a separate force: while from the extreme badness of the roads over the mountains, it was with the greatest difficulty that the necessary communications could be kept up, and in some positions it was quite impracticable by any means to communicate with the coast. Taking into consideration then all these difficulties, it was fair to anticipate a struggle fully as severe as that which now occurred.

BATTLES AT RONCESVALLES AND THE PASS OF MAYA,
25th July, 1813.

Lieutenant General Sir G. L. Cole with the 4th Division and a small corps of Spanish troops posted at the pass of Roncesvalles, was attacked this morning by Marshal Soult with forty thousand men, while a corps of twelve thousand under the French General Drouet, and another under General Clausel, attacked the heights of Maya and.

109

Echalar. Sir Lowry Cole defended the pass for some time, but after a very sanguinary contest which continued all the day, he was forced at length to yield to the enemy's superiority, and retired to Zubiri, in order that he might be succoured by other divisions.

Meanwhile the 2nd Division at the pass of Maya, unconscious of what was passing at Ronces Valles, received the enemy's attack with heroic firmness, and after one of the most sanguinary contests ever recorded, which lasted from 11 o'clock in the morning until 7 in the evening, they succeeded in repulsing the enemy and maintained their post. The defence of the pass had been specially intrusted to the 1st Brigade of this division, comprised of the 50th, 71st and 92nd regiments: these troops were encamped along the ridge of the heights of Maya, and were supported by the 34th regiment and some light troops of the other brigade posted a little to their right, in which quarter the attack first commenced.

No sooner had the enemy reached the heights than the 34th and 50th regiments charged them with the most devoted heroism, but were on the point of being surrounded, when the 92nd regiment arrived to their support, and the contest then became one of the most terrific ever known, insomuch that one wing of the 92nd regiment was almost exterminated, being for a very considerable time, with only 370 men, opposed to a French division of more than 2,000, whose attacks they sustained until their number had been reduced to 120 men, and all their officers excepting two had fallen or been borne from the field badly wounded.

These troops were at length so reduced that they were ordered to withdraw, while the 71st regiment with the remainder of the 92nd faced the enemy, whose numbers (notwithstanding their killed and wounded lay in heaps) seemed scarcely diminished: these regiments behaved with equal gallantry and devotedness, covering the retreat of the rest, who were ordered to take post behind a rock a little in rear of the pass, where they were shortly afterwards joined by the 82nd regiment, and subsequently by a whole brigade of the 7th Division: they then became the assailants, and drove the enemy back to the pass, until quite exhausted from the arduous exertions of this trying day, they were at length allowed to rest from the pursuit and lay down under arms; but at 10 o'clock in the evening accounts having reached Sir Rowland Hill of the attack at Roncesvalles, and the consequent retrograde movement made by the 4th Division, he was obliged to order his corps to retire from the heights they had so gallantly defended, and after marching all night through the valley of Bastan, they encamped on the morning of the 26th on the heights of Barrueta, in rear of Elizondo, the enemy shewing no inclination to follow or interrupt them.

July 26th. During the night, Sir Thomas Picton having heard of the events in front, the 3rd Division fell under arms, and at daylight this morning moved to the support of the 4th Division at Zubiri. Their arrival was very seasonable, as it enabled Sir Lowry Cole to keep the enemy in check at Zubiri almost all the day, and thus give time for the other divisions of our army in their isolated position to become acquainted with passing events, and for Lord Wellington to direct such operations and movements as he might deem requisite. Towards the evening, however, they both retired upon Pampeluna, and General Picton with the 3rd Division took post at Gorea, upon some rising ground about two miles on the right of Huarte, and four from the walls of Pampeluna, where he threw up some works, planted his artillery, and resolved to give the enemy battle: while the 4th Division passed over to the left, and was posted upon the heights above the village of Huarte, and in face of the mountains of Sauroren, to which place the French army had advanced, and from whence Marshal Soult wrote his dispatches to Buonaparte, detailing the operations of his army to this date.

27th. This morning Lord Wellington inspected the positions occupied by Generals Picton and Cole, and resolved to concentrate the whole army on this ground: the 2nd, 6th, 7th and Light Divisions were accordingly directed to pass the mountains of Lantz, and form on the left of the 4th Division, while orders were sent to the rear to bring up the cavalry under Sir Stapleton Cotton, who were to take post on the right of the 3rd Division. When the news of these operations reached St. Sebastian, Sir Thomas Graham suspended the siege, embarked the battering train, and stood in readiness with his two divisions to move as circumstances might require.

There was a very awful storm of thunder and lightning this afternoon, the effect of which was truly sublime, as the troops were crossing the mountains. Marshal Soult had been all day assembling his troops on the towering heights in front of us, and they were at intervals engaged with the 4th Division, disputing the possession of some posts between their respective positions,

This was a very beautiful morning. It was about nine o'clock when I joined the division at Gorea, having been sent on duty to the rear: the cavalry were now coming up, and as they arrived were posted on outright. The action had commenced, and the gallant 4th division was enveloped in fire and smoke on the mountains. Marshal Soult having assembled on the heights of Sauroren about thirty thousand men early in the morning, attacked this devoted corps, which had already suffered so much that it could scarcely occupy the extent of ground which it was necessary to cover: and the 3rd Division, incapable of moving from the position they occupied, saw with sorrow and alarm all the enemy's efforts directed against a corps which it was not possible for them to succour.

However, the orders given by Lord Wellington brought to their support the 6th Division, which had marched from Sant Estevan on the 26th, and now, by joining at the instant the attack commenced, saved the remnant of the brave 4th Division. The particulars of their interesting arrival, so unlooked-for by the enemy, and which was not known even to us until they were actually engaged, were related to me in the following manner. Last night they encamped in the mountains, scarcely knowing where they were, but supposing themselves to be in the enemy's rear.

This morning they continued their march prepared for whatever they might meet, when they discovered at a distance the 4th Division bivouac, and while they were endeavouring to ascertain whether it was a French or English camp, the bivouac was suddenly broken up, and the whole force seen falling under arms. It was then discovered that they were British, and that the enemy's columns were advancing to attack them. The division now hastening to their support, (in crossing a deep ravine which lay between them) very unexpectedly fell in with a strong division of the enemy in full march down the ravine, anticipating no opposition the light companies and Highland regiments were immediately engaged, and charging them with their usual impetuosity, drove them back with great loss, and thus afforded the 4th Division most seasonable support—the enemy's object in this movement having been to turn their position and surround them.

Marshal Soult, however, renewed his attack upon the 4th Division, determined to carry the hill which juts out from the rocky heights behind Huarte, and with this view, as fast as one column was repulsed another was ordered to advance, until the whole of the enemy had been driven down the hill three successive times with great slaughter: still, however, unwilling to yield, and knowing of what importance this position was to us, as our last refuge on this side of Pampeluna, he ordered all his troops once more to advance, and, it was said, offered instant promotion to every officer, and two Spanish *doubloons* (about £8 sterling) to every soldier who should succeed in forcing the British position and reach the plain, and that forty French officers sheathing their swords took muskets and led this last attack as a forlorn hope. In a contest in which so much devotedness was shewn on one side, and so much firmness on the other, the slaughter became terrific—the space of ground between the contending lines was already strewed with the unhappy victims of this unyielding strife, and it was now to be *heaped* with slain.

The French division advanced under cries of "*Vive l'Empereur!*" while the British and Portuguese waited for them with coolness and resolution, reserving their fire until the enemy had approached within a few paces, and then firing and charging them almost at the same instant, drove them down the hill in every direction; so that Marshal Soult was at length obliged to call off his men, and desist from such murderous assaults. Within these four hours he could not have sacrificed less than 4,000 men: our loss, too, was grievously severe. All the regiments in the 4th and 6th Divisions (Portuguese as well as British) were dreadfully cut up, and many distinguished officers had fallen, amongst whom was Colonel Le Mesurier, of the Portuguese service, who for some time commanded at Almeida.

Lord Wellington was on the spot directing the several movements, and encouraging the men. Colonel Gordon, *aide-de-camp* to the Field Marshal, was severely wounded, and His Serene Highness the Prince of Orange had a horse shot under him. Had the enemy succeeded in his attacks and carried this position, the army would inevitably have been divided, and it is not likely that the French Marshal would have rested satisfied with the relief of Pampeluna, when their park of 150 guns invited him to Vittoria, by recapturing which he would effectually have blighted the laurels of Vittoria, and retrieved the honour of the French arms. Nothing but views of such a nature, it was thought, could justify the sacrifice of lives which was made.

This afternoon an extraordinary thing happened in front of our division. A young French officer with a detachment of men entirely unsupported, ran cheering down the mountain and attacked our piquets. A party of the 88th regiment was immediately ordered out, one of which shot the French officer, and his men instantly retired. They were afterwards allowed to return with a flag of truce and take off his body, and we understood that he had acted entirely without orders. Nothing could be more extraordinary than the situation of the garrison of Pampeluna at this time: the army which had fought its way forty miles over the Pyrenees for its relief, had now been beaten before their face, and literally under the very walls of the town; they had been continually making signals to their friends on the heights, the distance being scarcely four miles from the walls to the mountains. The Spanish army continued to invest the town. We encamped on the position at Gorea, and I pitched my tent upon the green near to General Picton's quarters. All the mountains for many leagues round were covered with camp fires.

29th. The 2nd, light and 7th Divisions having all joined and taken post on our left, and our cavalry also having closed up from the rear, the French Marshal, without attaining any one of his objects, gave up the contest, and like his poor friends, whose conduct at Vittoria he had so much condemned, was obliged himself to submit to a similar defeat The whole of this day was accordingly spent by him in making preparations to retrace his steps into France. Lord Wellington came down to the right wing today, and rode over the position at Gorea and through the camp of the 3rd Division: he looked very much elated, and was heard to say, that nothing but a spirited pursuit now remained to complete the victory. I was very near falling into the hands of the enemy this afternoon, having gone some distance beyond our cavalry outlying piquet in search of supplies. Their foraging parties were in that part of the country, and the poor inhabitants of the villages were in a state of the greatest alarm.

RETREAT OF THE ENEMY
30th July, 1813.

Lord Wellington having made the necessary preparations for the attack, early this morning the 3rd, 4th and 6th Divisions were ordered to advance and drive the enemy from the mountains of Sauroren, where they now made but a slight resistance, the French Marshal's main object being to make good his retreat into France. Sir Rowland Hill having advanced upon their right so as to occupy the post of La

Zarza, which exceedingly cramped and impeded their movements, they attacked him in that position with above twenty thousand men, and this became the scene of a sanguinary conflict, which lasted all the afternoon.

The remains of the 34th, 92nd, 71st and 50th regiments were again engaged, and though they were forced to quit the village of La Zarza, the post to which they retired was at least an equal obstacle to the movements of the enemy, as all their attacks upon that post failed, so that at night they were obliged to desist, and the two forces encamped in face of each other. While the right wing of the French army had been thus engaged, their left and centre (weakened by the severe conflict which had taken place) offered but a comparatively feeble resistance to the divisions to which they were opposed, nevertheless, the contest here was still far from being bloodless, as it was found necessary to take several of the heights by storm, and some of our regiments in the 3rd Division suffered considerably; but they succeeded in making many prisoners, and in every direction drove the enemy before them.

31st. The French were in full retreat this morning pursued by our divisions through the passes of the mountains. Sir Rowland Hill falling in with a division of them strongly posted, he was once more engaged, and drove them from their post, making many prisoners and capturing a large convoy of provisions destined for Pampeluna.

August 1st. The 3rd and 6th Divisions marched for Roncesvalles, the 2nd division into the valley of Bastan, and to its old post at the pass of Maya, while the 7th Division under Lord Dalhousie, and the Light Division under Baron Alten, pursued the enemy by Echalar. Thus had the French (after seven days severe fighting) been forced to return to the lines they had so exultingly left, with the loss of about fifteen thousand men. Our loss in all these actions (which although they occasionally bear different names are generally classed into one great battle, called "The Pyrenees") was near six thousand men, a melancholy list, which threw many families in England and Portugal into mourning.

Major-General Pack was wounded on the 30th, upon which General Pakenham (the Adjutant-General) was sent to command the 6th Division, until the operations were ended, when he was relieved by General Colville. Lord Wellington now wrote his dispatches, and the Prince of Orange was selected to carry them to England. Headquarters were fixed at Lesaca.

	Killed	Wounded	Missing
British	381	2,449	404
Portuguese	167	918	50
Spanish	26	167	11
	574	3,534	465

Independent of the loss on the 30th, which amounted to 81 killed and 469 wounded of the British, the loss of the Portuguese being nearly double.

August 2nd, The 2nd Division resuming their old position at the pass of Maya, had the melancholy task of burying their dead which had been left upon the heights since the battle of the 25th; but the camp of this division being literally spread along the graves of their comrades so recently killed, the 3rd and 6th Divisions were ordered to exchange posts with Sir Rowland Hill, who in consequence marched his division to Ronces Valles.

10th. The 6th Division under the command of Major-General Colville, and the 3rd Division under Major-General Brisbane (General Picton having obtained leave to go to England), moving into the valley of Bastan, occupied Elizondo, Ariscon, Maya, and the heights above the valley, where it fell to the lot of the 91st regiment to encamp among the graves of the 92nd, Marshal Soult having thus received a repulse for the present, and our army being posted nearly as before the action, Sir Thomas Graham relanded the battering train, and in conjunction with the fleet resumed the siege of St. Sebastian.

12th. Being quartered in Ariscon, I rode this day to the camp on the heights of Maya, to see the fertile valleys of the Great Nation! From these heights the view into France of the ancient province of Gascony is beautiful beyond all description, and what was particularly cheering to us, we had a fine view over the Bay of Biscay, which our soldiers called the high road to England. From this time until the 31st nothing important occurred.

STORMING OF ST. SEBASTIAN, AND BATTLE OF IRUN,
31st August 1813.

The siege of the very important fortress of St. Sebastian had been carrying on since the early part of July, by the 5th Division of the army, under the immediate directions of Lieutenant-General Graham, and it was now to be brought to a close by storming the town. Lieutenant-General Sir James Leith having recently arrived from England, had resumed his command of the 5th Division, and the necessary dispositions being made by Sir Thomas Graham, the town was attacked this day at 11 o'clock in the forenoon, and after one of the most desperate struggles which have occurred during the war, was captured, and the garrison drove into the citadel.

The enemy made a most determined resistance, and the obstacles to which our troops were exposed were such as to require all their characteristic firmness and bravery to overcome. Sir Thomas Graham in his dispatches detailing the operations of the storm, says, "that at one point the difficulties were so great, that no man outlived the attempt to surmount them."

Lieutenant-General Leith lost an arm, Major-General Robinson commanding a brigade was badly wounded, and the division suffered so severely that some of the battalions were almost annihilated, one of them at the close of the storm being found under the command of a young lieutenant, all the field-officers and captains having fallen. In the 2nd battalion of the 59th regiment, out of 24 officers but five escaped unhurt.

The 1st regiment (Royals) suffered very severely, as did also the artillery and engineers. Colonel Sir Richard Fletcher, commanding officer of the latter, was killed. The operations of the army were aided by the fleet on that side of the town near the sea, and for whose services Sir Thomas Graham acknowledged himself much indebted. While this was going on at St. Sebastian, Marshal Soult attacked that part of our line where the Spaniards were posted, under their General Don Giron, between Iran and Echalar.

The French at first gained some advantages, and even pressed on towards the neighbourhood of Lesaca, so that the 1st and Light Divisions moved to the support of the Spaniards; but Lord Wellington perceiving that they alone would in this instance be able to cope with the enemy, would not allow the British troops to take part in the engagement further than to threaten the enemy's flanks.

After a sharp contest, in which the Spaniards sustained great loss, they succeeded in driving back the enemy, and obliged him to repass the Bidassoa.

Killed.	Wounded.	Missing.	
British	571	1,103	41
Portuguese	189	594	4
	760	1,697	45

September 1st. this morning the 3rd Division marched from Ariscon to Echalar (as it was presumed) to succour the Spaniards in the event of a more serious attack. In the afternoon I rode through the Spanish camp or bivouac upon the heights, which was certainly the finest and best arranged I ever saw: it formed three distinct and regular lines, the space between each being a fine beaten grass-*plat* strewed with leaves, and kept as clean as the Calle Mayor at Madrid.

3rd. The enemy shewing no disposition to renew his attack upon the Spaniards, we returned to the valley of Bastan.

8th The citadel of St. Sebastian, into which the garrison retired when the town was stormed, now surrendered, and thus closed the perilous and arduous services of the 5th Division against this fortress. Pampeluna, which it was the plan of Lord Wellington to starve into submission, continued closely invested by a large force of Spaniards.

October 7th. This morning we were all turned out of our quarters and cantonments to camp on the heights of Zugarrimurdi, between the passes of Echalar and Maya, our piquets extending down the mountain into the woods, in face of the enemy's position on the frontiers, and about a hundred paces to the front of the village of Zugarrimurdr, where General Brisbane was put up; while the 6th Division continued to occupy the heights of Maya, and the 7th Division those of Echalar. From this time until the evening of the 13th a series of partial but very severe engagements occurred, in which the Spanish and Portuguese troops were principally employed.

13th. A division of Spanish troops attacked and carried a redoubt at the foot of the high and rocky mountain of Le Rhone, not far from the village of Zarra. The Spanish General Sir John D—— had a horse shot under him, and was himself wounded in the affair. This officer, who is a native of Scotland, has in the course of a few years experienced a series of extraordinary adventures. When the Spanish revolution broke out he raised a regiment called the Legion of Estremadura, of which he was made Colonel by the Spanish *Junta*, and thus attached himself to the Spanish service.

His bravery and apparent devotedness to the cause, together with the attachment and partiality which he manifested towards everything Spanish, recommended him to the notice of the Spanish government, so that he was soon advanced to a command with the rank of Brigadier-General, and became so distinguished that the town of Seville presented him with the sword of the famous Pizarro, which he wears to this day. In one of his attacks against the enemy at Seville, he had been wounded and taken prisoner, on which occasion the French general in command suffered him to be most shamefully insulted and severely beaten, a treatment which he could never forget; and it was singular enough that upon his joining Lord Wellington last week, he happened to be posted in that part of our line where the same French general was opposed to him, upon learning which he sent a challenge to the Frenchman, offering to fight him in single combat in face of the two respective forces, but received no answer thereto. Sir John D——— is now in high favour at the Spanish court, and has been invested by the King of Spain with the Government of Seville.

When the division marched from Ariscon on the 7th from being attached to the divisional staff as well as the brigade of General Brisbane, I became entitled to quarters, and consequently obtained the same in Zugarrimurdi. At 10 o'clock at night on the 8th, however, I was turned out by a Portuguese colonel, and obliged to pitch my tent in a field outside the village. As it was a very dark and wet night it put me to great trouble and inconvenience, until the general was pleased on the 10th to give directions for my being provided with another place, which was done with great difficulty, the village being quite full. I have noticed this circumstance so particularly, because it was really a thing of some consequence to me, having a stable for my horses and a roof over my head during the five weeks we remained in this position.

The weather throughout this time was so wet and stormy that it was with difficulty the army on the heights could keep the field. One night a great part of the camp was inundated, and the brigade obliged more than once to change its ground, in order to seek shelter from the hills. In the camp of the 4th Division too, which was in a very exposed position, almost every tent was blown down for several nights successively, and great privation endured. The disputes and difficulties which were constantly arising about quarters are not amongst the least of the annoyances to which officers on service are exposed, and which no regulations of a commander-in-chief or general officer can altogether obviate, it being impossible to provide for every contingency of this nature which occurs during the active operations of an army.

18th. Buonaparte was on this day defeated in the grand battle of Leipsic in Saxony, by the Emperor of Russia and King of Prussia.

31st Pampeluna having been reduced by famine to a state of great distress, was surrendered, and the Spanish troops employed in the blockade being ordered to join the army in the field, preparations were now made for the invasion of France.

November 4th. We heard that the Emperors of Russia and Austria and the King of Prussia were advancing to the Rhine, and that Buonaparte was hastening to Paris. Lord Wellington was about this time almost constantly occupied in reconnoitring the enemy's fortified position; he was a long time one morning on some rising ground at Zugarrimurdi, making observations with his glass, which was carried after him by an orderly dragoon.

8th. Lieutenant-General Sir Rowland Hill having arrived with his corps in the valley of Bastan from Roncesvalles, which pass the snow had closed, the army now closed up and was formed into columns for the attack.

Left Column	Near the Sea.
Lieutenant-Gen. Sir John Hope, K. B.	
1st Division	Major-General Campbell,
5th Division	Major-General Oswald.
Right Column	Valley of Bastan.
Lieutenant-Gen. Sir Rowland Hill, K. B.	
2nd Division	Lieutenant-Gen. Sir W. Stewart,
Spanish Corps	Don Pablo Morillo
Centre Corps.	
Encamped on the heights of Maya, Zugarrimuidi, Echalar, &c.	
Marshal Sir W, C. Beresford, KL B.	
3rd Division	Major-General Colville,
6th Division	Lieutenant-Gen. Sir H. Clinton,
4th Division	Lieutenant-Gen. Sir G. L. Cole,
7th Division	Major-Gen. Le Cour (Portug.)
Light Division	Major-Gen. Chas Baron Alton.

A brigade newly formed, under the command of Major-General

Lord Aylmer, was posted near the left column, and the cavalry and Spanish armies at different points of the line.

Soon after midnight the army having fallen under arms without the sound of either trumpet or drum, began to descend the Pyrenean mountains by moonlight, by the passes of Maya, Zugarrimurdi, Echalar and Irun, and during the early part of the morning the several divisions were concentrating at the foot of the heights in the plains of Zarra and Ahhou, preparatory to the attack to be made at the break of day; whiles the baggage remained on the mountains, the tents standing and fires burning with the view of deceiving the enemy.

This grand movement was made with a quietness and secrecy almost incredible. The Portuguese brigade of the 3rd Division under Major-General Power, cantoned in Zugarrimurdi, turned out about half an hour after midnight, and shortly after the two British brigades under Major-General Brisbane and Colonel Keane descending from the heights. passed by and rested in a meadow on the skirts of the village. About this time we heard a gentle tinkling of arms on our right, which we supposed to be the 6th Division descending to their ground: by mistake a few fires were lighted, but they were soon extinguished; and so profound a stillness prevailed, that at Zugarrimurdi, while six thousand troops were passing under arms, their silent march was truly impressive.

Everything having been packed, and all persons prepared for duty, the scene was altogether so interesting, that it was impossible to resist the anxious feelings which it was calculated to excite. The village clocks striking the hours as they passed, increased the general anxiety for the break of day, when a signal was to be given for the attack, as our situation could not then for a moment be concealed, our very columns being in the woods within a few paces of the enemy's piquets. At length a grey streak, the harbinger of day appeared in the east, and almost instantly a cannon posted on the heights of Le Rhone was fired: this was the signal for a general attack, and all our columns rising from their ambushment, moved forward, when the French (taken by. surprise) were seen running to their posts in all directions.

The 4th Division which was nearest the enemy, now stormed a redoubt in front of Zarra, and in less than fifteen minutes this outwork was taken; the whole British line then advanced and drove in the enemy's piquets: a movement was made upon the village of Zarra by the 3rd, 4th and 7th Divisions, supported by the Spanish army, while the light division was seen moving over the heights of Le Rhone: all these forces continuing to advance, passed the frontiers, and moved against the centre of the enemy's fortified position, while the corps under Sir Rowland Hill from the valley of Bastan, and the 6th Division from the pass of Maya, marching against the enemy's left, prepared to attack the positions and fortified camps near Anhou.

A cannonade which sounded like thunder, was heard at intervals on our left, where Sir John Hope with the 1st and 5th Divisions was moving upon St, Jean de Luz, by the high road leading to Bayonne. By 10 o'clock, the village of Zarra had been taken, and the army was crossing the river Nivelle, which in its passage from the Nive to St. Jean de Luz, runs past that village at the foot of the enemy's grand fortified position. About this time Lord Wellington had taken post on a little eminence, but shortly after he galloped through Zarra, and passing the Nivelle, near the village, moved with the 4th and 7th Divisions: his staff and attendants on this occasion were so numerous, that at a distance I mistook them for a regiment of cavalry.

The 4th Division under Sir Lowry Cole and a Spanish force under General Giron now attacked and carried a position beyond the river, somewhat resembling the Arapiles in the plains of Salamanca; after which they made a short pause, while the 7th Division stormed a redoubt on a very high hill immediately on their right, which here seemed to be the key to the enemy's principal position: this redoubt had no sooner been stormed than we saw Lord Wellington moving in that direction, and he passed us as we were standing amongst the wounded and the dead on the hill which the 4th Division had just taken, and where I observed the 40th regiment had suffered very severely.

The following were amongst the officers of Lord Wellington's staff: Sir Edward M. Pakenham, Adjutant General; Sir George Murray, Quarter master-General; Lord Fitzroy Somerset, Military Secretary; His Serene Highness the Prince of Orange, *Aide-de-camp*; Marquis of Worcester, *Aide-de-camp*; Don Miguel Alava, Spanish service. He was followed by about seventy other officers and escorted by a, squadron of staff cavalry with their swords drawn. In passing a defile they were exposed to a fire of musketry, but Lord Wellington appeared to disregard it altogether, although his horse mended its pace a little.

We followed the staff to the hill, which commands a most extensive view on every side. At this moment Marshal Beresford came galloping up from the 3rd Division, which we had left passing the Nivelle near Zarra, and ascending the heights through the woods. This division under the command of the Hon. Charles Colville, after driving in the enemy's outposts in front of Zugarrimurdi, and co-operating in the attack at Zarra, passed the Nivelle near that town, and moving through the woods on the right of the 7th Division forced its way with its usual promptitude to the enemy's grand position, where it arrived before the rest of the line.

The right brigade under Colonel Keane of the 60th regiment supported by the left and Portuguese under Generals Brisbane and Power, forthwith proceeded to storm a strong redoubt situated about the centre of the enemy's line of fortifications and near the road leading to the town of St. Pe, in which the brigade suffered very much, particularly the gallant little battalion of the 87th regiment under Lieutenant-Colonel Gough, who was wounded, and the 94th under Lieutenant-Colonel Lloyd, who unhappily was killed, being shot through the body as he was leading and encouraging his men to the storm: on receiving his wound he staggered a few paces, and tossing his sword into the air, exclaimed, "It's all over with me:" he was instantly borne into a cottage near at hand, where breathed his last, and was that same hour buried under a large tree, together with an ensign of the 87th regiment, on the side of the very same hill which, but a few days previous to the action, he had in the course of conversation on the heights of Zugarrimurdi, pointed out to me as the post his regiment would probably have to attack.

While the 3rd Division were thus engaged, the 6th under Sir Henry Clinton were storming the redoubts and entrenchments at that point of the line near Anhou, where a very severe conflict was maintained for some time; but our brave battalions resolving upon victory, at length gained the ridge, and the enemy's huts were in a short time seen blazing like beacons all along that part of the line. The range of heights directly in front of us, the crests of which were crowned with French infantry, had now to be attacked. Lord Wellington (who was stationed on the hill, directing everything in person) accordingly ordered the 7th Division to move by one road, and the 4th by another parallel with it, each supported by a very large force of Spaniards.

These troops began to ascend the heights under a galling fire from the enemy, who on their approach suddenly fell into line, and their bugles sounding, a volley from right to left was fired upon the advancing columns: in a moment the enemy's line disappeared: our men now cheered, and continued their exertions to gain the summit of this stupendous hill; but before this could be accomplished (to our astonishment) the hostile line reappeared, and crowning the heights as before, their bugles were again sounded, and another volley fired: they then disappeared, and our troops gaining the ridge, drove them down the other side of the hill.

About this time we heard a very harmonious sound of bugles, and soon caught a view of the Light Division under Major-General Charles Baron Alten, which had moved over the mountains of Le Rhone, and were storming a strong redoubt about a mile on our left, where the whole of the French 88th regiment, by which it was defended, were made prisoners.—The enemy now fled from hill to hill, pursued by our victorious troops. The 3rd Division being ordered to march upon St Pe, came up with the enemy's rear-guard at that town in the evening, and a sharp affair which ensued, closed the operations of the day.

The baggage of the army, ordered to halt on the heights of the Pyrenees, had been packed and loaded ever since daylight; descending now from the heights they quitted Spain, and marched over the field of battle in the evening; but the moon not rising until late in the night, a great part thereof went astray and did not join the divisions until the next day. I encamped for the night upon the green of St. Pe: the 3rd Division were at bivouac in the woods near that place, with the 7th and 4th Divisions on their left and the 6th on their right. Thus ended the battle of the Nivelle, which (if not the most sounding of Lord Wellington's victories) was at least one of the boldest and most interesting operations of the Peninsular war, as the enemy occupied a tract of country not only exceedingly strong by nature, but fortified in a most extraordinary manner, every hill being crowned with a redoubt.

Their right rested on the sea coast near St. Jean de Luz, and their left on the River Nive near Cambo. The strength of the works which they had constructed at these two points made it impossible to turn either their right or left; Lord Wellington therefore resorted to the bold measure of attacking their centre, which was a perfect chain of redoubts and fortifications. The nature of this engagement, and of the ground upon which it was fought, did not admit of the cavalry being brought into action. The artillery was actively and warmly engaged as usual. There fell into our hands on this occasion, 51 pieces of cannon;

1500 prisoners, and a large quantity of ammunition, besides which, the enemy (it was calculated) lost upwards of three thousand men.

That very distinguished officer Colonel Barnard of the 95th (rifle corps) was so severely wounded as not to be expected to survive.

This battle bore several different names, according to the respective situations of the several corps engaged: for instance, the left column called it the battle of St. Jean de Luz; the right column, the battle of the Valle de Bastan; the 3rd Division, the battle of St. Pe; the 4th Division, the battle of Zarra; the 6th Division, the battle of Anhou: because these corps had been principally engaged at these several points. In England it was at first called the battle of St. Pe, because Lord Wellington dated his dispatches from that town; but it has since, very properly, been designated the battle of the Nivelle, from the name of the little river which the whole army had to pass in its advance against the enemy's grand fortified positions. The Marquis of Worcester was appointed to carry the dispatches to England,

RETURN OF THE KILLED, WOUNDED AND MISSING
IN THE BATTLE OF THE NIVELLE.

	Killed.	Wounded.	Missing.
British	277	1,777	58
Portuguese	66	501	15
	343	2,278	73

11th, The French continuing their retreat to the Nive, withdrew their right from St. Jean de Luz, retiring by the high road into their entrenched camp under the works of Bayonne. Much rain having fallen during the night and early part of the morning, the roads through the woods were very bad, by which the movements of the stores and baggage were much impeded, and it became difficult in some positions to supply the troops. About 10 o'clock at night I found the division at bivouac in a wood. General Brisbane was under a tree, without tent or baggage, there being no other shelter but such as the trees of the forest afforded. The arrival of a few tents however with the supplies was some relief, and my tent being amongst them, I encamped in the wood.

12th. This morning the baggage came up, and the troops moved forward about 10 o'clock. The French army having passed the Nive, and destroyed the bridges over it, now took post between that river

125

and the Adour, so as to cover Bayonne. We encamped this evening about a mile from the Nive, and not far from the village of Arrauntz. The rain fell in such torrents that it penetrated our tents, and put us to great trouble and inconvenience: mine having been inundated, I was obliged to rise in the night and leave it. The weather continued so wet that on the 18th we were allowed to go into quarters, and the 3rd Division occupied Arrauntz, where I got into a house without either inhabitants or furniture. The head-quarters of the army were stationed at St Jean de Luz.

December. About this time some severe and painful examples were made in order to preserve the strictest discipline and a due observance of the orders issued upon our entering the French territory, which strictly prohibited everything which might subject the inhabitants of the country to unnecessary inconvenience. The Spanish army, however, resolved to have some revenge, and shewing a determination not to submit to the severe discipline imposed on the British and Portuguese troops, was sent back into the Pyrenees for the present It was about this period that by the advance of the grand allied armies from the north of Europe, Holland was emancipated from the yoke of Buonaparte, and the hereditary Prince of Orange quitting this army for Holland embarked one morning at St. Jean de Luz under a royal salute: a British force under Lieutenant-General Sir Thomas Graham (who after the storming of St Sebastian had resigned his command to Sir John Hope) was also sent from England to assist the Dutch in recovering their fortresses and establishing their independence.

BATTLES OF THE NIVE.
From the 9th to 13th December, 1813.

The battles and operations connected with the passage of the river Nive, which commenced on the morning of the 9th and were not ended until the evening of the 13th December, 1813, occurred under circumstances of peculiar difficulty. Since the battle of the Nivelle, the army had taken up its quarters in as connected a line as was found practicable from the sea-side near Bidart to the banks of the Nive near Cambo. As the extent of this line was at least twenty English miles, and as each division, and particularly those in the centre, upon being concentrated for operations, formed a separate corps, the greatest generalship was requisite to post them properly and move them severally to each others' support as it became necessary to meet the manoeuvres and operations of the enemy.

At 10 o'clock in the evening of the 8th the train of pontoons passed through Arrruntz as quietly as possible, under cover of the night, and orders were given for the troops to turn out three hours before daylight. Accordingly about 3 o'clock on the morning of the 9th the divisions fell under arms, and began to concentrate. At day-break Lieutenant-General Sir Rowland Hill with his corps passed the river by a deep ford which had been found above Cambo, flanked the enemy's left by Urcuri, and forced his way into the great road which passes by there from St. Jean de Pied du Port to Bayonne, while the 6th Division passed the river by a pontoon bridge laid down at Ustaritz, and attacked the enemy's position about the village of Ville Franque, supported by the 3rd Division, which had also marched to Ustaritz, and passed the river by the pontoon bridge.

Soon after daybreak Lord Wellington, attended by his staff, passed through Arrauntz from St. Jean de Luz: he wore a large light drab-coloured cloak, which made him very conspicuous; and it is singular that at this action Marshal Soult (it was said) wore a similar one. The attack made by the 6th Division co-operating with the movements of the 2nd obliged the enemy to retire into his entrenchments and works near Bayonne, after a sharp engagement in which both parties sustained considerable loss. Sir Rowland Hill and Sir Henry Clinton with the troops under their command remained on that side of the Nive, but the 3rd Division being ordered to recross the river in the evening, we returned to Arrauntz, a part of our division occupying Ustaritz. Lord Wellington passed the night at Marshal Beresford's *château* near Ustaritz.

10th. The divisions were all under arms at the alarm-posts at break of day; but everything continued quiet with us until about 10 o'clock, when the division was hastily moved off to our left, and shortly after-wards the light division became severely engaged near a large *château* about four miles off between us and the coast. Lord Wellington gal-loped through Arrauntz almost covered with mud, inquiring for the nearest way to the *château*, followed at some distance by the Adjutant General, Sir Edward Pakenham, and the staff, whom his lordship had left at least a mile in the rear. Sir John Hope had been suddenly at-tacked on the coast with an immense force, which it appears the en-emy had drawn from his left and passed through Bayonne during the night.

The contest was maintained by the 5th Division supported by the

1st with the greatest valour, and after a most sanguinary struggle the enemy were repulsed and ultimately driven back upon Bayonne with great loss; but not without a painful loss on our part also, nearly two thousand of our brave fellows having fallen. Lieutenant-General Sir John Hope was wounded, and Major-General Robinson was carried off severely hurt. Had the enemy succeeded in the attack upon our troops on the coast (which he was very near doing) and taken St. Jean de Luz, we must all have been driven back into the Pyrenees and have perished: the whole of our divisions were drawing subsistence chiefly from our magazines at St. Jean de Luz, while from the severity of the season and badness of the weather, the roads were almost impassable, and the greatest difficulties experienced throughout the whole of these operations.

At night two German regiments in the French service deserted to us from the French lines, and they were sent to the coast to be embarked for England on their way to Germany. It proved a very wet and dreary night, and most of our troops were obliged to lay out without baggage on the heaths in face of the enemy.

11th. The enemy had been so roughly dealt with yesterday that they made but little noise today; but there was a good deal of skirmishing at different parts of the line, and they still appeared in force in face of Sir John Hope's column by the sea-side.

12th. The French renewed their attack upon Sir John Hope's column and the light division, trying to regain the ground they had lost on the 10th, but were repulsed in every direction. Early in the afternoon the 6th Division received orders to recross the Nive to the support of the 3rd and 7th Divisions, in face of which the enemy now shewed a large force, and their position was as usual strengthened with redoubts. Marshal Soult was practising some grand manoeuvres this evening with the view of deceiving Lord Wellington, knowing well that every stratagem was necessary to ensure any success against such opponents.

13th. Marshal Soult having in the course of the night marched through Bayonne almost all his forces, which had for the last three days been opposed to us on the coast as well as on our left and centre, very early this morning moved out of his entrenchments with forty thousand men, and made a most severe attack upon the corps of Lieutenant General Sir Rowland Hill, which had been left alone on the right banks of the Nive. This was a most masterly movement on the part of the enemy, and it required all the bravery and devotedness of Sir Rowland Hill's heroic band to counteract its effects: the crisis was awful beyond description: our brave troops assembled in haste to the number of about eight thousand, and (resolved to emulate the deeds of former days) stood firm to this unequal conflict.

No sooner had this movement become known than orders were sent to the 6th, 3rd and 4th Divisions to hasten to the support of the 2nd, and these troops were all the early part of the morning passing the river by the pontoon bridge, which (to facilitate the communication) had been brought from Ustaritz to Heroditz; but before our arrival the enemy had been repulsed and driven, back into his works with the loss of two pieces of cannon and five hundred prisoners, besides killed and wounded: our loss was of course very severe, Major-General Barnes of the British, and Brigadier-General Ashworth of the Portuguese service were wounded, and the regiments in general of the 2nd division sadly cut up

Our division joining about 10 o'clock, was posted on a height not far from the river where the light troops of the 2nd Division were skirmishing with those of the enemy all the afternoon. I was for about twenty minutes exposed to their fire this evening in passing a ravine enfiladed by the fire of their light troops) in a wood, and should probably have fallen into their hands but for the assistance of a piquet of the 2nd Division, who most readily advanced and extricated me from my perilous situation.

At night the enemy called in his light troops, and the action ceased. Our division slept upon the hill where they had been posted, but I returned to Arrauntz. Lord Wellington and Marshal Beresford were fording the river near Heroditz at the time I passed. The 4th Division were re-crossing the river all the evening by the pontoon bridge.

RETURN OF THE KILLED, WOUNDED AND MISSING
FROM THE 9TH TO THE 13TH OF DECEMBER INCLUSIVE.

	Killed.	Wounded.	Missing.
British	279	2,186	209
Portuguese	361	1,689	294
Spanish	5	21	—
	645	3,896	503

14th. Lord Wellington returned to St Jean de Luz this morning and the 3rd Division re-crossed the river to its former cantonments at Arrauntz, the 2nd and 6th Divisions occupying the ground taken from the enemy between the Nive and the Adour. Thus ended the operations connected with the passage of the River Nive, which although they may seem to bear nothing on the face of them to stamp them with the character of a decisive victory, had nevertheless in a military point of view been very important in their results. It is painful to advert to the severity of our loss, more than four thousand of our brave troops having been killed or wounded.

15th. This afternoon our division was ordered to cross the river at Ustaritz, and at night we were put up at Yatzu, where we halted three days. I had here a fireplace in my room, which was a great treat.

19th. The division inarched to Urcuri and joined the 2nd Division, which was in front of a division of the enemy near Hasparen.

27th. The brigade of Hussars under the command of Major-General Lord Edward Somerset coming up about this time and turning us out of our quarters, I got put up in a cottage near Hasparen, to which place the division advanced. The regiments generally assembled at daylight every morning at the alarm posts, as in their cantonments the troops were very much. dispersed.

1814

January 4th. The troops were all under arms at the alarm-posts this morning, and the baggage all ordered to the rear.

5th. During the night the 7th Division had been moved up to our support, and at daylight the baggage was ordered into the high road. Lord Wellington arrived at Hasparen this morning, and our old General Sir Thomas Picton rejoined the division from England.

6th. This morning our troops were all at the alarm-posts again before daylight, but no movement of importance occurred.

7th. This afternoon Sir Thomas Picton came up to the hill where the troops were all under arms, and we began to move forward, upon which the enemy called, in their piquets and retired pursued by our brigade until dark, when we took up our quarters in the *"Maisons des Campagnes"* which they had left. About this time His Royal Highness The Duc d'Angoulesme, one of the French Princes of the House of Bourbon, arrived at St. Jean de Luz from England, and we heard too this very evening that Lord Castlereagh had left England to join the head-quarters of the grand allied armies from the north of Europe, which were to pass the Rhine on New Year's day in pursuit of Buonaparte who had arrived in Paris. From this time until the middle of February we remained in our position near Hasparen.

February 14th. Lord Wellington having arrived at Hasparen this morning, Sir Rowland Hill with his corps, Sir Thomas Picton with the 3rd Division, and Lord Edward Somerset with the hussar brigade were ordered to advance, and the enemy retiring before them they encamped about eight miles in front of Hasparen,

15th. The division encamped this afternoon near a village called St. Martin, where I left them in the evening, intending to return to

131

Hasparen, but losing my way in the night, I was obliged to stop at a French cottage in the mountains until daylight.

16th. I was engaged all the morning at Hasparen: in the meantime the division had advanced as far as Masparte, where I joined them in the evening, and pitched my tent on a high hill. It was a very sharp frost and we suffered very much from the cold.

17th. Continuing to advance, the troops. encamped this afternoon in some fields by the roadside near Garis. We got into a house where there was plenty of hay, which was a great treat for our horses.

18th. This morning there was a heavy fall of snow. We marched through Garis, and the division encamped near St. Palais. I got into a French cottage: these are wretched habitations, with earth floors, and are better than a tent only from the facility which they afford of lighting a fire and cooking.

19th. The enemy having destroyed the bridge over the river Bidouse at St Palais, the troops were ordered to halt, and Lord Wellington went back to St Jean de Luz to direct the movements of the divisions left at Bayonne.

20th. Our division moved into quarters at Garis and St. Palais.

21st. Lord Wellington having returned to Garis, and the bridge over the Bidouse at St. Palais having been repaired, the troops began to pass the river.

22nd. We passed the Bidouse this morning, and were put up by the road side about four miles beyond the river.

23rd. The Light Division which had followed our movements from the vicinity of Bayonne and halted at St. Palais last night, just as we were turning out this morning! marched by our cantonments with their bugles playing, and followed the 2nd Division, while we marched over a large heath towards the River Gave near Sauveterre, and in the evening came to a small branch of that river running through a village: here the division halted, and the whole of the 45th regiment passed the stream to support the piquets who were now close up with the enemy. All the baggage was ordered to keep in the rear.

24th. We rather expected that another great battle would be fought today, the French having taken post on the opposite side of the river upon the high ground about the town of Sauveterre: their *vedettes* and piquets extending over the bridge which had been mined ready for explosion. About 10 o'clock our division advanced and drove the enemy's piquets across the river into the town; the bridge was then blown up before our faces, upon which a part of our right brigade under Colonel Keane gallantly plunged into the river attempting to ford or swim it, under a fire of musketry and artillery, but were forced to retire with the loss of about eighty men and an officer of the 94th regiment who was drowned. Meanwhile Lord Wellington led the 2nd, 6th and Light Divisions over the river by a pontoon bridge which had been laid down higher up, and marching upon the enemy's left while his attention was being diverted by the 3rd Division, compelled him to leave Sauveterre very precipitately.

25th. The movement made by the 2nd, 6th and Light Divisions having obliged the enemy to quit Sauveterre, they passed another branch of the River Gave near Orthez, and we saw them blow up the bridges at our approach. On our march this day we were met by the peasantry of the villages we passed through, bearing large branches of laurel, which they waved over our heads from each side of the road as we passed. The 3rd Division crossing the river at Sauveterre, encamped near Salis, where I joined them in the evening, and pitched my tent upon the heath: it rained most part of the night. Lord Wellington's head-quarters were in Sauveterre.

26th. Early this morning the 3rd Division marched through Salis, and passing the next river by a ford which had been discovered near the village of Prambos, were encamped on the road side about four miles from the town of Orthez. The 7th and 4th Divisions of the army which had moved from the vicinity of Bayonne about the time we passed the Bidouse, and followed the course of the Ardour, shewed their camp fires this evening on our left, while the 6th Division making a movement corresponding with that of the 3rd, encamped immediately on our right near the river, where a pontoon bridge was to be laid down during the night.

Sir Rowland Hill's corps occupied the banks of the river in face of the town of Orthez. I put up tonight at a *"Maison de Campagne"* near the ford where the 3rd Division had passed the river, and not far from the camp of the 6th Division. Thus had Marshal Soult (ever since our advance from Hasparen) been retiring before us, avoiding an action. He left in Bayonne a very strong garrison, in consequence of which Sir John Hope with the 1st and 5th Divisions was detached from, the rest of the army to blockade that place, and these divisions never joined us after; but the French Marshal having now fallen upon reinforcements seemed inclined once more to fight, and we could perceive him very distinctly both yesterday and today making his dispositions and posting his troops on the rising grounds and positions in the field of Orthez, his left resting on the town and his right extending along the heights, over which runs the high road to Dax upon the river Adour.

27th. (Sunday morning.) The enemy being found in the same position on the field of Orthez with the apparent determination to try the fortune of the day, the light and 6th Divisions crossed the river, and the army began to concentrate and close up for the attack, as near as I could observe in the following order.

On the Left.

4th Division	Lieutenant-Gen, Sir G. L. Cole, K. B.
7th Division	Major-General Walker,

In the Centre.

Light Division	Major-Gen. Chas. Baron Alten.
3rd Division	Lieutenant-Gen. Sir Thos. Picton, K. B.

On the Right   Near the River.

6th Division	Lieutenant-Gen. Sir H. Clinton, K. B.

Lieutenant General Sir Rowland Hill with his corps remained on the other side of the river opposite to the town of Orthez.

BATTLE OF ORTHEZ

Sunday, 27th February, 1814.

The troops of the 7th Division having some distance to march, did not come up until near 9 o'clock. The army had been for some time under arms awaiting their arrival, and, orderly officers were sent down the road to hasten them; but for these there was no occasion, as they themselves were as anxious to get up in time as the rest were for their appearance: at length they announced their approach by a loud cheering, and the engagement then commenced with driving in the enemy's piquets.

The 6th Division under Sir Henry Clinton, supported by the Hussar Brigade and some guns, moved by the high road upon Orthez, while Sir Thomas Picton, supported by two guns (leaving the road) marched his division left in front towards the enemy's centre position, and posted it in a ravine under cover of a little hill, ready to attack the French at that point as soon as circumstances should require; but Marshal Beresford with the 4th Division, supported by the 7th, was first to attack the right of the enemy, while the light division moved up a deep ravine between these corps and the 3rd Division, with the view of aiding and supporting the operations of either.

For a considerable time the 4th Division was severely engaged, endeavouring to turn the enemy's right; from the nature of the ground, however, it was found impracticable to effect this, which I believe prevented our troops from deploying properly into line. From half-past nine until eleven o'clock a severe conflict was maintained at this point, the enemy darkening the air with their shells, some of which were carried to the hill where we stood.

Major-General Ross commanding a brigade in the 4th Division was brought off the field wounded in the head, and Lieutenant-General Sir Stapleton Cotton at this moment galloping out of the battle joined the Hussar Brigade, which was instantly in motion, and advancing by a brisk trot upon the town of Orthez, where the 6th Division had by that time commenced their attack: but the brunt of the day was on this occasion reserved for the 3rd Division, under Sir Thomas Picton, who was now ordered to attack the enemy's centre, which occupied a vast track of broken and uncultivated ground, forming as it were three tongues of land pointing obliquely to the high road, connected with each other at several points by a cross range of hills intersecting the ravines.

The left brigade under Major General Brisbane led the attack, supported by the rest of the division. The engagement now became general along the whole of the line. Our left column appeared to be rather losing ground, and was suffering very much; the Light Division was also severely engaged, and the English brigade of the 7th Division moved down into the ravine to their support a loud cheering (audible notwithstanding the roar of the cannon and rattling of the musketry) at this time drew general attention to the 3rd Division, which was forcing its way to the enemy's main position, enveloped in fire and smoke: the cavalry trumpets too were sounding near Orthez, and the French drums beating on the ridge above the town, which appeared completely darkened with their troops.

Nothing decisive could be effected until the 3rd Division should have finished its task of forcing the enemy's centre positions, which could not have been confided to better hands; and in justice to the "Fighting Division," the whole army were ready to acknowledge that if human efforts could effect it they would do it. All the eleven regiments forming this division were desperately engaged, carrying hill after hill until they were at length observed climbing the enemy's grand position, under a loud cheering and the sound of light infantry bugles.

A sharp struggle ensued on the ridge, and the French cavalry charged, while their infantry fled over the vast track of level ground which lay in their rear, until they reached some rising ground near a chapel, from which point, across a deep ravine, may be seen the town of Orthez: there they attempted to rally: but Lord Edward Somerset brought up the Hussar Brigade, and the 7th Hussars under Colonel Kerrison charged and brought in some prisoners. The enemy now formed into squares, but our artillery being also up and our infantry advancing, they fled, and were followed by our divisions in triumphal march. In the meantime Sir Rowland Hill had passed his corps over the river above Orthez, and marching along some heights in the enemy's rear compelled them to quit the road and fly over the fields towards the Adour, until passing some streams which had been swollen by the late rains, they destroyed the bridges to arrest our pursuit, and we lost sight of them once more.

Thus had another bloody battle been fought, and another victory obtained, at the price of 2,000 men *hors de combat*; and though the enemy suffered in proportion, it is to be deeply deplored that such sacrifices of human life should be requisite, and they were now become so frequent, that however devoted the officer or soldier might be, he could not but wish that some limits were put to this reign of slaughter, for otherwise no one could hope to outlive it, and a man only escaped today to fall tomorrow: this, however, was the impression upon my mind, when the division mustered on the camp ground this evening, and we found so many missing.

Of the two thousand men killed or wounded in this action, eight hundred, including 70 officers, were of the 3rd Division; so that General Picton could not complain of having been left out, which at the commencement he appeared to be very fearful would be the case. Colonel Taylor commanding the 88th regiment, Lieutenant-Colonel Forbes of the 45th, Lieutenant-Colonel Carr of the 83rd, and Major Debarres of the 87th were all wounded, and these regiments sustained severe loss, as did also the Portuguese regiment of Cayadores in our division under Colonel Kelshaw, who was killed.

It was about 3 o'clock when the enemy's last post was carried and the victory gained: and the pursuit continued until late in the evening, when I left the division still marching, and returned to the field of battle to meet the baggage and stores, which I had the good fortune to prevent going astray, as they were taking the road to Dax. We reached the camp ground about 10 o'clock and I pitched my tent near the cottage occupied by General Brisbane.

We were about twelve English miles beyond the field of battle, and ten from the town of Orthez. The Spanish forces had all been absent from this action, but they were now moving out of the Pyrenees to assist in the blockade or investment of Bayonne, and a division under Don Manuel Frere had been ordered to join us forthwith. All our heavy cavalry too had been in the rear ever since July, in cantonments on the river Ebro in Spain; but they were now marching through the Pyrenees to join us.

RETURN OF THE KILLED, WOUNDED AND MISSING,
IN THE BATTLE OF ORTHEZ.

	Killed.	Wounded.	Missing.
British	207	1387	38
Portuguese	66	503	38
	273	1,890	76

28th. As the troops were getting under arms this morning, Lord Wellington rode by the camp: he had been slightly wounded in the action by a musket ball, but did not quit the field. I had to go back to the field of battle, but I joined the division in the evening in the camp of St Severs; it was a very wet and dreary night and there was no shelter saving what a tree here and there afforded, the 4th Division having got the wood and the baggage having been unable to pass the waters, which in some places had so inundated the road that it was impossible to pass them in the night

March 1st The troops falling under arms as usual, this morning marched through St. Severs, and passed the river Adour, which is here very deep, and several women and children with the baggage were drowned. This was a very wet and cold night; we encamped in a field near the village of Grenade, and were very miserable.

2nd The division marching through Grenade and Cazeres encamped near Ayr. We got into a poor dirty little cottage in a lane near the camp ground, where the people were as uncivil and uncouth as possible: the only answer we could obtain to any question was, "*n'y pas*" or " *nai n'y pas*," by which they meant to say, "there is nothing for ye."

3rd. During the night some snow had fallen, and this morning it blew very hard with rain and sleet, so that it became necessary to allow the troops to go into quarters, and they were put up in the huts and cottages about the country, the division head-quarters and the Portuguese brigade occupying Cazeres.

12th. When we passed the Adour at St. Severs last week, Marshal Beresford with the 7th Division marched upon Mont de Marsan, where he made some large captures of public stores, and then prosecuting his march to Bourdeaux, he entered that city this day in triumph, the people hoisting the white cockade and declaring for the Bourbons, upon which the Duc d'Angoulesme repaired thither, and administered the oaths of fidelity in the name of Louis XVIII. The 7th Division never joined us after, but remained on duty at Bourdeaux under the command of Lord Dalhousie, who soon rejoined them from England; and Marshal Beresford again joined Lord Wellington.

14th. Don Manuel Frere with his division of Spaniards having formed a junction with us, the British troops advanced to Barcelona, and Lord Wellington's head-quarters were fixed at Ayr on the Adour. Our heavy cavalry also now arrived in fresh and excellent condition, and were posted near to Sir Rowland Hill's corps.

15th. Marshal Soult having (as was supposed) fallen upon some reinforcements near Tarbes, returned and threatened our position near Ayr; in consequence of which the 3rd Division turned out to camp on the left of the river, and the Spaniards moved up to Barcelone in triumphal march. I would not for a trifle have missed seeing the entry of the Spanish General into the petty and insignificant town of Barcelone this evening; it was ludicrous enough. Amongst his attendants was a knight in armour. Our old General Sir Thomas Picton stood in the square smiling ironically, but the *Don* sent word to him that he must turn out, as the Spanish head-quarters would occupy the town.

17th. Whether it was the arrival of the Spaniards and the sound of their trumpets, or (what is much more likely) Britannia's crowded camps, which dismayed the French Marshal, I do not presume to decide, but he this day called in his piquets and retired.

18th. The army moved forward this morning in two grand columns, one on each side of the Adour, the French retiring before us. We encamped for the night on some heights near Porvis, the hills opposite being covered with the enemy's fires.

19th. As we were now close up with the enemy the baggage was directed to move about a mile in the rear, until about 12 o'clock when it was halted, and the division ordered to close up.

AFFAIR OF VIC BIGORY
March 19th 1814.

This morning the brigade of German Heavy Dragoons, a troop of horse artillery and the light troops led the march, followed by the rest of the division in close order. About mid-day we passed through a town where the road enters a wood: upon leaving the wood a perfect forest of vineyards (extending several miles every way, and encircling the town of Vic Bigory) presented itself; this forest being held by the enemy's light troops, who lined the avenues on every side, it was found quite impracticable to advance by the high road until the vineyards on the right and left should be cleared.

Orders were therefore given for the baggage to fall back a little, and the troops to close up for this attack, which wore the appearance of as disagreeable an affair as the division had ever encountered. The enemy were so completely concealed, and had so much the advantage from the avenues being known to them, that I have since often wandered that they should so soon have been compelled to quit their ground. We were now all lying at the corner of the wood, concealing ourselves as well as we could behind a few cottages and the trees, while Lord Wellington and Sir Thomas Picton with a squadron of the German dragoons and our light companies, were reconnoitring the ground, the cannon balls dancing over the plain.

A singularly shocking instance of sudden death occurred on the spot where I was, and where we thought ourselves sufficiently concealed. An artilleryman was struck by a cannon-shot, and so dreadfully mangled and disfigured, that it became necessary to bury him instantly, and it was done so quickly that many who were near, knew not what had happened. An order now came for two guns to debouch from the covert, and presently we heard their discharge, which was like a single shot, when they were instantly galloped back into the wood, The division now advanced, the light companies being in the vineyards skirmishing with the enemy.

About this time Colonel Arbuthnot, the quarter-master-general of our division, came riding out of the vineyards wounded in the arm: he had been reconnoitring the avenues and leading on the troops. The cavalry now began to move along the high road, and we all marched through the vineyards to Vic Bigory. As we were passing through the *grande place* the enemy (having ascended some heights) threw some shells into the town, two of which burst in the square, creating some alarm and frightening the cavalry horses. Our light troops continued to clear the vineyards, and at night the division encamped about two miles beyond Vic Bigory on the road to Tarbes.

The loss which we sustained fell principally on the light companies, and the Portuguese brigade. We saw many of them lying in the vineyards most dreadfully wounded, indeed this field was remarkable for horrid wounds, which may perhaps be accounted for from the victims having been (in many instances) taken by surprise, and shot even at the cannon's mouth, which was the case with some of the French; and I remember their own country-people came to look at them with an air of perfect indifference, and actually refused to grant the poor creatures shelter from the night air, though in more than one instance we begged it of them as a favour.

Affair of Tarbes
March 20th, 1814.

Early this morning the column of Sir Rowland Hill which had marched round the vineyards on our right was seen filing over the fields of Vic Bigory, and joining the 3rd Division they moved upon Tarbes, which town is here seen at the distance of about six miles. it is beautifully situated in the plain at the foot of the loftiest mountains of the Pyrenees, the tops of which are throughout the year covered with snow. Beaten out of the vineyards yesterday by the 3rd Division, the enemy had now taken post upon the heights on the other side of the Adour, above Tarbes, his rear-guard still occupying the town. Thus had Marshal Soult been leading us up from the coast along the margin of the Pyrenees and the course of the Adour (which river rises in the mountains not far from this place), probably with the view not only of drawing us from our resources and making us a burthen to the country, but of removing us also from our corps at Bayonne and Bourdeaux, from which, in the event of disaster, we could now receive no immediate succour.

This was a most beautiful morning, and the scenery before us exceedingly romantic. We were in full march upon Tarbes by the high road, and our light companies in front were beginning to deploy into position under cover of our barrage which topped the hills in a cloud of smoke; upon which our light troops entered Tarbes driving the enemy through the town, and our artillery firing down the streets, the French all passed the river and took post on the heights which here present themselves.

The 2nd and 3rd Divisions then marched through the town in triumph, with their bands playing and bugles sounding: the inhabitants, who appeared to be chiefly women, assembled in the streets to see the novelty of a British army, crying "*Vive les Anglaises!*" and "*Vive l'Angleterre!*" but there was no cry of "*Vive les Bourbons.*" We were informed that the French marshal had declared he would fight on the heights to his last man, so that it was doubtful to whom the town would belong that night. This however was soon decided; for our battalions had scarcely time to pass the river before the enemy commenced a retreat, pursued by our divisions in a sort of triumphal march: this march continued until dusk, when the troops encamped in the mountains about five miles from Tarbes.

Our division had just began to light their fires, when the enemy (thinking us too near neighbours) very maliciously brought some guns up to a height and cannonaded our camp, which obliged the troops to move back a little to another range of hills. I was not present when this took place, being out in quest of the supplies, which with all the baggage had (as usual) gone wrong. The Spaniards having moved up in our rear, passed Tarbes in triumphal march and followed Sir Rowland Hill's corps. I passed through their camp and that of the 2nd Division about 9 o'clock, and reached the division about 10.

It was a fine starlight night but rather cold, and mine was the only tent standing in the field. Nothing could possibly exceed the romantic grandeur of the camp scene this night; the whole face of the country (which of itself is extremely picturesque) was covered with camp-fires as far as the eye could reach in every direction, and the Spanish and Portuguese camps at different points resembled towns on fire: for (not content with the common bivouac lights) the Spaniards in particular had set fire to some ruins of houses, some piles of wood, and even straw-stacks, which illumined the whole face of the country for many leagues round; and being on the edge of the Pyrenean mountains, the green sides of which were partially covered with snow, exhibited as romantic a scene as the most fertile imagination could possibly conceive.

21st About 11 o'clock last night, while I was conversing with some officers of the 45th regiment, we observed that most of the enemy's fires and even their piquet-lights were going out; and this morning it was found, that they had decamped altogether. Soon after daybreak we moved forward and came into the high road to Toulouse, by which the enemy had retreated. We continued to advance all day under a heavy and cold rain, which made us very miserable, having no other shelter for the night but a cold and wet camp.

22nd. We had a very wet march again today, and the division encamped early in the afternoon. I got shelter in a very wretched habitation near the camp.

23rd. In this day's march the division turned off the high road, and at night was put up in several small villages not far from a little place called Boulogne, where I passed the head-quarters of the army just as it was getting dark. In passing the Spanish camp I inquired of a sentry which road the 3rd Division had taken. My friend concluded that I meant the 3rd Division of the Spanish army, and when I undeceived him, he observed very significantly, that he knew nothing of the English army, but that " *no doubt it was in the rear!"* Now this was excellent, for they themselves were actually moving three leagues in our rear, and were this very evening encamped not far from the ground we left in the morning.

24th. We were put up this night at a village called Anan, where a couple of fowls sold for sixpence; but the price was soon raised.

25th. We halted this afternoon at the village of St. Martin: the master of the cottage which fell to my lot was so very rude and uncivil, that I could not refrain from telling him, that he deserved to be properly introduced to the *Dons,* who were coming, and who I was sure would not study his accommodation so much as I did.

26th. The division moved forward this morning, but I was too unwell to keep up with them any longer. About 12 o'clock the Spaniards arrived, when I was obliged to move off and leave my cross landlord to them, who doubtless made him know who were the best guests— the English or Spaniards. I slept in a house at Sizes where the people were very civil.

27th. Upon joining the division this morning at Fonchaub, I got into a little *château* near the village, which proved by far the best quarters I had occupied in France.

28th. The division moved up to Plaisance, and I was obliged to quit my *château*, for a miserable room at a blacksmith's.

29th. The troops were ordered to halt, as we were now once more up with the enemy, who occupied the town of Toulouse, about five miles distant from this place. On reconnoitring their position it was found that the great bridge over the Garronne was so strongly *barricadoed*, and the suburbs of the town on this side of the river so covered with works and fortifications, as to render them perfectly unassailable. Our divisions therefore now branched off to the right and left of the road, and spread themselves along the banks of the river, leaving us in the centre at Plaisance, with the Spanish army in our rear at Fonchaub and its vicinity.

31st. At daylight this morning we were turned out, and marched off to the right to support the 2nd Division, which had been directed to cross the river. The division remained under arms all the morning on its banks, a little above the bridge. In the afternoon we were ordered into quarters at Cogneaux and some other little villages on the spot, but the troops were to be kept as much in marching order as possible. It was reported in the camp this evening that the Russians and Prussians had entered Paris; that Buonaparte was dethroned, and the war over.

About 9 o'clock, as I was spending the evening with some of the 45th officers, the general's *aide-de-camp* came in with the news that tomorrow would probably be another bloody day, and shortly afterwards the serjeant called with the orders, which confirmed what had just been said. The division was to assemble on the green two hours before daylight, in marching order, with the left brigade in front, the ammunition to follow the column, but all baggage to remain loaded in the rear. Thus interrupted in our conviviality, we soon separated, and retired to rest.

April 1st The division was under arms by, about 3 o'clock, and assembled on the green at Cogneaux, where (in constant expectation of orders to advance) we remained all the morning: in the afternoon we were ordered again to our quarters. Sir Rowland Hill, it now appeared, had passed the river by a bridge of pontoon, and was returning, having found the roads, in that direction impassable for artillery.

It had also been discovered that the enemy's army occupied a very formidable position covered with redoubts, and scarcely inferior in point of strength to their chain of field-works on the Nivelle.

2nd. The 2nd Division, after marching all night, arrived this morning at Cogneaux, and we moved back to Plaisance.

3rd. This afternoon Lord Wellington's head-quarters marched through Plaisance, moving from the right wing of the army to the left, and at half-past 11 at flight, when we were gone to rest, our bugles sounded to assemble, and the division falling under arms marched at midnight under torrents of rain.

4th. Soon after daylight we fell in with the 4th, 6th and Light Divisions, all moving in the same direction, and about 11 o'clock came to the banks of the river not far from a small town called Grenade, where Lord Wellington had fixed his head-quarters: here we found a pontoon bridge just laid down, and the troops began to pass the river in presence of Lord Wellington in the following order.

Colonel Vivian's brigade of Hussars. Horse Artillery.
6th Division of Infantry under Sir Henry Clinton.
Foot Artillery.
4th Division of Infantry under Sir Lowry Cole.
Foot Artillery.
Major-Gen. Lord Edward Somerset's brigade of Hussars.
Horse Artillery.
3rd Division of Infantry under Sir Thomas Picton.;
Foot Artillery,
Six regiments of Heavy Cavalry.

The passage of the cavalry and artillery was particularly tedious, every man being obliged to lead his horse in single file over the bridge, and the guns and carriages were dragged over by men, the horses being led singly after the carriages. By the time the above force had passed over the evening came on, and operations were of course suspended: there still remained on this side of the river, the light division of infantry, the Spanish army, a considerable force of cavalry, all the reserves: and of course all the baggage of the army, also the 2nd Division under Sir Rowland Hill; posted as a corps of observation in face of the bridge and town of Toulouse near Plaisance. The rain had ceased since the morning, but now night came on with stormy and wet weather, which caused so great a swell in the river that the pontoons were taken up for the night.

5th. The river was found too high and its current too strong this morning to bear the bridge, notwithstanding the efforts of the engineers, which were repeatedly made in presence of Lord Wellington during the day. In the meantime the enemy having discovered our situation filled the river with trees and large pieces of timber, which the tide floated down, and about 11 o'clock a large boat filled with stones came down with great rapidity and created a great degree of anxiety, as the bridge was down at the time, and the width of the river was such as to require every pontoon to form the bridge, so that any damage or loss would have been severely felt.

The swell of the river however was so great, and the cables very fortunately so loose, that the pontoons rode safely over the boat, which now under a loud cheering from us all pursued its hasty course for Bourdeaux, where I suppose it would arrive in the evening, and from thence, if not arrested in its course, pass into the Bay of Biscay. It was followed by a great many other things of less magnitude in quick succession, but no damage was done to the pontoons as the bridge was now taken up: thus however the army became completely divided, the one half being separated from the other by a wide river perfectly impassable. It was calculated that in the present reduced state of our divisions, we had over the river about twelve thousand bayonets, four thousand swords, and twenty pieces of cannon.

6th. It had ceased raining, but the effect produced on the river was such that the bridge could not be laid down, so that it was naturally expected that the, enemy would attack that portion of our army which had passed, over, and Sir Thomas Picton (who as senior officer held the command) haying expressed his apprehensions that a blow would be struck, early this morning Lord Wellington and Marshal Beresford crossed the river together in a little boat, mounted dragoon horses on the other side and joined the troops. Considering the enemy's vast superiority in point of numbers, it is surprising that, they did not come out of their works and attack, this small force, whose very ammunition they might have exhausted. Lord Wellington and Marshal Beresford returned in the evening, leaving Sir Stapleton Cotton and Sir Thomas Picton in command.

7th. Notwithstanding the weather had cleared up it was still found impossible to lay down the bridge. I was generally at the waterside most part of the day, the 46th regiment being on duty there with the engineers. Lord Wellington came down as usual this mornings and went off to Sir Rowland Hill's corps: returning in the evening, he passed our camp on the hill.

8th. Shortly after daybreak this morning Lord Wellington came down to the waterside, and the bridge having been laid down according to the directions he had given the preceding evening, the Spanish army had began to pass, and about 8 o'clock Lord Wellington himself passed over, leading his own horse, which he refused to let his orderly take. As I knew the Spaniards would suffer no other interruption while they were passing, I crossed at the same time.

Having to go to Fronton, in the direction of Montauban, I did not join the division until late in the evening: they had advanced since the morning along the banks of the river, and were encamped in some meadows about two miles from the town of Toulouse, with their piquets in some shrubberies or plantation round a neat little *château* near a fortified bridge over a canal. The report that the allies were in Paris was revived again this evening, but very few of us believed it.

9th. The pontoon bridge having been moved higher up the river this morning and laid across about two miles in rear of our camp, the light division passed over and joined the army, which now advanced, spreading itself along the front of the enemy's fortified position.

The town of Toulouse is seated on the right banks of the river Garronne, over which there is a handsome stone bridge of seven arches, which together with the suburbs of the town on the left banks of the river, had been fortified and *barricadoed* in such a manner as to render it proof against every assault. On this side of the river the canal of Languedoc, in the form of a crescent, encircles the town, being cut along the margin of the suburbs. It falls into the river about half a mile below the great bridge, and in its course to this point skirts the park on the other side of the town, and then passes close under a vast range of heights, over which runs the high road to Paris, and which here separates from the town.

The banks of this canal were for the most part lined with batteries or breast-works, every road or pass enfiladed, and all the bridges over it *barricadoed* and fortified. In addition to these, the range of heights above-mentioned, as separated from the town by the canal, was one perfect chain of redoubts and other field-works, capable of affording cover to fifty thousand men with a hundred pieces of cannon: indeed at this distance .they resembled so many castles, and were all connected with each other by covered ways, double tiers of breast-works encircling the declivities of the hills, and all the houses on the heights being loop-holed for light infantry: in short such a field for assault had seldom been seen.

Notwithstanding all these obstacles, however, the storm (for I can call it by no better name) was resolved on, and our divisions were moved and posted this evening in face of their several points of attack. Thus after all the delay arising from the weather and other impediments, which seemed almost to have conspired to prevent the effusion of more blood, we were on the eve of another sanguinary conflict, which was greatly to be lamented, as it afterwards proved that at Paris hostilities had long since ceased. However, no information of this event having been obtained, the troops from the rear were all ordered to close up, and the 45th regiment joining the division in the evening marched through the camp with their band playing, and Colonel Forbes at their head: they had scarcely taken their ground when Lord Wellington galloped through our camp and the day closed.

BATTLE OF TOULOUSE,

LEFT COLUMN.

Marshal Sir W. C. Beresford, K. B.

4th Division, Sir G. L. Cole
6th Division, Sir H. Clinton
} To pass the river Ers, carry the village of Montblanc, and attack the right and centre redoubts of the enemy's grand fortified position.

LEFT CENTRE COLUMN.

Lieutenant-General Don Manuel Frere.

Spanish Army of Gallicia
} To attack the left wing of the enemy's fortified position and join our left column on the heights.

RIGHT CENTRE COLUMN.

Lieutenant-General Sir Thomas Picton, K. B.

Light Division, Baron Alten
3d Division, Sir T. Picton
} To observe the enemy in the suburbs near the canal, and to threaten the canal bridge and the town near the river.

147

Lieutenant-General Sir Rowland Hill, K. B.

2d Division, Sir W. Stewart Spanish Corps, Don P.Morillo	On the left banks of the Garronne, assisting by a cannonade across the river the operations of the 3d division, and to threaten the great bridge.

The cavalry and artillery supporting the infantry in their attack at different points of the line.

Easter Sunday, 10th April, 1814.

Awakened this morning by the rolling of the enemy's drums on the heights, I rose by starlight, and walked about the tented field: our camp were all at rest, regardless of the approaching hour of strife, until the day at length appearing, the bugles all through our extended camp sounded the old well known tune to assemble, and the troops taking their arms began to fall in.

As the sun rose over the hill about seven o'clock, the columns were all on the move, and marching over the fields of green corn which were fanned by the morning breeze, with their colours flying and light infantry bugles sounding the advance. The Spanish General, Don Manuel Frere, first marched by on our left, and moved upon a redoubt at this point of the enemy's position, supported by the Light Division posted a little under the hill, upon which Sir Thomas Picton forming our division into three separate bodies, posted the left (Colonel Keane's brigade) in face of the canal near the light division, supported by the Portuguese on their right; the brigade of Major-General Brisbane being to move along the banks of the river up to the plantations and *château* before mentioned, as occupied by our piquets, and there conceal itself for the present behind a mud-wall and the cottages of a little village, the 60th (rifle companies) occupying some houses near the river, and skirmishing with the enemy across the canal.

While these operations were carrying on at our point of the line, the left column of the army under Marshal Beresford, consisting of the divisions of Sir Lowry Cole and Sir Henry Clinton, having passed the Ers and carried the village of Montblanc, was moving against the enemy's grand fortified position, the other extreme point of which we heard them now attacking under a tremendous cannonade, which seemed to be the signal for the Spanish attack, as they now began to ascend the hill under a galling fire.

This conflict at the two extreme points of the French position had continued about the space of one hour, during which many valuable, lives were lost, and great sufferings endured, when the Spaniards gave way, and we saw them hastening down the hill into the plain pursued by the enemy, who quitted their works, and making terrible slaughter seemed resolved to exterminate the poor fellows altogether, until our light division shewing itself, prepared to take the task off the hands of the Spaniards, when the enemy fled back into his redoubts and entrenchments to avoid a British charge.

It was now about 11 o'clock, and the engagement was suddenly suspended. We could not account for this unexpected pause, otherwise than in a persuasion that our left column had sustained a repulse similar to that of the Spaniards; but all our fears and doubts of their success were groundless. The brave 6th Division (as Lord Wellington called it in his dispatches) supported by the 4th, after a most sanguinary struggle, had taken the principal redoubt on the enemy's right, and were now only resting until some guns could be brought up to cover their ulterior operations.

The failure of the Spaniards having left a dreadful task for our left column, Sir Thomas Picton determined upon creating some diversion in their favour, and General Brisbane with our brigade moving from his concealment advanced to the canal, and attempted to storm the bridge, while Sir Rowland Hill's corps kept, up a heavy fire from across the river, with the view of aiding this attack: unhappily, however, they cannonaded some of the houses which had afforded cover to our light troops standing on our side of the canal, and the enemy opened upon us such a blaze of musketry and artillery (chiefly grapeshot), that the brigade was not suffered to persevere in the storm. General Brisbane had his hat carried off by a cannon-ball, and was shortly after brought off wounded in the arm.

Poor Colonel Forbes of the 45th was killed, and this devoted regiment sadly cut up. When this assault commenced I observed Sir Thomas Picton ride off towards the plantations. The command of the brigade having devolved upon Colonel Taylor of the 88th regiment, he called off the troops, and placed them in concealment as before. This attack, which had lasted about half an hour, although it appeared to have failed in its object, certainly drew the enemy's attention to that point for the moment, by which a seasonable diversion was created in favour of our left column, or at least a short respite or breathing time gained for them.

These operations were scarcely over before a most afflicting contest recommenced on the heights, the whole range of which appeared as one vast mass of fire and smoke. The 6th Division (as I have before observed) having established itself on the enemy's right was now moving along the ridges of the hills storming the redoubts, fortified camps and houses in succession, a task so terrific that it lasted them all the afternoon, and the few who outlived the storm could hardly tell. how it had been done. Lord Wellington knowing under what advantages the enemy fought in his works, adopted his old system of exposing as few men as possible to their fire at once, by not sending two to perform what could possibly be effected by one.

Although this system does certainly tend to diminish the slaughter, yet it renders the task doubly severe upon those to whose lot it falls to be engaged, and never perhaps might this observation be better applied than at the Battle of Toulouse, for it may almost fairly be said that the 6th Division and a portion of the 4th alone gained the victory, as (if we except the Spaniards, who were unsuccessful) we had at no one time more than 12,000 men actually engaged.

Every effort had been made to rally the Spaniards and lead them back to the attack, but by the time they were again advancing, the 6th Division had carried all the redoubts, camps and *châteaux* from right to left, and joining the Spaniards in their second attack, stormed for them the very last redoubt, and planted the Spanish colours on the parapet, their own having (as I understood) been necessarily sent off the field in consequence of the reduced state of the regiments, and lest a sufficient number of men should not be left to guard them; and this observation applied particularly to the 42nd, 79th, 36th and 61st regiments, which were reduced to perfect skeletons.

The enemy now retired across the canal into the town, under cover of the fortified bridges. From the nature of this engagement, their loss, I should conceive, could bear no comparison with ours, which was deplorably great, as appears by the following statement:

RETURN OF THE KILLED, WOUNDED AND MISSING
IN THE BATTLE OF TOULOUSE

	Killed	Wounded	Missing
British	312	1,795	17
Portuguese	78	529	—

Spanish	205	1,722	1
	595	4,046	18

I had been most part of the day at a *château*, where we had some artillery, and where our 5th regiment was posted: at intervals I had been under fire, but that for a few minutes only. Many distressing scenes took place here owing to the baggage-camp being so near the field of action. The women could not be prevented from coming up from the rear to look out or inquire after their husbands, and our sufferers today were so many of them married men, that most of the women who came found their husbands either killed or wounded. One particularly affecting scene occurred.

An artilleryman having died of his wounds in the *château*, his wife (who was present) became so frantic that she ran into the field exposing herself to the enemy's fire, until she was dragged off to the rear by a serjeant. While they were putting this poor fellow underground, another man who had just fallen was carried to the spot to be buried. At this moment several women were weeping at the grave, one of whom soon discovered the corpse now brought to be that of her own husband, and she prevailed in her entreaties that it might not be buried until she had wept over it awhile, and had put a clean shirt upon it and some socks.

All this happened about 12 o'clock, during the pause in the engagement. It had just got dark and the firing had ceased, when I was proceeding to join the brigade near the plantations, but mistaking the way in the dark, I got into a lane leading down to the canal. I had rode but a very short distance when a gun immediately in front of me was fired, but the ball very providentially passed some distance from me, and struck the ground in my rear. Of course I soon faced about, and retreated along the ditch, and I joined the brigade just at the time the 45th regiment were burying poor Colonel Forbes, whose body they had obtained leave to bring off from the spot where he fell, in front of the fortified bridge over the canal.

The colonel had a presentiment of his fate from the time that the regiment received orders to join the division yesterday; and as soon as it was known that a battle would be fought he became visibly depressed, and could not divest himself of the idea that he was doomed to fall. We were all much grieved to see the melancholy by which he was depressed as he rode round the camp last evening, as though he was taking a last farewell of his regiment. He left a widow and family in England to lament his fall.

My friends M. and B. of the regiment had again escaped unhurt; O. F. had been on baggage-guard, but Major Lightfoot, upon whom the command had devolved when Colonel Forbes had fallen, having been carried off the field severely wounded, as next in command he quitted his post in the rear and joined the regiment. Captain M. had brought it off from the attack. All the houses and cottages here were full of the wounded of the 3rd Division. We entered one where poor Little of the 45th was dying—the scene was very distressing. The brigade went into bivouac behind a large empty *château*, orders having been given for the tents and baggage to continue in the rear.

I remained with them until about 10 o'clock, and then returned to the baggage camp. B's servant having been wounded, I endeavoured to find him out at the hospital, in the ruins of a large deserted *château*, where a most shocking scene presented itself. Several of the poor fellows were dead, and others dying, while the wind whistling round the turrets, of the mansion, seemed to mock the moans of these poor victims of fame, who were extremely destitute, and in most of the rooms had no other light but what the moon afforded, which served to increase the horror of the scene. I went to my tent greatly discomposed in mind: the camp-fires of our left column were glimmering over the field of battle on the heights, lighting many a sad and tragic scene.

THE FIELD OF TOULOUSE
A Sketch.

Nay! go not, go not to the field,
Unless thy heart's to pity steel'd:
I would not view that deadly dance,
For all the treasures once in France.

But now I ventured out to see
If any living there might be;
I passed along all silent dead,
They rested on their grassy bed.

Oh! but it was a fearful sight
To see that field in the lonely night;
Just one wild wand'ring glance I threw,
And closed my eyes to shun the view.

A murmuring sound stole on my ear.

It seemed the sigh of someone near:
I called, but no reply was given—
A soul had wing'd its flight to Heaven.

Again, again, a low strange sound!
'Twas the blast of night as it swept the ground,
Lifting the plumes all bloody and low,
That once waved bright on the warrior's brow.

Then Julian came, and we went on
In vain—there was no living one;
But many an English mother's care,
And many a lady's love lay there.

There was one spot where something bright
Was glittering in the pale moonlight:
Oh! blessed Virgin, who might be
Unmov'd, that mournful sight to see.

'Twas a warrior youth, whose golden hair
All lightly waved in the dewy air,
And the moonbeam resting on his face,
Gave it a sad unearthly grace.

A broken sword beside him lay—
It failed him on that desperate day:
Slumbering he seem'd ,but drew no breath,
His sleep was the heavy sleep of death.

Nay! go not, go not to the field,
Unless thy heart's to nature steel'd:
For all the treasures once in France,
I would not view that deadly dance.

Hawarden, 1814

11th. The enemy being still in Toulouse, encircled by his fortified
bridges over the canal and the river, our divisions fell under arms this
morning, and were assembled in columns on the hills and along the
plain, while Lord Wellington sent a flag of truce into Toulouse requiring the enemy to evacuate the town forthwith; and intimating that if
they did not it should be laid in ashes by the rocket brigade, which
had been brought up to the heights. An order was now also given for
the army to wear laurels for the victory.

The day was spent in burying the dead, and over the graves we
planted laurel boughs, which however the French peasantry tore up as

soon as our backs were turned. Colonel Coghlan of the 61st regiment, the first officer in rank who fell, was buried on the field of battle with military honours, the whole procession being crowned with laurels, and the band playing the "Dead march in Saul." In the afternoon an order came down to the 3rd Division to throw up works round a: *château* near our camp, and at night the 45th regiment and the three companies of the 60th were shut up in the *château*, the rest of the division lying in the field a little in their rear.

12th. At daylight this morning it was discovered that the bridge over the canal had been evacuated, and that the enemy had (during the night) quitted Toulouse. Lord Wellington touched the right string in threatening to burn the town. The National Guards, there was good reason to believe, had until then sided with Marshal Soult, but now that their property was at stake or endangered, they soon mounted the white cockade; the tri-coloured flags were hid, and the white brought forward, and all was "*Vive les Bourbons!*" and "*Vive le Roi!*" There is little doubt in my mind that these people had for some days known the fall of Buonaparte, for many of them without hesitation declared their belief that the allies were in Paris.

Triumphant Entry into Toulouse.
12th April, 1814.

Lord Wellington entered Toulouse in triumph this morning about 10 o'clock. He was met at the gate by the local authorities, civil and military, headed by the mayor and commandant of the national guards, and escorted from thence down the principal street into the "*grande place*" or square, one entire side of which is occupied by the "*Capitole*" or "Hall of the *Municipalite*," a very large building of white stone, on the top of which they had hoisted the white flag; but it was curious to observe that it waved over a bust of the Emperor Napoleon, which I suppose they had either forgot to remove or had not had time to take down.

All the balconies round the square, every window, and even the housetops were crowded with well-dressed females, crying "*Vive le Roi!*" and "*Vive les Bourbons!*" The National Guards with the white cockade and colours paraded the streets, and in the square two regiments of British cavalry were drawn out to receive Lord Wellington with due honours. About half past 9 o'clock our old general Sir Thomas Picton rode across the square with laurels in his hat: he was greeted as he passed, and shortly afterwards, the approach of Lord

Wellington being announced, the cavalry trumpets were sounded and swords drawn, while the procession entered the square in the following order.

The Spanish General Alava,
In Spanish uniform, crowned with laurels.
Field Marshal Wellington,
In a blue surtout coat, white waistcoat, and cocked hat,
Without laurels..
The Adjutant-General. The Quarter-Master General.
Three General Officers.
Lord Fitzroy Somerset, Lord W. Russell, Lord G. Lennox.
Twelve *Aides-du-camp* and twenty other Staff-Officers in
uniform, (All crowned with Laurels.)
British, Spanish, and Portuguese Dragoons.

The Mayor of Toulouse in full dress, with white sash, rode on the right of the profession: the air rang with cries of " *Vive Lord Wellington!*" " *Vive le Roi!*" and " *Vive les Bourbons!*" Lord Wellington was rendered very conspicuous by the restiveness of his horse, which on entering the square reared on its hind legs and literally danced over the ground. His Lordship carried his hat in his hand, the whole of the time, and bowed to the people until the procession had entered the court yard of the " *Capitole,*" where he was received by the principal inhabitants of the town, and the ceremony ended.

As yet we knew nothing of the restoration of the royal family at Paris, and Lord Wellington had given orders that no officer should for the present accept from the people or wear the white cockade: the people however spared no pains to compliment us, for several of them fixed little black cockades on their white to indicate an union. Sir Rowland Hill with his corps now marched over the great bridge and through the town, following the French army which had gone in the direction of Ville Franque, a place about eight leagues distant, where (it was said) they had another fortified position.

The rest of our army encamped on the field of battle, our division spreading along the banks of the canal. I pitched my tent on a grass-plat near the river, and close to the ruins of some houses which had been burnt during the action. At 5 o'clock in the afternoon dispatches arrived from Paris by an officer, who as he passed through the town to Lord Wellington's quarters, announced the news of peace; and shortly afterwards the following particulars being made public and proclaimed throughout the town, soon reached us in the camp, where they created the most lively sensations.

Substance of the Bulletin published at Toulouse on the evening of the 12th April, 1814.

On the 30th March, the grand allied army, under the Emperor of Russia and King of Prussia, having arrived in the vicinity of Paris, a battle was fought on the heights of Belle Ville and Mont Martre, in which the allies were victorious, and Paris surrendered by capitulation.

On the 31st March, the Emperor of Russia and King of Prussia entered Paris in triumph at the head of their victorious armies, with Marshals Blucher and Swartzenburgh.

On the 1st April the Emperor Napoleon being declared prisoner at Fontainbleau, the national guards and people of Paris offered their allegiance to the royal house of Bourbon, the authority of which was now restored under an executive government. Hostilities ceased, and an embassy was dispatched to England to invite Louis XVIII. to return to the throne, of his ancestors. Marshals Berthier, Massena, Ney, Marmont, Victor, Jourdan, Mortier, Macdonald, &c. &c. declared for the new government, and the armies were mounting the white cockade.

At the theatre the bulletin was read from the stage, and Lord Wellington from his box displayed his hat, bearing on the English cockade the Spanish on one side of the loop, the Portuguese on the other, and the white in the centre. The officers of the army were now ordered to wear a white favour upon their black cockades, which made us all look very gay.

We come now to advert to a circumstance which seems to require some explanation. How comes it that the events which took place at Paris on the two last days of March and first of April were not known at Toulouse on the 10th? The distance may be about three hundred miles, and (to say nothing of telegraphs) the common communications by the regular channel pass in the space of three nights and days.; but this news, which was of such vital importance to us, had actually been published in London seven days prior to its being known here, and five before the cruel battle which had been fought

The French army had consequently been fighting for and the British against a government which had ceased to exist. Every exertion possible had undoubtedly been made by Lord Wellington previous to

156

the action to obtain information, but his operations were necessarily to be continued or suspended according to those of the army to which he was opposed; and no messenger could reach us over land from Paris without passing through the French lines. True it is that we obtained the victory: notwithstanding this, however, the results were by far the most painful on our side. The French lost but a few hundred men, and these for the most part men of desperate fortunes, without a home or any social principles: whereas we lost thousands of gallant fellows, whose worth the tears of their disconsolate widows and friends will best attest, and to whom it would prove but a poor consolation that another leaf had been added to the already swollen laurel-wreath of these campaigns.

April 13th. When the news from Paris reached Lord Wellington last evening, he sent an account thereof by a flag of truce to Marshal Soult; but we understood the answer to be, that he and his army could for the present at least recognize no authority but that of the Emperor Napoleon. This afternoon the people of Toulouse took down the bust of Buonaparte, which I have before mentioned as being on the "*Capitole*," and dashed it to pieces.

14th. Immediately on the arrival of the dispatches from Paris on the evening of the 12th, Lord Wellington sent by express to Sir John Hope commanding at the siege of Bayonne, orders to suspend hostilities; and the messenger reached that camp last evening: upon which General Hope sent a flag of truce into Bayonne with the account, proposing to the French General that hostilities should be suspended, and all effusion of blood stopped on both sides, until further accounts should arrive: to this fair and equitable proposal we heard the Frenchman replied, that he would give a definitive answer on the following morning, and so indeed he did, for between two and three o'clock this morning more than five thousand men from the garrison made a sortie upon our camp, putting to the sword and bayoneting all before them.

Our poor fellows, elated with the news of the past evening, and relying upon the honour of the enemy, were rather off their guard. The confusion and alarm (according to all accounts) was dreadful: most of the camp were undressed; many in the front were murdered in their sleep, and those who were awake obliged to fight naked. The generals and other officers hastening up in the dark, several fell into the hands of the enemy, and amongst them Lieutenant-General Sir

John Hope himself, who was wounded and dragged into the town. Major-General Hay of the 5th Division was killed, and what rendered this officer's fall particularly distressing was, that his lady and family had just joined him from England, and had probably that very evening been fondly anticipating his glorious and happy return.

The French had everything their own way until our troops could form, when they were driven back into the town at the point of the bayonet. This man, however, not only escaped punishment, but was (I believe) confirmed in his rank and command. The line of policy pursued by the allied cabinets towards France at this period was of so conciliatory a nature, that no harsh measure, however just, was suffered to disturb the jubilee of the French King's restoration.

16th. Another messenger arriving from Paris, the following account was published.

The Emperor Napoleon abdicates the crowns of France and Italy for ever, and retires to the isle of Elba in the Mediterranean on a pension.

The messenger also brought dispatches for Marshal Soult, which were, sent into the French lines.

17th. Marshal Soult, notwithstanding all that had passed, still refusing to recognize the changes effected at Paris, or to suspend hostilities, the divisions which had encamped on the field of battle were ordered under arms this morning, and the 3rd Division soon after sunrise marched through Toulouse with their bands playing, and moved by the road to Villefranque, to join Sir Rowland Hill, the 6th, 4th and Light Divisions marching along the banks of the canal on our left. We had proceeded about three leagues, beyond Toulouse, when we met a carriage escorted by French lancers and some English dragoons, preceded by a flag of truce; it contained the French General, Count Gazan, whom Marshal Soult had deputed to wait upon Lord Wellington. We continued marching until we came to the village of Bassieges, where we encamped, hanging our hats with the white cockade on the outside of our tents.

18th. We expected to move forward again this morning, but our march was suspended. Marshal Soult having at length agreed to a suspension of hostilities, General Gazan in concert with Sir George Murray, appointed by Lord Wellington, made all the necessary arrangements, and fixed the line of demarcation. I had the misfortune this morning to lose my best horse, which had cost me sixty guineas.

19th. The army having been ordered to fall back into the line of demarcation, we marched back to Toulouse, and were put up in the suburbs on the left of the Garronne.

20th. The divisions moved into the cantonments allotted them as follows:

2nd Division	Toulouse and suburbs.
3rd Division	Grenade and adjacents.
4th Division	Condomme and adjacents.
6th Division	Auch and adjacents.
Light Division	St. Jory and adjacents
Cavalry	Fronton, & Mont deMarsan.
Heavy Artillery	Plaisance.
Head Quarters	Toulouse.
7th Division	Bourdeaux.
1st Division	Vicinity of Bayonne.
5th Division	Vicinity of Bayonne.

The Spanish armies commenced their march for Spain,

On this same day (April 20th) Louis XVIII, entered London in grand procession, and was received there by his Royal Highness The Prince Regent. On the 23rd the King of France embarked at Dover in the royal yacht of England, and the Prince Regent dined on board with his Majesty. On the 24th (Sunday morning) the King of France and his suite, escorted by an English and Russian fleet, under his Royal Highness the Duke of Clarence, crossed the channel and landed at Calais.

29th. Having been relieved in my duties with the 3rd Division, to which I had been attached ever since December 1812, I left Grenade and joined head-quarters at Toulouse. About this time an expedition for America assembling at Bourdeaux, several infantry regiments were ordered to embark for that country, among which were the 5th and 88th in the 3rd Division. Generals Brisbane and Power also joined this expedition.

May 3rd. Louis XVIII. entered Paris, Buonaparte having previously quitted for Elba,

13th. Lord Wellington having been to Paris, returned to Toulouse this evening, and on the day following set out for Madrid. Ferdinand the VIIth had arrived in Spain, Buonaparte having given him his liberty before his abdication.

30th. The general peace having been signed and ratified at Paris on this day, the Emperor of Russia, the King of Prussia, with old Marshal Blucher and a most princely retinue proceeded to England, upon a visit to the Prince Regent, where they were received and treated with the most generous and enthusiastic admiration. His Serene Highness Prince Leopold of Saxe Cobourg Saalfield was in this company, and it was said that he bore a letter of introduction to the Princess Charlotte of Wales from her uncle the Duke of Brunswick.

I remained in Toulouse all the month of May, billeted at No. 325, 11th section, near the canal. The weather was delightfully fine, and I often rode over the field of battle. The snowy mountains of the Pyrenees hear Tarbes are seen very clearly from here, which must have been a great consolation to our friends the Spaniards, inasmuch as they had yet a distant view of that "*buena tierra, Espana.*" About this period the Commissary General and the department generally were occupied in winding up the accounts, and settling such claims amongst the French people as had not already been liquidated.

It certainly is a just subject for exultation to Great Britain, that under the protracted difficulties and accumulating embarrassments of a twenty years' war, carried on in the face of all Europe, a line of policy should have been adhered to, even to the last, so highly creditable to and worthy of the generous and exalted feelings of the nation. By the at most unlimited sacrifices made, and unexampled devotedness displayed by the people of England throughout this arduous contest, our government had been enabled to add to its consistency and moderation that dignified spirit of firmness and good faith which, while it raised the astonishment and admiration of Europe, produced that confidence in us as a leading power, best calculated to lead to a general and lasting peace.

The British army throughout its operations in the Peninsula, and especially in France (contrary to the conduct not only of the French, but of every other military force), had taken the greatest pains not to be a burthen to the country. All public as well as private debts were everywhere as honourably and as punctually paid as circumstances would admit, and care taken to soften the rigours of war as much as possible, by making a fair remuneration to those who were sufferers by our presence.

Considering then that ours was a conquering and victorious army, sent from countries which had been insulted, threatened and impoverished, and some of them even plundered and laid waste, it was to be expected that our marching thus peaceably through France would have produced a laudable spirit of emulation amongst the inhabitants, which would at least have shielded us from base impositions and abuse: but their conduct was so opposite to any things of this nature, that it was a thankless and disgusting task to distribute amongst these people the hard-earned treasures of England.

It would be a tedious task to relate the various attempts at fraud and imposition, or the ignoble advantages taken by the people of this country of the latitude given to their meanness, by the liberal nature of the orders and regulations. Enormous demands were made (but very properly rejected) even for the marks left by encampments, whereas in almost every instance, and always when possible, the troops encamped on heaths and uncultivated ground.

When we entered upon the French territories many new orders were circulated, one. of which directed every English commissary passing through a town or village to call upon the mayor or chief inhabitant of the place to know if he or his neighbours had any claims unsettled, or any complaints to prefer, and if so such officer was bound to pay such claims instantly, if practicable, or at all events put them in a channel for liquidation. Under such regulations, the country, so far from suffering, was actually enriched in every direction that we moved, and the people generally, on that account, were glad to see us. About this time the cavalry commenced their march through France, to embark at Calais and Boulogne. The infantry were to embark at Bourdeaux.

June 4th. We left Toulouse this morning, and in the evening encamped at l'Isle en Jourdan. On the day following we marched to Auch; on the 6th to Condomme; on the 8th to Castel-Jealous; on the 9th to Bassage; on the 10th we reached Bourdeaux, and the next day Lord Wellington arrived there from Madrid. On passing Bassage on the 9th, we came up with the 3rd Division, the Portuguese of which were about to be separated from their British companions, probably for ever. Our men were treating the poor *Jozes*, for which purpose each man had received an advance of money.

The soldiers of the two nations were walking about together, and the parting next morning was very affecting, having been arranged and ordered as fellows: the Portuguese brigade marching out first formed on each side of the road, and as the British passed presented arms and dropped their colours, their bands playing "God save the King"; and the men with tears in their eyes cheering in the British style: the English troops having passed were then formed on the road, while the Portuguese brigade marched past them under the same salute, our bands playing a Portuguese national air and the men cheering.

The Portuguese then branched off by the road leading to Spain, and the British pursued their march for Bourdeaux, but while they continued in sight of each other, there was a cry of "*Viva os Inglezes!*" on the one part, and "Portugal forever!" on the other, It was here too that I bid a final *adieu* to the old 3rd Division, and to my friends of the 45th, M——, O'F—— and B——, all of whom had been carried through these perilous campaigns. O'F. had been wounded in the dreadful night of Badajos, and M—— in the storming of Ciudad Rodrigo; left in a hopeless state amongst the dead, his recovery was considered a perfect miracle: but B——, who had been in the heat of every engagement from the first landing of the army in 1808, up to the battle of Toulouse, had never once been wounded: he had seen three commanding officers fall in the field; nearly every other officer in the regiment, I believe, had been wounded, and the regiment had lost six times its original strength since he had joined during this long and arduous service he had never been absent from his duty even a day under any pretence whatever, which, considering the dangers, fatigue and privations to which he had been exposed, was very wonderful. I had often experienced great pleasure in seeing them come safe out of action, and now I wished them a happy return to old England.

16th. Lord Wellington after reviewing the divisions in the camp of Blanquefort, where they had assembled for embarkation, left the army this morning for England by way of Paris, and having landed at Dover at 5 o'clock in the morning of the 23rd from the Rosario, he arrived in London at 6 o'clock that same evening, after an absence of five years, having never been to England since he left it as Sir Arthur Wellesley in 1809. The troops for America having sailed from Bourdeaux and gone to assemble at Cork, the embarkation of the regiments for England now commenced.

During the time that we remained at Bourdeaux a great many quarrels occurred, and several duels were fought between the British and French officers, who obtained leave to come in from their cantonments obviously for the purpose of creating disturbances, particularly at the theatre, where the presence of the commander in chief, Lord Dalhousie himself, whose judicious measures often restrained them, was not sufficient to repress them altogether, and it rendered our stay here at times intolerably disagreeable.

23rd. The troops having all embarked, Lord Dalhousie and the British staff left Bourdeaux this morning, and the French army marched in.

August 7th. (Sunday.) At 7 o'clock this evening I embarked in the river Garonne on board a Swedish vessel bound to England. On the 12th we joined the convoy at anchor in Verdun roads, and after a calm and quiet passage, at 2 o'clock in the afternoon of the 23rd, came to anchor in Plymouth Sound, under Mount Edgcumbe; and at 3 landed at Plymouth Dock.

> *Breathes there the man with soul so dead,*
> *Who never to himself hath said,*
> *'This is my own, my native land!'*
> *Whose heart hath ne'er within him burn'd,*
> *As home his footsteps he hath turn'd,*
> *From wand'ring on a foreign strand?*
>
> W. Scott.

In our passage over the Bay of Biscay on the 18th, a vessel overtook us from Bourdeaux, with orders for me amongst some others to proceed direct to Cork, and join the troops assembling there for America; in consequence of which I was obliged to pack up and prepare for this new service: but when, on the morning of the 22nd, the signal was made for officers under orders for America to proceed on board the frigate, about to part convoy for Cork, and a boat was put out from the frigate, it blew so hard and the sea was so rough, that it could not come along side; and the frigate being already very much crowded, after laying to for the space of one hour, during which I was standing at the gangway with my baggage, we were permitted to proceed for England, and upon reporting myself in London I was placed on half-pay.

Prize money allotted me for the Peninsular campaigns, £27 5s. 1d sterling.

His Royal Highness the Prince Regent resolving to confer some high marks of his favour upon those officers who had held the most important commands in the Peninsular War, the following were raised to the dignity of Peers, with the titles respectively annexed :

Field-Marshal the Marquis of Wellington, KG. to be
Duke of Wellington.
Lieutenant-General Sir John Hope, K. B. to be
Lord Niddry.
Lieutenant-General Sir Thomas Graham, K.B. to be
Lord Lynedoch of Barrosa.
Lieutenant-General Sir Rowland Hill, K.B. to be
Lord Hill of Almaraz.
Lieutenant-General Sir Stapleton Cotton, K. B. to be
Lord Combermere.
Marshal Sir William Carr Beresford, K. B. to be
Lord Beresford of Albuera.

The order of the Bath also was extended and formed into three classes, *viz.*

1st, Knight Grand Cross of the Bath, K. G. C. B.
2nd, Knight Commander of the Bath, K. C. B.
3rd, Companion of the Bath, C.B.

Oh! it is transport to the heart to dare
All haunts of peril, so renown be there.
But does not pity's eye with horror shrink,
And pity's soul in deep dejection sink,
To note what enterprising thousands fall,
And mark how soon oblivion shrouds them all:
How many a Briton's high career is o'er
Who never, never shall bethought on more!
Let Lusia's thousand streams with blood that swell
Of Britons, who for Lusia's freedom fell,
And let Iberia's earth to shame the Iberian tell.
Yet each of these was wont to look on high
To Fame, through Fancy's telescopic eye,
E'en when the last inevitable stroke
The glittering bubble of expectance broke.
Still the fond thought came thrilling to his heart,
Not unobserved at least shall I depart.
Though here far far from home my bones must rest,
My name shall shelter in my country's breast.
Vain thought! of all yon scattered host

Select the death that lives in story most,
And think although that claim was bought so dear,
How few the tale have heard, or care to hear.
What though the warrior left a halcyon home,
Beneath inhospitable climes to roam—
What though he boldly braved a triple league,
Encircling danger, famine and fatigue,
And found at last the heroes boasted doom
Amid a heap of foes—a crimson tomb!
His fete at best a day's attention draws,
A feint short gust of popular applause,
That with light pinion quickly brushes by,
And hurries onward to the next that die.

Zuillianam.

1815

The torch of war had scarcely been quenched when it was again lighted by the reappearance of Buonaparte in France at the head of an armed force. Having quitted Elba on the last day of February and landed at Antibes, he marched for Paris, claiming the crown of France, and being joined on his march by all the French troops he met with, together with those sent out to oppose him, and also most of the French marshals, amongst whom were Ney, Soult and Massena, he entered Paris on the 20th of March, obliging the King and royal family to take refuge in Belgium, where an auxiliary force of about ten thousand British troops had been providentially left, under the command of the young Prince of Orange. Buonaparte, upon his abdication, was no longer to be regarded as a prisoner, and consequently could not be treated as such; and although not much reliance could be placed on his *parole d'honneur*, yet the apparent spontaneous burst of loyalty which had displayed itself in France, appeared of itself to be a sufficient security against any machinations from him and his adherents.

It was for France, however, on this occasion, to exhibit to the world a specimen of dissimulation which should astonish all Europe. Louis XVIII. had received into his favour and confidence all the French Marshals and Generals as they submitted to his government, especially the Marshals Ney, Davoust, Mortier, Macdonald and Soult, the latter of whom was at this time minister of war. All these professed their attachment and devotion to the King in the warmest terms, and Marshal Ney being chosen to lead the forces against the usurper, on being presented to his majesty and invested with the command, declared to the king that " he would bring the rascal (Buonaparte) to Paris in an iron cage," by which he meant (as it afterwards proved), surrounded by the guns placed under his command!! The troops marched out of Paris crying "*Vive le Roi!*" no doubt smiling ironically at the credulity of their King, for they had in their knapsacks tri-coloured cockades, which they afterwards boasted of having kept all along.

Now these things must have been seen by the officers in their common inspection of the men's equipments. Davoust, while in office for the King, issued secret addresses to the troops in Paris in favour of the Pretender; false signals were also made by the telegraphs; and Soult with fifty other officers quitted Paris in one morning to join Buonaparte, and Ney of course followed their example. In fact almost every officer of rank and influence seemed to stand by the King only so long as they were able to deceive him and serve the cause of Buonaparte; so that altogether there is not perhaps on record, in the annals of Europe, so base a combination of perjury and treason as the conduct which the French armies and France generally exhibited on this occasion: nor is its temerity as respects the insult offered to the powers of Europe, to be less regarded.

The French armies could now scarcely expect to intimidate all the nations of Europe with their cries of "*Vive l'Empereur!*" nor could the French people for a moment Suppose that the allied potentates would quietly put tip with such an insult or suffer themselves to be thus overreached. I presume not to say anything of the choice the people of France are disposed to make between the Bourbons and Buonaparte, and shall consequently confine my observations chiefly to the means they used to effect this extraordinary change, which according to my humble judgment were such as should never be permitted to triumph. The reign of Buonaparte had by dear-bought experience been found to be of that ferocious nature that it endangered the very existence of all the neighbouring states.

The powers of Europe too, by an alliance best calculated to preserve the public tranquillity, having bound themselves to support that state of things which had produced the peace, it would have been as impolitic as unjust to have swerved from these engagements, by acquiescing in a measure which promised at once to undo all that had been done, and which would have left every country of Europe, but especially England, at any future day exposed to the assaults of a faithless and inveterate enemy. The part, therefore, taken by the British cabinet on this trying occasion was not only such as it became them to. take, but such as was dictated by the soundest policy; and by the unhesitating course adopted, they effectually guarded the pass, and England became, once more, the guardian of astonished Europe.

All was now bustle and exertion to reinforce our little army in Belgium, and the Duke of Wellington who was at Vienna, was ordered to repair to Brussels to take the command. This change in affairs called us all from our half-pay homes; so that on the 20th of March I received orders to hold myself in readiness, and on the 25th was placed on full-pay, with orders to join the army in the Netherlands,

April 1st. I embarked at 6 o'clock this evening at Woolwich, in the *Traveller* transport, *No. 829.* We weighed anchor at 8 o'clock the next morning, and at night anchored off the Nore. On the 3rd we put our pilot on shore at Broadstairs, and steering put to sea, at sunset we lost sight of England.

4th. We passed Ostend early this morning, and scudding along the Dutch coast, we reached the mouth of the river Scheldt in the evening, and anchored off Flushing.

5th. A party of us went on shore this morning at Flushing, and hired a vehicle, with which we proceeded to Middleburg: these two towns are amazingly strong: from the parapets of either may be viewed the whole island, which lies so low that a great part thereof is generally covered with water, and its level appears to be beneath the surface of the sea, from which it is walled or banked off with great labour and trouble. The road from Flushing to Middleburg, however, is notwithstanding raised, and paved in such a manner as to make it admirable.

These towns too are not only well built, but the streets and houses in general kept so clean as to bespeak the industry of their inhabitants. Here they have a curious custom of placing at their windows little mirrors, which pointing up and down the street exhibit to the persons seated within, all that passes within their reach: almost every house at Middleburg has them. We returned to Flushing in the evening, and were on board our ship again at 7 o'clock.

From this time until the evening of the 10th we remained at anchor off Flushing, when we were ordered to put back to Ostend. It seems that this vessel, having ordnance stores on board, was at first bound to that port, but upon our leaving the Thames, a report prevailed that Ostend had been surprised by the enemy; So that all vessels of this description were ordered for the present to rendezvous at the mouth of the Scheldt

12th. We were landed at Ostend this morning, and at 4 o'clock in the afternoon set out in the barge: for Bruges. These barges are a very easy, pleasant and cheap conveyance, and provided with three cabins, one of which is very neatly furnished. Dinner, coffee or almost any other refreshment may be had on board at a reasonable rate, and seats are fixed on deck for fine weather. We reached Bruges about 7 o'clock; the distance from Ostend being about twelve miles, for which we paid 22 *sols* (11d.) each, and a trifle for our baggage.

13th. At 9 o'clock this morning We got into the barge for Ghent, and arrived at 6 in the evening; the distance being about thirty miles. The course of the canal from Bruges to Ghent runs through a rich but very level country. We experienced some difficulty in .finding accommodation in the hotels, Louis XVIII. with his court and staff having taken up their residence here: but at last we got into the Flanders Hotel, where three of us slept in beds made up in a large dining-room.

14th. We remained at Ghent today to purchase horses and such other equipment as we wanted to carry us on to Brussels, as the canal here turns off to Antwerp. Ghent is a very large town, insulated and divided into several parts by the numerous branches of canals which pass through the town. It is indifferently called Gand or Ghent, but the former seems to be preferred, from its being French, to which custom the people in general appear altogether the most habituated and attached.

15th. Left Ghent early this morning, and at night put up at Asche.

16th. Arrived at Brussels, and was ordered to join the 7th Hussars as soon as they should have arrived from England.

20th. Left Brussels this afternoon, and the next morning returned to Ghent, where I was to await the arrival of the regiment The King of France was still here, attended by the Marshals Marmont, Victor, Jourdan, Berthier and such few others who had not deserted him in his misfortunes.

24th. I joined the 7th Hussars under the command of Colonel Sir Edward Kerrison, C. B. at the village of Everingham, The driver of the cabriolet or chaise which I hired from Ghent had been a dragoon in the French army, and had served in Spain against the English.

25th. The regiment marched to Deynse on the river Dendre, and the next day went into cantonments at Haerlebec and the villages near Courtray, where the 2nd Hussars of the King's German Legion and the 35th Foot were posted. This place is only a few miles from the frontiers, and five leagues from Lille. During the few days we remained here, several French deserters came in from the enemy's lines, wearing white cockades, as a badge of their loyalty. They gave rather a formidable account of the warlike preparations happening in the French camp, where fresh troops continued to arrive from the interior of the country every day, being forwarded from Normandy and other distant provinces in wagons.. All France had declared for Buonaparte; even our friends at Toulouse and Bourdeaux, who had changed their cry of "*Vive le Roi!*" for that of "*Vive l'Empereur!*" At the latter of these places the presence and extraordinary efforts of the Duchess d'Angoulesme to quell or repress rebellion had proved fruitless.

May 1st. This afternoon the regiment marched from the vicinity of Courtray, and on the day following was put up at Ninove and some villages adjacent. We passed Oudenarde this evening, a place rendered famous by a victory gained there by the Duke of Marlborough in the reign of Queen Anne.

4th. I was put to considerable expense and trouble about this time from not being properly mounted and equipped, my horse not having yet reached me from England; and we were continually afraid lest the campaign should open before we were ready. Having occasion to go to Brussels today, I hired a *cabriolet*, which on my return to Ninove in the night broke down near Alost. My driver had been a French dragoon, and had fought against the English at the battle of Fuentes d'Onor, Salamanca and the Pyrenees. As he Spoke Spanish a little we conversed in that language. He called Buonaparte a brigand, Lord Wellington a pretty. good general, and the Spanish patriots rebels: he had all the self-sufficiency, *gasconade* and impertinent freedom of a French soldier, and endeavoured to persuade me that the French armies had never been fairly conquered. We reached Ninove about two o'clock in the morning, and I was obliged to pay him 30 *francs* for the journey.

11th. The head-quarters of the regiment having been removed from Ninove to Schendelbeke, I was put up at a farmhouse in that village.

29th, All the cavalry and horse-artillery of the army were reviewed this day in the plains of Grammont, by Field-Marshals the Duke of Wellington and Prince Blucher: they had been ordered to assemble by 10 o'clock, and were by that hour accordingly formed into three lines, the first being all Hussars, the second, all Heavy Dragoons, and the third all Light Dragoons, Horse Artillery being posted between each line, and ten guns planted on each wing to fire the salute when the Field-Marshals arrived. The day was very fine, and being the 29th May, the troops, horses and guns were crowned with oak boughs, presenting altogether a most imposing spectacle. It was calculated that no less than 13,000 English horses were on the field, and being fresh from England they appeared in the highest order.

At 11 o'clock the Field-Marshals passing through Schendelbeke were seen descending into the plain, escorted by a squadron of the 7th Hussars, and attended by at least 150 General and Staff-Officers, British and Prussian, wearing the stars and other decorations of the several orders to which they respectively belonged. Amongst them I observed Lord Hill and the Prince of Orange. The Duke of Wellington wore the uniform of a Field-Marshal of England, with the Bath star and a Wellington hat without a feather, and was mounted on a fine little horse with plain appointments; by his side rode the veteran Blucher in Prussian uniform, and his breast almost covered with stars.

The trumpets now sounded, and the guns were fired, while the Earl of Uxbridge, who as lieutenant-general and chief of the cavalry held the command, directed the movements. After the inspection of the lines, the troops all marched round the field, and passed in open squadrons, commencing with the life guards and ending with the 18th Hussars. As the regiments passed, they left the field, and Lord Wellington and Prince Blucher afterwards set out for Ninove to dine with the Earl of Uxbridge. Captain T. of the 14th and a few other officers dined at my quarters in Schendelbeke.

Two months had now elapsed since Buonaparte entered Paris, during which time the moist active preparations had been making on all sides for war. The armies of Russia, Austria and Prussia which had returned or were returning to their respective countries, had been ordered to advance again to the Rhine, and a strong corps of the latter nation, under Field-Marshal Blucher, was already posted at Namur and upon the Sambre; while in England the most vigorous measures were adopted to reinforce our little army in Belgium, in which direction the greater part of the French armies, it was obvious, were assembling.

Every disposable regiment in England, Scotland and Ireland was sent out, and orders dispatched to America to bring home those veteran troops who had been so victorious in the Peninsula, nine thousand of whom were at this moment preparing to cross the Atlantic

Ocean: lest these, however, should not arrive in time, transports had also been sent to Lisbon, to bring round a body of Portuguese troops. Reinforcements of men and horses arrived daily from England, but the allies from the north of Europe, it was thought, could not possibly arrive until late in June.

In the meantime the British and Hanoverian army, which had been consolidated in the same manner as the British and Portuguese had formerly been, together with the Dutch and Flemish forces, united under the command of the Duke of Wellington, and the corps of Prussians on the Sambre under Prince Blucher, held what may fairly foe teamed the post of honour, in face of the enemy, who were said already to have assembled fifteen thousand cavalry and one hundred thousand infantry: everything indeed seemed to portend that the day of trial was not far distant, and that the troops already assembled must meet the first shock, for all accounts agreed in the fact that Buonaparte was about to leave Paris for the army, and that Marshal Ney had already joined the camp near Lille. An order was now sent round for all our cavalry swords to be sharpened and pointed, according to a pattern sent to each regiment.

The following distribution of the Army into Brigades and Divisions, with their respective Commandesr, all under the immediate command of the Duke of Wellington, will be found to be correct.

CAVALRY.
Lieutenant-Gen. the Earl of Uxbridge.

Major-General Lord Edward Somerset, K. C. B.

1st Brigade of Cavalry	1st Life Guards
	2nd Life Guards
	Royal Horse Guards (Blues)
	1st Dragoon Guards

Major-General Sir William Ponsonby, K. C. B

2nd Brigade of Cavalry	1st Dragoons (Royals)
	2nd Dragoons (Scots Greys)
	6th Dragoons (Inneskillens)

Major-General Sir William Dornberg, K. C. B.

3rd Brigade of Cavalry	1st Light Dragoons, K, G. L.
	2nd Light Dragoons, K. G. L.
	23rd Light Dragoons

Major-General Sir Ormsby Vandeleur, K. C. B.

| 4th Brigade of Cavalry | 11th Light Dragoons |

12th Light Dragoons
16th Light Dragoons

Major-General Sir Colquhoun Grant, K. C. B.

5th Brigade of Cavalry   7th Hussars
15th Hussars
2nd Hussars, K.G.L.

Major-General Sir Richard Hussey Vivian, K. C. B.

6th Brigade of Cavalry   10th Hussars
18th Hussars
1st Hussars,; R. G. L.

Colonel Sir F, de Arentschildt, K. C. B.

7th Brigade of Cavalry   13th. Light Dragoons
3rd Hussars, K. G.L.

Major-General Victor Baron Alten.
Hanoverian Cavalry.

INFANTRY.

Major-General Peregrine Maitland.

1st Brigade of Infantry   2nd Battalion 1st Guards
3rd Battalion 1st Guards

Major-General Sir John Byng, K. C. B.

2nd Brigade of Infantry   3rd Batt. 2nd Guards (Coldstream.)
2nd Battalion 3rd Guards

Major-General Frederick Adam.

3rd Brigade of Infantry   1st Battalion 52nd Foot
2nd Battalion 95th Foot
71st Foot

Colonel H. Mitchell.

4th Brigade of Infantry   3rd Battalion 14th Foot
23rd Foot
51st Foot

Major-General Sir C. Halkett, K. C. B;

5th Brigade of Infantry   2nd Battalion 30th Foot
2nd Battalion 69th Foot
2nd Battalion 73rd Foot

Major-General Johnston.
6th Brigade of Infantry   1st 2nd 3rd & 4th Battalions,K.G.L

Major-General Duplat.

7th Brigade of Infantry	2nd Battalion 35th Foot
	2nd Battalion 59th Foot
	1st Battalion 91st Foot
	54th Foot

Major-General Sir James Kempt, K. C.B.

8th Brigade of Infantry	1st Battalion 79th Foot
	95th Foot
	28th Foot
	32nd Foot

Major-General Sir Dennis Pack, K C. B.

9th Brigade of Infantry	3rd Battalion 1st Foot
	2nd Battalion 44th Foot
	42nd Foot
	92nd Foot

Major-General Sir John Lambert, K. C. B.

10th Brigade of Infantry	1st Battalion 4th Foot
	1st Battalion 27th Foot
	2nd Battalion 81st Foot
	40th Foot

The 1st Division of Infantry consisted of the 1st and 2nd Brigades, under the command of Major-General Cook

The 2nd Division consisted of the 3rd and 7th Brigades and 3rd Hanoverian Infantry Brigade, under the command of Lieutenant-General Sir Henry Clinton, K. G. C. B.

The 3rd Division consisted of the 5th British, 1st German Legion and 1st Hanoverian Brigade, under the command of Lieutenant-General Sir Charles Baron Alten, K. C. B.

The 4th Division consisted of the 5th and 6th British and 6th Hanoverian Brigades, under the command of Lieutenant-General Sir Charles Colville, K. G.C.B.

The 5th Division consisted of the 8th and 9th British and 5th Hanoverian Brigades, under the command of Lieutenant-General Sir Thomas Picton, K. G. C. B.

The Infantry were divided into two corps. The 1st corps composed of the 1st, 3rd and 5th Divisions, was under the command of his Royal Highness the Prince of Orange, K.6.C.B.

The 2nd corps consisted of the 2nd and 4th Divisions, under the command of Lieutenant-Gen. Lord Hill, K. G. C. B.

The Royal Artillery (about 150 guns) commanded by Colonel Sir George Wood.

The Royal Engineers commanded by Colonel Carmichael Smith.

Adjutant-General of the army, Major-General Sir Edward Barnes, K. C. B.

Quarter-Master-General of the army. Colonel Sir William Henry De Lancey, K. C. B.

June. On the 10th of this month Buonaparte left Paris for the army, accompanied by his brother Jerome Buonaparte and Marshal Soult, and as soon as he arrived in the camp the French army began to concentrate and close up for operations, in face of the Prussian corps posted on the Sambre.

Statement of the French Army under the Command of Napoleon Buonaparte.

1st Corps of Infantry	General the Count d'Erlon.
2nd Corps of Infantry	General Count Reille.
3rd Corps of Infantry	General Count Vandamme.
4th Corps of Infantry	General Count Gerard.
6th Corps of Infantry	General Count Lobau.
	Imperial Guards.
15,000 Cavalry.	300 pieces of Cannon.

The 1st and 2nd Corps formed their left wing, under Marshal Ney.

The 3rd and 4th Corps formed their right, under Marshal Grouchy.

The 6th Corps and Imperial Guards formed their centre, under Napoleon himself, Marshal Soult being Adjutant General. Jerome Buonaparte had the command of a division, two of which, I believe, formed a corps.

The 5th Corps remained in France, probably with the view of covering the frontiers and guarding their rear.

COMMENCEMENT OF HOSTILITIES
June 15th, 1815.

There was a sound of revelry by night,
And Belgium's capital had gathered then
Her beauty, and her chivalry, and bright

The lamps shone o'er fair women and brave men;
A thousand hearts beat happily, and when
Music arose with its voluptuous swell,
Soft eyes look'd love to eyes which spake again,
And all went merry as a. marriage bell;
But hush! hark! a deep sound strikes like a rising knell!
Did ye not hear it? No; 'twas but the wind,
Or the car rattling o'er the stony street;
On with the dance! let joy be unconfin'd;
No sleep till morn when youth and pleasure meet
To chase the glowing hours with flying feet—
 But hark! that heavy sound breaks in once more,
As if the clouds its echo would repeat;
And nearer, clearer, deadlier than before!
Arm! Arm! it is—it is—the cannon's opening roar!

Within a window'd niche of that high hall
Sate Brunswick's feted chieftain—he did hear
That sound the first amidst the festival,
And caught its tone with Death's prophetic ear;
And when they smiled because he deem'd it near,
His heart more truly knew that peal too well
Which stretched his father on a bloody bier,
And rous'd the vengeance blood alone could quell:
He rushed into the field, and foremost fighting, fell.

Ah! then and there was hurrying" to and fro,
And gathering' tears and tremblings of distress,
And cheeks all pale, which but an hour ago
Blush'd at the praise of their own loveliness;
And there were sudden partings, such as press
The life from out young hearts, and choking sighs
Which ne'er might be repeated; who could guess
 If ever more should meet those mutual eyes,
Since upon night so sweet such awful morn could rise?

And there was mounting in hot haste; the steed,
The mustering squadron and the clattering car
Went pouring forward with impetuous speed,
And swiftly forming in the ranks of war;
And the deep thunder peal on peal afar;
And near, the beat of the alarming drum

Rous'd up the soldiers ere the morning star;
While thronged the citizens with terror dumb,
Or whispering, with white lips—"the foe!
they come, they come!"

And wild and high the "Cameron's gathering" rose
The war-note of Lochiel, which Albyn's hills
Have heard, and heard too have her Saxou foes:—
How in the noon of night that pibroch thrills,
Savage and shrill!—but with the breath that fills,
Their mountain-pipe so fill the mountaineers
With the fierce native faring which instils
The stirring memory of a thousand years.
And Evan's, Donald's fame rings in each clansman's ears!

And Antennas waves above them her green leaves,
Dewy with nature's tear-drops as they pass,
Grieving, if aught inanimate e'er grieves,
Over the unreturning brave—alas!
Ere evening to be trodden like the grass
Which now beneath them, but above shall grow
In its next verdure, when this fiery mass
Of living valour, rolling on the foe
And burning with high hope, shall moulder cold and low.

Last noon beheld them full of lusty life,
Last eve in beauty's circle proudly gay,
The midnight brought the signal sound of strife,
The morn the marshalling in arms,—the day
Battles' magnificently stern array:
The thunder clouds close o'er it, which when rent,
The earth is covered thick with other clay,
Which her own clay shall cover, heaped and pent,
Rider and horse,—friend, foe,—in one red burial blent!

Lord Byron.

The advanced guard of the Prussian army under General Von Zi-ethen, posted on the Sambre, being attacked this day by Buonaparte, Marshal Blucher turned out his troops, and ordered them to assemble with all possible haste at Ligny and Sombrief, upon which point General Ziethen retired in the evening, followed by Buonaparte as far as Charleroi. Messengers by express were immediately sent to Brussels, to inform the Duke of Wellington of these momentous events, and the first intimation of this actual commencement of operations was received there about 10 o'clock at night.

There had been a very splendid ball at Brussels the preceding evening, which it was intended to have repeated this evening; but the important news which now arrived at once suspended all merry meetings. Orders were circulated for the troops to be in readiness to turn out; all officers absent from their posts or regiments were directed instantly to join; and expresses were sent off in every direction over the country to assemble the forces, as not a moment was to be lost. None of the grand allied armies had yet joined, and the head of the nearest Prussian column was five marches distant: not a man had yet arrived either from America or Portugal, and from the dispersed nature of the cantonments, it was not possible to assemble the troops in the country in less than twenty-four hours.

All the divisions and brigades, however, had been roused during the night, and the officer who brought our orders galloped through Schehdelbeke about daybreak. In Brussels the bugles sounded and drums beat to arms at midnight, and the 5th Division marched out on the road to Waterloo about 2 in the morning. Our brave troops were now all hastening up by Waterloo, Nivelle, Genappe, &c. from every quarter towards the scene of operations, and were ordered to assemble at the farm of Quatre Bras or Four Arms, a house so named from its situation at the meeting of four roads, about four miles on the right of the Prussian army. Lieutenant-General Sir Thomas Picton just arrived from England, having been appointed to the command of the 5th Division, left Brussels in the night, and was one of the first who arrived at Quatre Bras, where the Prince of Orange with some Belgic troops, and the Duke of Brunswick with his Brunswickers, had already posted themselves.

BATTLES OF LIGNY AND QUATRE BRAS
June 16th, 1815.

The French army having passed the Sambre in the night, Buonaparte advanced this morning from Charleroi, and assembled his forces in face of Marshal Blocker's position at Ligny,, whose right rested on the village of St Amand, It was about 3 o'clock in the afternoon when the attack commenced upon the Prussian right wing, and the village of St. Amand, after an obstinate defence, was carried; Marshal Grouchy with his wing of the French army being ordered at the saw time to attack the principal post at Ligny, where Blucher waited for him without flinching. For five hours the battle here raged with the greatest violence, both sides receiving from their reserves a constant succession of fresh troops, actuated by a, spirit of the most dire hatred towards each other, produced by the recollection of private insults and public injuries on one part, and a sense of disappointed ambition on the other.

All the unhappy feelings of animosity of which the human mind is capable, seemed here to combine to render the conflict as terrific as possible, neither party (it was said) gave or asked for quarter. The veteran Blucher, at his advanced age (upwards of seventy years), headed his cavalry in their charges, in one of which he had his horse shot under him, and the Prussians being at that instant obliged to fall back, had not time to remount him; one of their officers who saw him fall, instantly threw himself by his side, determined to share his fate; but the French were so eager in the pursuit, that they passed by the Prussian Field-Marshal without discovering who he was, and being shortly afterwards in their turn forced to retire, he was safely rescued from their hands, and soon again at the head of his gallant army, which continued to defend itself against the furious attacks of the enemy all the afternoon, under the impression that they were opposed to the whole of their force, and should therefore be shortly succoured by the English army: but no sooner had the Prussian right wing been dislodged from St. Amand, than Buonaparte dispatched Marshal Ney with a large force of cavalry, fifty pieces of cannon, and two entire corps of French infantry (and here it should be observed that in the French army a corps of infantry comprises at least twenty thousand men) to march by Quartre Bras into the rear of the Prussians, or at all events take them in flank, if they could not surround them altogether.

The French Marshal supposing that there had not been time for the English to have assembled in sufficient force to check this movement, moved on with confidence, little suspecting that the handful of men we haft collected would attempt seriously to obstruct his progress: he was, however, soon undeceived; and he and his legions found it necessary to fight with all the fury and courage they could exert. Their first attack was upon a small force of Belgians headed by the Prince of Orange; but these being soon joined by the 5th Division under General Picton, and the troops of the Duke of Brunswick from Brussels, about 3 o'clock a most serious contest commenced, in which the division of General Picton covered itself with glory.

The 28th, 32nd, 79th and 95th regiments, formed the brigade under Major-General Pack in the 5th Division, in which were the 42nd and 92nd Highlanders: these troops on this occasion surpassed all their former deeds of heroism, having to sustain the shock of this terrific conflict until they were joined by the 1st and 3rd Divisions successively, who as they arrived on the right of the 5th Division, immediately took part in the contest, which by that time had become one of the most murderous and terrible ever recorded in history. From the great distance which our cavalry had to march, not a regiment of them had arrived, so that the only mounted force at hand was a regiment of Dutch dragoons (which, I heard, was completely cut to pieces), and those of the Duke of Brunswick, which about 4 o'clock advanced and charged the enemy, but sustaining an irreparable loss in the fall of their gallant Prince, and suffering very severely, they were obliged to be withdrawn again to the rear: this left the enemy at liberty to renew his attacks upon our gallant infantry with such a preponderating force of horse and foot, that it was impossible to repel their assaults without the most distressing loss.

The carnage was dreadful, every man's part became a forlorn hope, and for awhile no efforts, either individual or collective, promised success. The losses in the two Highland regiments abovementioned were beyond all precedent; both their colonels had fallen, and the field was strewed with their dying and their dead. The 42nd had to sustain several most severe charges from the enemy's cavalry, in which they had nearly lost their colours; an occurrence which under such circumstances could have been no disgrace; yet few men of the regiment, I believe, would willingly have outlived their loss. After falling from one hand to another, they were at length seized by a French dragoon, who attempted to escape with them into the forest. Sir Robert Macara, their colonel, who was then stretched on the field severely wounded, perceiving the desperate state of affairs in which his brave regiment was involved, ventured to wave his hand for their encouragement, upon which he and several others of the poor wounded were barbarously hewn to pieces by the French cavalry: this produced such a frantic spirit that no quarter was given on either side, add the field soon became heaped with slain.

Amid this strife, however, the Highlanders recovered their colours, and the daring individual who had ventured to seize them was literally torn to pieces. When the 3rd Division arrived it marched to the left of the 5th, and the 1st occupied a wood on their right hear the farm of Quatre Bras: against this post the enemy renewed his attacks until late in the evening, when he was driven back upon his reserves at all points, and as Buonaparte in his account of the action said, "The British at Quatre Bras not content with repulsing the Marshal Duke of Elchingen (Ney) actually assailed his position at Frasne;" and our troops bivouacked on the hills which at the commencement of the action had been occupied by the enemy. In the meantime the battle at Ligny had continued wife the same terrific violence.

The village of St. Amand was in part retaken in the evening, when the Prussian cavalry posted behind the village were overthrown by the French cavalry, and a body of their infantry also getting unobserved into the Prussian rear, the day turned against the Prussians, notwith-standing all the noble efforts they had made, and the success which had attended the British at Quatre Bras.

Blucher was therefore compelled to yield the field to his antago-nist, and retreat upon Wavre. Buonaparte in his account of these op-erations, says, the Marshal Duke of Elchingen lost four thousand two hundred men, and he estimates the English loss at five thousand: and then turning to the battle of Ligny, he says, the Prussians lost fifteen thousand men; and estimates his own loss there at only three thousand: but considering the desperate valour with which the Prussians fought, and how long the day was undecided, there was every reason to be-lieve that this estimate was considerably underrated, particularly as the brave Prussians were considered really to have lost upwards of ten thousand men. The account of our loss, however, was nearly correct, one third of our force having suffered. He called the Prussian army ninety thousand strong, whereas it did not I believe exceed 50,000, General Von Bulow with his corps not having joined.

Our brigade having marched from Schendelbeke early in the morning, had passed through Grammont, Enghein, &c. and early in the afternoon we same within hearing of the cannonade. Just as it was getting dark an order came down the road for the cavalry to come up with all possible speed; which soon brought us to Nivelles, Where another order met us, directing us to go forward, and passing through the town, the streets of which were crowded with wounded men, we reached the field of battle about midnight.

Immediately after passing Nivelles the troops were ordered to file off to the right and left of the road, so as to leave the "*pave*" in the centre clear for the poor wounded who were coming from the field, Strewing the road with their blood: they were chiefly of the 1st and 3rd Divisions, particularly the 33rd regiment and the guards, and by whom Captain Elphinstone, of our regiment, was informed, upon inquiry, of the death of his brother, Colonel Elphinstone, who commanded the 33rd; but happily it afterwards proved that this gallant officer had been wounded only. We were almost stunned by the noise of the hospital spring-wagons passing us at full speed along this stony road.

The news had just been received that the day had turned against Marshal Blucher, and that he was falling back, in consequence of which our troops would be obliged to change their position also: every effort was therefore to be made during the night to bring off the wounded and move them to the rear. When we reached the field of battle we passed by the dying and the dead, and turned into a field where there was not a tree or bush for shelter: it was a cold and cloudy night, during which neither baggage nor supplies appeared, so that the troops had to suffer serious privations. I went back to Nivelles, and about 3 o'clock in the morning got my horse into a stable, and lay down upon a wooden form in a room of an *auberge*, which was too much crowded even to afford me a blanket.

Events of the 17th June

All the cavalry and a part of the 2nd Division of infantry had arrived during the night, and the remainder of our army, together with the Dutch and Flemish troops, were coming up: but the retreat of the Prussians upon Wavre rendering a corresponding movement on our part necessary, orders were given for the town of Nivelles to be cleared as speedily as possible of the wounded, and the baggage and stores of the 4th Division and cavalry which were moving upon this town from Enghein and Grammont were ordered to cross the country by Hal, and make the best of their way to Antwerp or Brussels, while the divisions began to retire from the field of Quatre Bras towards the village of Waterloo, the cavalry covering the retreat.

During these operations the enemy never offered us the least molestation, either because they were not prepared to advance or that they were unacquainted with the nature of our movements until the whole of our army had fallen back with the exception of the 7th Hussars, which had been left as a kind of piquet to watch their motions. No sooner, however, had the last division of our cavalry receded than the French lancers and *cuirassiers* began to file out of a wood in face of the 7th Hussars, upon which the regiment retreated in good order as far as Genappe, through which town passes the high road from Quatre

Bras to Waterloo.

The French being close at their heels they had scarcely cleared the town when the enemy marched through, and our rear squadron had but just time to face about before they were charged by a mixed force of *cuirassiers* and lancers, against which they found it impossible to make head: the squadron was almost annihilated. Major Hodge and the adjutant of the regiment were instantaneously unhorsed and killed, and Captain Elphihstone being severely wounded and made prisoner with a number of his men, was carried directly before the Emperor, with whom he had an interesting interview and conversation.

Buonaparte was standing upon a hill wrapped in his cloak and encircled by his staff: it was then raining very fast. In the meantime the regiment retiring before their too powerful assailants were at length succoured by the Life Guards, which regiment Lord Uxbridge had ordered up to their support, and the enemy's cavalry were then called up from the pursuit. At the time the retreat from Quatre Bras commenced I was in Nivelles, when a part of the 4th Division under Sir Charles Colville, amongst which was the 14th regiment, about 3 o'clock in the afternoon passed that town in their way to the position appointed them. The enemy's piquets were then approaching the town, and Sir Charles Colville, who soon recognised me as belonging to the old Peninsular 3rd Division, cautioned me against remaining there any longer. Such part of the baggage of these divisions which had reached this town joined that of the cavalry and other divisions on the road which in its way to Waterloo crosses the position the army was now to occupy, and passes but a few paces from the farm of Hougomont.

I never shall forget the scene which this road exhibited from the town of Nivelles on the hill to the village of Waterloo in the plain (a distance of about five miles): the warlike train of cavalry, artillery, ammunition and baggage wagons, in some places four and five deep, seemed to form an unbroken chain all in full speed upon Waterloo: our brave infantry were taking up their ground on the hills and in the cornfields in every direction as far as the eye could reach, and some guns were being drawn up to the eminences.—About 4 o'clock I passed the large old *château* of Hougomont, which stands a little off the road on our right as we pass from Nivelles, around the walls and premises of which our troops were then posting themselves; but at this time it did not possess that interest which it has since acquired.

A thunder-storm which had been gathering all the morning by

this time had so darkened the horizon as to form one perfect black canopy over the field of Waterloo. We had for some time heard the murmuring of thunder at a distance, and it now rolled in awful peals over our heads; the lightning became exceedingly vivid, and the storm at length burst in torrents of hail and rain. It was at this moment that the charge at Genappe took place, during which we could scarcely distinguish between the sound of the cannonade and that of the thunder.—At 5 o'clock I arrived in Mont St. Jean, one mile below which, and just on the verge of the forest of Soignies, stands the once obscure and simple, but now the far-famed Waterloo, At Mont St. Jean the road from Quatre Bras and Genappe joins that from Nivelles.

On the eve of being enrolled in the annals of fame, this village as well as that of Waterloo had been deserted by their inhabitants, several of whom had only time to hide themselves in the forest, and some of the houses which happened to be nearest the field were being taken to pieces for fuel The confusion here was quite terrific. All the baggage of the army having now to retreat by one road upon Brussels, in passing through the forest got so crowded and entangled, that for some time not any part of it could proceed, which afforded an opportunity to some ill-disposed or cowardly persons (principally natives of the country with some Belgic troops, and doubtless with the view of aiding the enemy) to create a panic, by spreading false alarms during the whole of the night and following day, by which they rendered the rear of the army a scene of almost as much peril and confusion as the field of battle itself.

The forest of Soignies, whose dark foliage in some parts entirely excludes the rays of the sun, casting an awful gloom over the road, conspired with the pelting storm which beat upon our heads to render the scene truly terrific. Towards dark, as I was riding down to Waterloo, in company with some wounded officers; the Duke of Wellington passed by; he was noticing some stragglers of the Belgic army who had left their regiments, and were endeavouring to conceal themselves in the forest. At this instant an orderly dragoon came galloping up to the Duke, and delivered him a note, which appeared to be of some importance, as he immediately faced about and returned to Mont St, Jean.

A cannonade was now heard in front, and the alarms in Waterloo and the forest increased. Some few of the inhabitants who had not fled were in great consternation, and were closing their houses and evidently preparing for the entrance of the French. I endeavoured to obtain the assistance of a man who was closing his doors against us, to dissuade from flight some country people with their horses which I had under my direction; but he quickly replied that he would have nothing to do in the business, as he was no "*homme des guerres*," (no man of wars.)

While I was thus occupied, the Duke of Wellington returned, and passing close by us he went into a farmhouse nearly opposite, where I believe he remained all night Amongst the officers of his staff I was surprised to see the famous Spaniard, Don Miguel Alava, not knowing that he was in this country. It appears that he had arrived as ambassador from the court of Spain to that of the Netherlands, but finding affairs here in so critical a state, he awaited their result before he delivered his credentials. It was now getting quite dark: the rain continued to fall in torrents, and the road laying low was in some places actually knee deep in mud and water.

The crests of the heights were crowned with cannon, and all the fields round Waterloo and Mont St. Jean were full of troops, exposed to the accumulated privations of this trying night. About 10 o'clock I left Waterloo for Brussels. I do not remember having ever been out on so truly awful a night: the wind and rain continued unabated, and with so much violence that at times it was impossible for our horses to proceed: the atmosphere was a perfect mass of fog and vapour, which rendered it as cold as in December. We found the road choked up with broken carts, wagons and other wrecks of the baggage, while some foreign troops and artillery meeting in the dark had got mixed in such confusion, that we were obliged to leave the road and wind our course through the forest, where some of our cavalry, in search of shelter and refreshment, were bending their march upon Brussels, but with orders to be at Waterloo again early in the morning. I fully expected that my baggage was all lost, as I could neither see nor hear anything of it.

Soon after midnight I arrived at Brussels, which but a few evenings previous had been the seat of revelry, and the cheerful residence of many English as well as native families of distinction, but now presenting a most melancholy contrast. The streets were crowded with baggage, and wagons full of wounded moving in sad procession towards Antwerp, while here and there carriages with English families were seen posting through the town in the greatest haste and alarm for Ostend, from whence to escape to England; and such was the difficulty experienced in obtaining conveyance, that one hundred Napoleons, I heard, were offered for a *chaise* from Brussels to the coast. I went to the inn where I had formerly put up, but could gain no admittance: however I at length succeeded in getting my horse into a stable in another part of the town, where I also procured for him a feed of corn, and then lay down in my wet clothes until daylight, when I set out again for Waterloo, and fell in with the same brigade of cavalry marching out of Brussels which I had passed in the night

BATTLE OF WATERLOO
18th June, 1815

And Harold stands upon this place of sculls,
The grave of France—the deadly Waterloo.

Lord Byron

(*Sunday morning.*) The following was the disposition of our troops on this eventful day. The centre of the army occupied the high ground above Mont St. Jean, with its reserve in the village: the left rested on the farm of Ter la Haye, and the right ran along the ridge as far as Brain le Leud, between which place and the farm of Hougomont it crossed the Nivelles road: the ground in front of this position sloped gently towards the valley, and in the same easy manner ascended on the other side, where the French army was posted at the distance perhaps of about 1,200 paces from ours.

The 1st Division occupied that part of the position denominated the right centre, in front of which is situated the farm of Hougomont, in the orchard and gardens of which were also posted some foreign troops: the 3rd Division under Sir Charles Alten, formed the left centre, and occupied the farmhouse of La Haye Sainte: the 5th Division was posted on the left of the third, the 2nd Division on the right of the 1st and the 4th on the right of the 2nd. Sir John Lambert's brigade of infantry and a large force of Belgic troops formed our extreme left, and kept open our communication with Wavre by Ohain. Our cavalry were for the present in rear of the infantry at different points of the line, and the foreign troops, some of them chequered with the British, and the remainder in reserve about the villages of Mont St. Jean and Waterloo.

From this statement it will be found that the 1st, 3rd and 5th Divisions, forming the corps of his Royal Highness the Prince of Orange, occupied that part of our position which was immediately opposed to the enemy, while the corps of Lord Hill, particularly the 4th Division, forming our extreme right, was thrown back across the Nivelles road, so as to form a kind of support to the right of our centre, and one brigade of this division had been posted near Hal with the view of blocking up a road which passes there from Nivelles to Brussels.

Buonaparte after his success at Ligny on the evening of the 16th, concluding that the Prussians had, at least for the present, been disabled, ordered one corps of his army, under the directions of Marshal Grouchy, to follow them to Wavre and observe their movements, while he himself should advance with the rest of his forces to fight the Duke of Wellington, Marshal Ney having taken possession of Nivelles last evening shortly after we had left it, approached the British position from that quarter. Jerome Buonaparte held a command in the right of their centre, and Napoleon's head-quarters were at a farm near Planchenoit, which appears a little off the great road from Waterloo to Genappe, about a mile in rear of the French position.

Such was the disposition of the two armies on the morning of this memorable day, which was occupied in awful preparations for the tremendous conflict. From the retrograde movements we had made yesterday, Napoleon, it seems, had rather expected that we should this morning have commenced our retreat; for when information was brought to him early that the British were still on the field of Waterloo, he exclaimed, "Ah! I have caught these English then:" upon which Marshal Soult, who was then near to the Emperor (it was said), observed with a smile, "that there was now no fear of our running away." I can easily imagine with what a consciousness of knowing the British troops Soult could make this observation.

Buonaparte throughout his enterprising life, it would seem, had studiously avoided meeting a British army, or opposing himself personally to any of our troops. It was now, however, his fate at last to meet them plumed with laurels which were yet green, from the Egyptian, Indian and Peninsular gardens. The heavy rains which had continued to fall throughout the night, and to which the troops of both armies were equally exposed, had so softened the ground, the greatest part of which was ploughed soil grown over with rye and other grain, that in some parts of our position the men were nearly up to their knees in mud and water, and even where the ground was more elevated, none could stand long in one place without sinking ankle deep into the clay-cold earth.

Under such circumstances, and exposed as they were to the severe inclemencies of so dreadful a night, it will readily be imagined that the cavalry and artillery found the greatest difficulty in keeping their horses alive, and turning them out this morning in any sort of order: but difficulties and privations of this nature, severe as they were, soon prepared to vanish before the scenes of life and death which were now at hand. From the time the rain had ceased the men had been cleaning their arms and appointments, and where it was practicable, by lighting a few camp-fires, endeavouring to dry their clothes, until about 11 o'clock, when the French army was observed to be falling in, and in line of battle preparing to advance from the opposite hills.

The Duke of Wellington and the several general and other officers quickly repaired to their posts. *Aides-de-camp* were seen passing our lines in every direction with orders for the regiments to stand to their arms, and the bugles and trumpets sounding, the divisions all fell in and took their posts with cheerful hearts. The battle now began with a furious attack upon our troops posted in the *château* and gardens of Hougomont, while the enemy's cavalry crowning the ridge on their side the valley, began to advance by the highway, supported by a terrible fire from an immense quantity of artillery extremely well served.

The situation of the *château* of Hougomont in front of our right centre was such as rendered it of that importance that it was termed the key to our position in that quarter, and the defence of it was specially confided to the two brigades of foot-guards under Major-Generals Byng and Maitland, the light companies of which, together with some Belgic and a few Brunswick infantry, lined the avenues and plantations round the house: these were the troops first attacked: they defended the post with great gallantry, until they were nearly surrounded, and absolutely obliged to fall back, when they retired in good order towards the house: the conflict then became very terrific: the *château* and premises were attacked by thirty thousand men, under cover of a fire from fifty pieces of cannon: all the gates and avenues leading to the mansion were assailed at once, and from half-past 11 until near 1 o'clock it was impossible for a spectator at any moment to say in whose possession the premises were; so nobly did the British guards defend this post, that they called forth the just admiration of the whole army and the highest encomiums from the Field-Marshal.

Every tree in the orchards and gardens had been sharply contested for, and the troops in the house having loop-holed the walls poured forth such an incessant shower of musketry, while those at the gates charged with the bayonet, that the most terrible carnage spread itself on every side, and all the approaches to the *château* were heaped with slain. In the meantime the right and right centre of the French having crossed the ravine between the two armies, had attacked our left, and left centre, and there the conflict was throughout the day. of the most murderous and terrific nature.

The enemy's attacks were made by such immense columns both of infantry and cavalry, sometimes together and sometimes separate, that it required all the skill and exertions of the generals and commanding officers, and all the characteristic devotedness of both officers and soldiers, to bear up against them. No sooner had one body of troops been repulsed than another advanced. The French cavalry charged our squares of infantry time after time with the most frantic valour, shouting *"Vive l' Empereur!"* and notwithstanding the terrible defeats they sustained still returned to the attack, and being met by our cavalry a most terrific scene of havoc and confusion prevailed on all sides, and thousands of men and horses fell.

The armour of the enemy's *cuirassiers* received no impression either from our volleys of musketry or cavalry swords, and thus defended, they were dealing destruction in every quarter, and galloping round our hollow squares sometimes charged all four faces of them at once. Our men were ordered to fire low, this together with the bayonets of the front line brought down many horses and hurled their riders to the earth. At length our heavy cavalry appearing through the clouds of fire and smoke, suddenly charged them with all the weight they could carry, which brought several squadrons of them at once to the ground with a tremendous crash, and for the moment cleared that part of the field: still however the battle continued with the same terrific violence.

Two, three and four o'clock came and found things in the same undecided state, notwithstanding that the enemy had again and again attacked the ridge occupied by the 3rd and 5th Divisions, and after a most dreadful contest had taken the farm of La Haye Sainte. This post from the commencement of the conflict had been gallantly defended by a part of the King's German Legion and some Hanoverian troops sent from the 3rd Division. The French had for two hours been directing their chief attacks against it, by which the ammunition of the garrison being exhausted at a time when it was impossible to send them a fresh supply, they were compelled to surrender or sell their lives as dearly as they could, and they chose the latter; for when the gates of the farm were carried by the enemy a sanguinary contest with the bayonet was maintained in the yard and house as long as there was a German left upon his feet.

By the loss of this place the position occupied by the 3rd and 5th Divisions had become seriously exposed, and the enemy under a heavy cannonade was now preparing to attack the heights near the highway above Mont St. Jean, where the veteran warrior Sir Thomas Picton, with his invincible division, was posted. Regardless, though not altogether unconscious, that this would prove his dying hour, with calm composure he viewed the storm approach, and resolved to meet it like a man ready to die for his country.

The French were crossing the ravine in solid squares, their cavalry and artillery moving by the highway: for a while their march was considerably impeded by a destructive fire from our artillery posted behind a hedge on the left of our position and some Belgic troops on the slope of the hill; but these being at length compelled to give way, the shock of steel now awaited the 5th Division, which at first fell into squares to receive the French cavalry, and then into line to meet their infantry. The French troops advanced with their drums beating, colours flying and eagles soaring over their heads, the cries of "*Vive l'Empereur!*" resounding from every mouth as they approached the British columns.

But on the British heart were lost
The terrors of the charging host;
For not an eye the scene that view'd,
Chang'd its proud glance of fortitude.

Walter Scott.

At length after a terrible carnage the enemy gained the ridge, where Sir Thomas Picton: had formed the whole of his division into one grand line for a charge with bayonets. A shock then took place too dreadful to contemplate, in the midst of which General Picton fell; a musket-ball which passed through his head closed his warlike career. For a quarter of an hour it was not known that the General had fallen, so close and terrific was the fight. Hundreds were falling around him; and his *aide-de-camp*, poor Captain Chambers, who was also with the old 3rd Division in the Peninsula, fell by his side. For some time the work of destruction was such on all sides, that it was impossible to say which way the scale of success would turn, and the oldest officers could not but look forward to the issue of this struggle with terror and alarm.

While these dreadful events were passing with the divisions of Picton and Alten, a scene no less appalling presented itself at Hougomont, the towers of which edifice (from the shover of shells and cannon-balls poured down upon it) were now on fire, and the whole mansion soon after became one mass of smoking ruins: at the same time the enemy surrounded the court yard and gardens, and attempted to carry them at the point of the bayonet. The Field Marshal himself being on the spot rallied the troops around the burning edifice, and in person led on the guards to a charge in which they drove back the enemy with dreadful carnage.

In the meantime Marshal Ney after several attempts had succeeded in penetrating to that part of the ridge where the 2nd Division was posted, and with a very large force of cavalry attempted to carry those heights. The only British regiments in this division were the 52nd, 71st and 2nd battalion of the 95th, all Light Infantry; these together with the 7th brigade (Germans) and a corps of Hanoverians now maintained a most terrible conflict. The Duke of Wellington, who throughout this day as well as the 16th was always to be seen where the danger was the greatest and his presence most wanted, repaired to the spot, and (I heard), was once compelled to take refuge in one of our hollow squares, which was charged repeatedly by the French cavalry; in all their attacks, however, they were beaten back, and sent reeling down the hills by our cavalry, in which the brigade of household troops and the 1st Dragoon Guards under Lord Edward Somerset performed most important service and were highly distinguished.

During this struggle a brigade of the 4th Division moved up to the support of the 2nd, but the fire from the enemy's artillery was found so destructive that as soon as they could be spared they were again withdrawn into the ravine. The 23rd Fusiliers here lost their distinguished commanding officer, Sir Henry Ellis, K. C. B. and the field was covered with killed and wounded. The engagement in this quarter although still maintained, had become less violent and destructive before the contest had been decided on the heights of Mont St. Jean, where a perpetual succession of French troops arrived as they were called off from the attack at Hougomont.

At length the British flag waved triumphant in that quarter also, for the enemy finding all their efforts fruitless, began to give way, and soon took completely to their heels, pursued by our cavalry. The brigade of heavy dragoons under Sir Wm. Ponsonby, composed of an English, Scotch and Irish regiment, as they galloped by the 5th Division, shouted "England, Scotland and Ireland forever!" which thrilled the senses of every man present, and produced such a feeling of attachment to their country as effectually cheered them in this trying hour.

The charge of this brigade was so tremendous, that those who witnessed it from the hill declared that they actually cut through the enemy's columns as far as the valley between the two positions, and then wheeling about charged back again, dealing death and destruction on every side, by which heroic conduct they captured two eagles and secured two thousand prisoners, some of whom refusing to march to the rear they were obliged to cut down, as fresh columns of the enemy were descending the ridge to their assistance.

It is supposed to have been in one of these charges that Major-General Sir William Ponsonby fell; but the confusion was such that no one knew what had befallen him until after the battle, when his body was found shockingly mangled upon some very heavy, ground, by which it was, supposed his horse had been impeded and finally arrested in its career at a moment of imminent danger, probably when the French were attempting a rescue of their prisoners: by his side also lay his *aide-du-camp*, within whose clenched hand I have been told was found a miniature portrait of Lady Ponsonby, which the General was accustomed to wear in his bosom.

It was conjectured that he had given it to his *aide-de-camp* when he found himself wounded and likely to fall into the hands of the enemy, by whom he was sure to be plundered; but to fall into the enemy's hands at such a moment was to fall into the very jaws of death; and the General not only by sad experience found this to be the case, but his *aide-de-camp* too it appears had not time to escape, and shared his fate. By this time the field of battle at all points had assumed a horrid aspect, the hills and ravines in every direction (but particularly the slopes of the hills along the front of our position) were so covered with the mangled corpses of friends and foes, that neither man nor horse could in some places pass without treading upon them.

Those of the wounded who could not crawl from the groaning field, were in perpetual danger of being struck by the showers of shot firing over them, or trodden to death by the charging squadrons. The cries of these poor fellows were lost amid the clashing of arms, and roar of 400 pieces of cannon which spread death in every direction, and absolutely shook the ground: in some quarters the shots flew so thick that many of them must have struck each other before they reached the ground. The defeat which Buonaparte had just sustained had so deranged his plans as to cause a temporary suspension from these murderous attacks, during which however preparations were obviously making for a renewal of them, and the cannonade was continued without intermission.

Not more than half an hour had elapsed before another terrible struggle commenced; the enemy's infantry advancing in solid columns with their flanks protected by a large force of cuirassiers and lancers and an immense artillery, once more attacked the whole extent of our line, but after some terrific charges both of cavalry and infantry they were again sent reeling back upon their reserves. This dreadful work of destruction had now continued for the space of six hours, and on a space of ground not exceeding two miles in length, were heaped the bodies of more than twenty, thousand victims: the loss of human life was, as usual, no consideration with Buonaparte, who knowing that his *all* was at stake had sent upwards of seventy thousand men into action at once, a force calculated to overwhelm all resistance: but every acre of ground was to be covered with slain before it was yielded, and then disputed for again.

Still, however, Buonaparte conscious of his superiority in numbers (notwithstanding that fifteen thousand of his men were already stretched upon the plain), remained unshaken in his resolution to carry our position; and when Marshal Ney sent him word that he could not advance by reason of an English battery which threatened his utter destruction, and asked for orders, the reply was, "*take the battery!*" when he doubtless himself knew that it was an absolute impossibility; and added, "tell the Marshal that the day must and shall be ours." His friend Marshal Soult, who it would appear was remarkably quiet on the occasion, I dare say could by this time have told him a very different story. It was now past 6 o'clock, and the loss which we had sustained was beyond all precedent.

Upwards of ten thousand of our brave officers and troops had fallen, and still the day was not over: it seemed almost that no man was to outlive it, and that all parties had met to die together; for now the bloodthirsty Napoleon perceiving that affairs were come to such a crisis, that in the short space of one hour more all must be lost or won, resolved to set the fate of the day and that of all parties once more at issue, by one most awful effort, which though it should fail of success would yet afford him and his soldiers the bloody satisfaction that their falling spears had to the last drank deep in British gore, and pierced every heart in England.

Finding that all his attempts against our troops at Hougomont had failed, he gathered his whole force, including all his reserves, into such order, that by a simultaneous movement they bore down upon our little devoted army with such savage rancour and despair, as for the moment; threatened to render the victory again doubtful, for there was not a sufficient number of British and Hanoverian troops left to hold the position, one half of the former having fallen, and it was considered dangerous In the present juncture of affairs to bring forward those Belgic regiments which had been left in the rear, as almost every man of them had formerly been in the service of Buonaparte. Just at this critical moment a tremendous roar of cannon upon our left, in the direction of Aguiers, announced the arrival of the Prussian army, which was now forming upon the enemy's right flank, with the view of marching into their rear.

Marshal Blucher immediately on his arrival at the head of his troops (although they were not all up), perceiving the dreadful crisis to which affairs were brought with the English army, and as he himself nobly expressed it, "knowing that with whatever firmness the British maintained the conflict it was impossible but that all their heroic efforts must have their limits," resolved instantly to commence the attack, which we had been most anxiously looking for all the afternoon. It appears by Buonaparte's account that the Prussians had attacked him in this same quarter about 4 o'clock, but that the 6th Corps of his army under Count Lobau, which was then in reserve, soon defeated and drove them back.

Now this was nothing more than the advanced guard of the Prussians, who had marched from Wavre as soon as it was light, with the view of joining us soon after the contest should have commenced; but from the badness of the roads, which the heavy rain had broken up, and the difficulties they experienced in passing a defile, they had been so retarded in their advance that the British had been sustaining the heat of this unequal and awful conflict for four hours before even the Prussian advanced guard arrived.

Unequal as this heroic little band was to the task of giving their friends that effectual aid of which they stood so much in need, while the enemy had still so large a force in reserve ready to oppose them, they viewed the scene (it was said) with tears in their eyes, and struck with admiration at the firmness and constancy with which the English army defended the great cause, endeavoured to create a diversion in our favour: but Buonaparte having with his reserves driven them back, then concluded that he had once for all done with the Prussians, especially as he had left, what he considered a sufficient force with Marshal Grouchy to keep them in checks

This officer appears to have received but very imperfect information, however, respecting Prince Blucher's movements, for his attack upon the corps left at Wavre was made too late in the day to be of any service to Buonaparte, who imagined that either he was engaging the attention of the Prussian army at Wavre, or that, if their grand force was marching in this direction, he also was making a corresponding-movement.

Fully impressed with this persuasion, and perceiving that nothing but the most preponderating force could make any impression on the British, regardless altogether of the Prussians, in his last attack he brought forward all his reserves, by which though he certainly caused us dreadful loss, he effectually paved the way to his own complete overthrow; for now that the Prussian army was really advancing and had commenced its attack, he had no disposable force left to oppose it, and he was so astonished that for a time he would not believe but that they were his own troops under Marshal Grouchy. Lord Wellington perceiving that the Prussians were now really up and had commenced their attack, ordered our reserves to close up, and the whole line being formed for offensive operations, the trumpets and bugles Sounded for the advance, and the air rang with shouts of victory all through the field.

The French Imperial Guards destined to defend the Emperor's person and their cavalry then threw themselves before our line with the view of covering their retreat. Our cavalry now again came into action, and broke the enemy's squares in every direction; but Lieutenant-General the Earl of Uxbridge whose services had been of the most brilliant nature throughout the day, was struck by a cannon-shot, by which he lost his leg.

The Imperial Guards who had again attacked the post of Hougomont were once more met by our guards and light brigade, by whom they were charged over the ravine between the two armies, and Buonaparte not only acknowledges this, but attaches to it such importance, that by it, he says, his whole army were panic struck, and to this he attributes the rout and confusion which ensued; but as he must, in conformity with his general maxim, in the first instance claim the victory, he wanted an excuse for the loss of it, though I must own he appears to me to have chosen a very poor one.

Our victorious army now advancing from the field of desolation which they had so well defended, carried by a sort of triumphant attack the position of the enemy just as it was getting dark, and the Prussians headed by Marshal Blucher having got into the high road in their rear, their whole army (as Buonaparte in his own account says) became one perfect mass of confusion: all the soldiers of different arms were mixed pell-mell, and it was utterly impossible to rally a single corps, cries being heard in every quarter of "all is lost! all is lost!" "*sauve qui peut!*" "save themselves who can!"

All their guns (more than 300), ammunition wagons, baggage, and in short everything was abandoned. A division of Prussian light troops, part of the corps of General Von Ziethen, overtook at Genappe Buonaparte's head-quarters baggage. His carriages (from one of which he himself escaped without hat or sword), all fell into their hands, and even his famous travelling chariot in which he had travelled to Moscow and through all his celebrated campaigns, and which had often brought him home in triumph to Paris. It is singular enough that this carriage was some years ago built at Brussels; and feeing a great curiosity it was sent to England and exhibited in London.

The Prussian army having come up fresh from Wavre, where it had also been joined by the corps of General Von Bulow, undertook the pursuit of the enemy, and the British army bivouacked on the French position at 10 o'clock. About this hour the two Field Marshals, Wellington and Blucher, met at a farmhouse on the field, which is called La Belle Alliance, where they mutually exchanged congratulations, and Blucher said he had sent forward every man land horse under his command, with orders to pursue the enemy by day and night.

Throughout this glorious and eventful day I was posted in rear of the army, and most part of the time on the road leading from Waterloo to Brussels, and consequently not exposed to danger further than in that degree to which we should all have been liable had the enemy proved victorious, for then escape would have been out of the question, and it had been said from the very commencement of these operations, that the French soldiers were fixed in their intention, upon gaining the victory, to give no quarter and make no prisoners of any sort, but to put every man to the sword without distinction; and their conduct during the last three days seemed fully to justify this assertion; for besides the instances already mentioned of poor Sir Robert Macara and the Highlanders on the field of Quatre Bras on the 16th, there was but too much reason to fear, that Major Hodge and the adjutant of the 7th Hussars who were lost on the 17th, were murdered after they were taken: they certainly fell alive into the enemy's hands: and the people of Genappe afterwards affirmed that some English officers had been put to death there by the French soldiers that night.

One can hardly be too backward or cautious in giving credit to reports in their nature so revolting to every feeling of humanity and honour; but I am sorry to say that these impressions received but too much confirmation from the very few prisoners which the French took, under circumstances where they could have done it with safety and saved many lives, and from the cruel conduct of their lancers in particular on the field of battle, one instance of which has been already brought before the public.

Colonel P. of the 12th Light Dragoons (who happily recovered, and was providentially restored after all the horrid sufferings he endured) having in a charge made by his regiment in the early stage of affairs been severely wounded, was lying on the field of battle in great distress, when he was passed by some French lancers, one of whom seeing him still able to move, cried, *"Ah cochon vous n'etes-pas mort, eh!"* (Ah you dog or pig you are not dead, eh!) and with a thrust of his lance added another dreadful wound, and then left him for dead: he was afterwards most unfeelingly mocked and insulted by others as they passed, one of whom made his body a rest for his musket while he fired; and them is no doubt that many of our poor wounded men had their deaths hastened by such inhumane treatment;

It appears, however, that this conduct was by no means sanctioned by Buonaparte, for Captain Elphinstone and such other prisoners as were taken before him (I believe) bear testimony to the lenity with which he treated them; but no sooner had they left the Emperor's presence than they were most grossly insulted and ill-treated by the soldiers, who affirmed as they marched them to the rear, that they had secret orders to put all the prisoners to death, and that consequently they might prepare. This barbarous conduct of the French soldiers led in some degree, in the heat of the action, to a retaliation on our part, by which, in one or two instances, they were severely chastised.

They had (as already observed) on the 16th roused the mountain rage of the Highland regiments, particularly of the 42nd, who (as I was told) at the close of that day petitioned General Picton to afford them an opportunity (should one offer) of taking signal vengeance. The old General, with whom the French were no greater favourites than with them, in one of the earliest attacks made upon him on the 18th, by the following stratagem gave these troops satisfaction.

The Hanoverian brigade of the division was posted in front to receive the enemy, while the Highland regiments were placed in ambush along the slope of a little hill in their rear: the French columns advanced under their usual cries of "*Vive la Gloire!*" and "*Vive l'Empereur!*" when the Hanoverians, as they had been instructed, after receiving and returning the enemy's fire, faced about and fled in apparent dismay and confusion.

The French seeing this, and perhaps also taking them for British, their dress being scarlet, believed that they had made a serious impression, and rushed forward with great impetuosity; but in the blaze of musketry and clouds of smoke in which they were enveloped, they passed the ambushment of the Highlanders without discovering it. About 9,000 of the enemy (it is supposed) had thus passed, when the "*Sans culottes*," as the French term them, arose like fierce lions from their ambushment, fired a destructive volley and then dashed in amongst them with fixed bayonets.

The French in this perilous situation soon cried out for quarter, but were answered by the appalling cry of "no quarter!" "where's Macara?" and such others as had been murdered by their cavalry on the field of Quatre Bras, until it became necessary for our officers, from a sense of humanity, to interfere in favour of the French, and they did all that was possible to restrain the fury of their men, often at the imminent peril of their own lives.

An officer of the Highlanders who had passed through the perils of this sanguinary day, in relating to me these particulars, declared that he never saw our men so savage, and that for awhile it was impossible by any efforts to curb their fury, while there was such a general shout of " no quarter!" and that the soldiers were more like lions than men. I trust the French with all their temerity, will not be over ready again to rouse the hardy vengeance of these British mountaineers. It was said too that when the cavalry charged there was a cry of "no quarter!" "no prisoners!" certain it is that our troops were very much exasperated, from an impression that the enemy intended to shew no mercy.

Towards the close of the day, however, this spirit subsided, and on every occasion, where any of the French surrendered, all hostilities against them ceased; notwithstanding which, the French prisoners in many instances refused to march to the rear, and seized every opportunity that offered of assaulting their guard. The ferocity of one party of them exceeded anything of the kind I had ever seen: they were marched through Waterloo on their way to Brussels under an escort of Hanoverian cavalry, in number I think they exceeded 2,000: their conduct was extremely indecorous and even outrageous, insomuch that the escort had great difficulty in guarding them, and they were obliged to shoot some by the road side to preserve order.

They had almost all been wounded, generally with the sabre or sword, some had lost their ears, others their noses, and the faces and hands of all were besmeared with blood, exhibiting altogether a very terrific scene: it was not advisable to approach them without your sword drawn or pistol cocked. I must own I was astonished as well as shocked at their conduct, as it would seem they had set out with the resolution of rendering the contest a war of extermination, a spirit so different from that of the army to which they, were opposed, for I was myself witness to many acts of extreme kindness on the part of our soldiers towards the wounded French after the battle; and one instance in particular I ought to have mentioned before.

On the night of the battle of Les Quatre Bras, a house had been filled with wounded men, chiefly of the Guards, amongst whom a few French also had crept in for shelter: the English rations of provisions were brought, when our men asked if there were any for what they called the poor French, and being answered no, they immediately shared their own small allowance with them. It certainly was not to be expected that much feeling or humanity would be evinced by what might justly be termed a furious *banditti*, who had by their unprecedented crimes carried misery and desolation into the bosoms of all the nations of Europe, excepting our own, and who had repeatedly set at defiance all laws social, moral and divine; but the barbarous conduct of the French army generally throughout these operations was such as was not only shocking to honour and humanity, but in some instances revolting to human nature itself.

Sad and terrific then would have been the consequences to England and to Europe had these unprincipled ruffians proved victorious and successful. Vain would be the attempt here to relate the various acts of heroism or the many instances of suffering which this eventful day presented; but they are recorded in the rolls of fame. We have only to look at the magnitude of this conflict, at the interests at stake, and the decisive shape which the victory took, to estimate the exertions of those to whose lot it fell to effect this great and most glorious achievement.

INFANTRY.	CAVALRY.
4 Battalions of the Guards *	1st Regiment of Life Guards *
1st Regiment (Royals) *	2nd ditto*
4th ditto *	Royal Horse Guards (Blues)*
14th ditto	1st Dragoon Guards *
23d ditto (Fusileers)	1st Dragoons (Royals) *
27th ditto	2d Dragoons (North British) *
28th ditto *	6th Dragoons (Inneskillens) *
30th ditto *	7th Light Ditto (Hussars) *
32nd ditto	10th ditto (Hussars)
33rd ditto *	11th Light Dragoons
35th ditto	12th ditto
40th ditto	13th ditto *
42nd ditto (Highlanders) *	15th ditto (Hussars) *
44th ditto *	16th Light Dragoons
51st ditto (Light Infantry)	18th ditto (Hussars)
52nd ditto (Light Infantry) *	23rd Light Dragoons *
54th ditto	1st Hussars (K. G. L.)
59th ditto	3rd ditto (K. G. L.) *
69th ditto	1st Light Drag* (K. G. L.)*
71st ditto (Light Infantry) *	2nd ditto (K. G. L.) *
73rd ditto *	
79th ditto (Highlanders) *	
91st ditto	
92nd ditto (Highlanders) *	
95th ditto (Rifles) *	

Note.—Those marked thus * were principally engaged and suffered most. The 35th, 54th, 59th and 91st regiments were posted near Hal and not engaged. The 81st foot were on duty at Brussels, and the 2d Hussars, K. G. L. absent on duty near Courtray.

We come now to the mournful task of recording a list of the killed and wounded.

BRITISH AND HANOVERIAN:

Killed.		Wounded.	
Lieutenant-Generals - -	1	Generals - - - - - - -	1
Major-Generals - - - -	1	Lieutenant-Generals -	2
Colonels - - - - - - -	5	Major-Generals - - -	7
Lieutenant-Colonels - -	8	Colonels - - - - - - -	12
Majors - - - - - - - -	10	Lieutenant-Colonels -	50
Captains - - - - - - -	49	Majors - - - - - - - -	33
Lieutenants - - - - - -	40	Captains - - - - - - -	162
Ensigns - - - - - - - -	23	Lieutenants - - - - -	280
Cornets - - - - - - - -	3	Ensigns - - - - - - -	84
Adjutants - - - - - - -	5	Cornets - - - - - - -	9
		Adjutants - - - - - -	21
		Volunteers - - - - - -	5
	145		**684**

Non-commissioned Officers, Rank and File:

	Killed.	Wounded.	Missing.
British - - -	2,180 - - -	8,040 - - -	830
Hanoverian -	450 - - -	1,330 - - -	970
	2,630	**9,370**	**1,800**

Killed, Wounded and Missing.
Dutch and Belgic loss: 4,000 - - - Brunswick loss: 2000

Prussian Losses:
Ligny, 16th June, 12,000 - - Waterloo, 18th June, 4,000

Amongst the Officers of rank, killed and wounded, were the following.

Killed.

His Serene Highness the Duke of Brunswick-Oels

Lieutenant-General Sir Thomas Picton, K. G. C. B.

Major-General Sir William Ponsonby, K. C. B.

Colonel Sir William Henry De Lancey, K. C. B. Quarter-Master General

Colonel Sir Henry Ellis, K. C. B. 23d Foot (Fusileers)

Colonel Morrin, 69th Foot

Colonel Duplat, King's German Legion

Colonel Ompteda, ditto

Lieutenant-Colonel Sir Robert Macara, K. C. B. 42d Foot

Lieutenant-Colonel Sir Alexander Gordon, K. C. B. Aide-de-camp to the Duke of Wellington

Lieutenant-Colonel Miller, C. B. 1st Guards

Lieutenant-Colonel Cameron, C. B. 92d Foot

Lieutenant-Colonel Canning, Aide-de-camp to the Duke of Wellington

Lieutenant-Colonel Currie, Lord Hill's staff

Wounded.

General His R. H. the Prince of Orange, K. C. B. severely

Lieutenant-General the Earl of Uxbridge, K. G. C. B. leg amputated

Lieutenant-General Sir C. Baron Alten, K. C. B. severely

Major-General Cook, arm amputated

Major-General Sir Edward Barnes, K. C. B. Adjutant-General, severely

Major-General Sir James Kempt, K. C. B. slightly

Major-General Sir Colin Halkett, K. C. B. severely

Major-General Sir William Dornberg, K. C. B. severely

Major-General Frederick Adam, severely

Major-General Sir Denis Pack, K. C. B. slightly

Colonel Sir John Elley, K. C B. Deputy Adjutant General

Colonel Harris, 73d Foot

Colonel Quintin, C. B. 10th Hussars

Colonel the Honourable F. Ponsonby, C. B. 12th Light Dragoons

Lieutenant-Colonel Lord Fitzroy Somerset, K. C. B. Military Secretary

Lieutenant-Colonel Sir Robert Hill, C. B. Royal Horse Guards

Lieutenant-Colonel Sir G. H. Berkley, K. C. B. Assistant Adjutant General

Lieutenant-Colonel Waters, C. B. Assistant Adjutant General

Lieutenant-Colonel Norcott, C. B. 95th Foot

Lieutenant-Colonel Adair, C. B. 1st Foot Guards

Lieutenant-Colonel Hamilton, C. B. 30th Foot

Lieutenant-Colonel Vigoureux, C. B. 30th Foot

Lieutenant-Colonel Hay, C. B. 16th Light Dragoons

Lieutenant-Colonel Wyndham, 1st Foot Guards

Lieutenant-Colonel Abercromby, C. B. Assistant Quarter Master General

Lieutenant-Colonel Bowater, 3d Foot Guards

Period of honour as of woes,
What bright careers 'twas thine to close!—
Mark'd on thy roll of blood, what names
To Britain's memory, and to Fame's,
Laid there their last immortal claims!
Thou saw'st in seas of gore expire
Redoubted Picton's soul of fire—

Saw'st in the mingled carnage lie
All that of Ponsonby could die—
De Lancey change Love's bridal wreath,
For laurels from the hand of Death—
Saw'st gallant Miller's failing eye
Still bent where Albion's banners fly,
And Cameron, in the shock of steel,

203

Die like the offspring of Lochtel;
And generous Gordon, 'mid the strife,
Fall while he watch'd his leader's life,
Ah! though his guardian angel's shield
Fenced Britains' hero through the field,
Fate not the less her power made known,
Through his friend's hearts to pierce his own!

Forgive, brave dead, th' imperfect lay!
Who may your names your numbers say?
What high-strung harp, what lofty line,
To each the dear-earn'd praise assign,
From high-born chiefs of martial fame
To the poor soldier's lowlier name?
Lightly ye rose that dawning day,
From your cold couch of swamp and day,
To fill, before the sun was low,
The bed that morning cannot know.
Oft may the tear the green sod steep,
And sacred be the heroes' sleep,
Till time shall cease to run;
And ne'er beside their noble grave,
May Briton pass and fail to crave
A blessing on the fallen brave
Who fought with Wellington!

Farewell, sad field! whose blighted face
Wears desolation's mournful trace;
Long shall my memory retain
Thy shatter'd huts and trampled grain,
With every mark of martial wrong,
That scathe thy towers, fair Hougomont!
Yet though thy garden's green arcade
The marksman's fatal post was made,
Though on thy shatter'd beeches fell
The blended rage of shot and shell,
Though from thy blacken'd portals torn
Their fall thy blighted fruit-trees mourn,
Has not such havoc bought a name
Immortal in the rolls of Fame?
Yes—Agincourt may be forgot,

And Cressy be an unknown spot,
And Blenheim's name be new;
But still in story and in song,
For many an age remember'd long,
Shall live the towers of Hougomont,
And field of Waterloo!

Look forth, once more, with soften'd heart,
Ere from the field of Fame we part;
Triumph and sorrow border near,
And joy oft melts into a tear.
Alas! what links of love that morn,
Has war's rude hand asunder torn!
For ne'er was field so sternly fought,
And ne'er was conquest dearer bought:
Here piled in common slaughter sleep
Those whom affection long shall weep;
Here rests the sire, who ne'er shall strain
His orphans to his heart again;

The son, whom on his native shore
The parent's voice shall bless no more;
The bridegroom, who has hardly press'd
His blushing consort to his breast;
The husband, whom through many a year
Long love and mutual faith endear.
Thou can'st not name one tender tie,
But here dissolv'd its reliques lie!
O! when thou see'st some mourner's veil,
Shroud her thin form and visage pale,
Or mark'st the matron's bursting tears
Stream when the stricken drum she hears;
Or see'st how manlier grief, suppressed,
Is labouring in a father's breast,—
With no inquiry vain pursue
The cause, but think on Waterloo!

Walter Scott.

June 19th. The field of battle and village of Waterloo exhibited a
most affecting scene this morning. The royal wagon train and commissariat wagons had been out all night, and were still employed in taking
up and bringing off the wounded. In riding down Waterloo about 9

o'clock, I passed an open carriage, in which lay Lord Uxbridge bound up, a staff-surgeon was seated by his side. His Lordship had undergone the operation of amputation, besides which there was a deep sabre cut down his face: he appeared to be asleep, and in order that he might not be disturbed, the whole train of baggage, &c. moving along the road was halted, and ordered to keep silence while the carriage passed slowly by for Brussels: following this at a short distance, was a vehicle conveying the corpse of our poor old General, Sir Thomas Picton, under an escort of infantry. His body was carried to England and privately interred in his family vault at Paddington.

I have been informed from very credible sources, that the General had a full presentiment of his fate. At the time he received his orders from the war-office to join the army in this country, he was amongst his family in Wales, where he had purposed after his long and arduous services to end his days in peace. Although he certainly could have avoided this service, yet considering himself in honour bound to answer the call, he cheerfully obeyed the summons; but before he left Wales he arranged his affairs in such a manner as shewed his apprehensions that he should return no more, and to a particular friend even expressed as much, concluding with these remarkable words: "When you hear of my death, expect to hear also of the most glorious yet most bloody day England ever saw."

It was painful, beyond all conception, to view the field of battle, and every eye seemed to avoid it as much as possible; for it was enough to make the stoutest heart shudder to look towards the hills or fields in any direction. Parties were out shooting such of the wounded horses as were yet alive, which at a distance sounded like skirmishing, while preparations were making to burn the dead. The Duke of Wellington wrote his dispatches this morning in Waterloo, and Major the Hon. Henry Percy, of the 14th Light Dragoons, was the *aide-de-camp* selected to carry them to England. It was a singular coincidence that the officer who carried home the Duke of Marlborough's dispatches from Blenheim, in the reign of Queen Anne, was also a Percy.

The 2nd and 4th Divisions marched through Nivelles about noon, with their bands playing, accompanied by Lord Hill, at whose safety everyone seemed to rejoice. They were followed by the cavalry; and the pleasure of meeting my Peninsular friends after a battle, was never exceeded by that which I experienced when the 7th Hussars marched by, at seeing at their head my Colonel, Sir Edward Kerrison, but who had not 200 men left under his command. Besides Major Hodge, the adjutant, and Captain Elphinstone, whom they had lost on the 17th, all the captains and almost every other officer had been wounded on the 18th. The horse which the colonel rode at the review on the 29th of May, and which I believe he valued at 300 guineas, was shot, and the general of our brigade, Sir Colquhoun Grant, had no less than four horses shot under him. The cavalry on this occasion suffered much in the same proportion as the infantry.

Both the brigades of heavy dragoons had been thrown into one, under Lord Edward Somerset, and now did not muster the original strength of either singly: the sufferings of these and of the brigade under Colonel Arentschildt, consisting of the 13th Light Dragoons and 3rd Hussars of the King's German Legion, were the greatest. In the infantry the guards and Highlanders on both days were desperately engaged: the 95th regiment lost in killed and wounded on the 18th forty-two officers: the royal artillery also suffered very severely.

The cavalry marched this morning after the Prussians, to know if they were likely to want any support, and to inquire after the enemy; but we returned to Nivelles in the afternoon, and the army encamped again for the night about that town. In passing the 4th Division bivouac I saw Captain T. of the 14th, who had happily got safe through the day: the regiment having been posted on our extreme right, which was thrown back near Merke Braine, had not been much engaged. We were at bivouac this night in a little wood between Nivelles and Quatre Bras, about seven miles in front of the village of Waterloo.

20th. At daybreak this morning the whole army advancing moved upon the town of Mons, which had a Dutch garrison. We halted in the evening at a village where a corps of the Prussian army crossed our line of march, singing songs of triumph, This is a custom very general amongst the German troops, and was practised by our Hanoverian cavalry throughout their march to Paris.

21st. We Arrived at Mons early this morning. The infantry were marching through the town, and were to assemble at night at Malplaquet, famous for the great victory gained there over the French army by the Duke of Marlborough and Prince Eugene on the 11th of September 1709. The cavalry were ordered to pass the frontiers near Malplaquet, and to continue marching until it became dark, the Prussian army being already in France. In the evening it began to rain, and it proved a very wet night, It was nearly dark when I passed through Malplaquet, which is nothing but a row of miserable huts and cottages, with one or two wretched farmhouses. The old field of battle is now covered with a wood at least that part of it where the English fought and suffered so much.

At the instant I was passing Malplaquet, the infantry (who after their long march had just halted and were beginning to light their camp-fires) were hastily ordered to fall under arms, in consequence of a sharp firing which was heard in a wood a little in our rear: it proved, however, to be nothing more than some of our foreign troops discharging their pieces. Our poor fellows, I remember, were very angry at this interruption, after the fatigues of a march of unusual length: it was nevertheless highly necessary to be on the alert, as no one yet knew what direction the French corps under Marshal Grouchy had taken. I joined my regiment at a town a little in front of Malplaquet, and got into quarters.

22nd. Before sunrise we were all again on the march, and passing the frontiers into France about noon, were quartered in a village near Le Cateau.

23rd. The regiment having no orders to move this morning, I went into Le Cateau, which was now the army head-quarters. The old King of France, Louis XVIII. had just arrived from Ghent, where he had been during the whole of the late operations. His Majesty and his loyal followers must have been in no small degree of anxiety and alarm at the time of the battle. His carriage and attendants were throughout the day in a state of readiness to convey His Majesty to the coast, which was no unwise or premature precaution, as the enemy's cavalry could have reached Ghent from the field of battle in little more than two hours.

I have omitted mentioning that when we were proceeding to Ghent in the barge from Bruges, in April last, we met with a French royalist officer, who assured us that they would not require the assistance of the allies in this affair, as they were themselves strong enough to bring the contest to a favourable issue! for that it was only a few *"desperadoes"* who had joined Buonaparte, and that these would never fight for him. The royalist officers, however, appeared to think very differently now; they gazed in silent admiration at our troops, and seemed to look upon a British officer as a prodigy of valour.

In the afternoon Lieutenant-General Sir Charles Colville with a part of the 4th division, a train of artillery and our brigade of cavalry, was ordered to march against Cambray, while the 1st Division and the rest of the army moved against Peronne, St. Quinten, &c. The approaches to the place having been reconnoitred, it was judged advisable to send for more troops, and we bivouacked for the night a few miles from the town.

25th. The remainder of the 4th Division having joined early in the afternoon, General Colville ordered the troops again to approach the town, and sent in a flag of truce, demanding the surrender of the place by sunset, until which a truce was granted: the signal was a white flag fixed upon one of the sails of a windmill, upon the taking down of which hostilities were to commence. It was fully expected that the town would be surrendered without the effusion of blood, as notwithstanding the strength of the works, it was not in any way provided for a siege, and succours were quite out of the question.

Five and 6 o'clock however came, without any satisfactory reply from the enemy; so that our troops and guns began to encircle the town, while the infantry with their ladders were descending into the ditches to escalade; the cavalry being posted in the fields at a convenient distance to be ready to assist in the event of a sortie. The enemy answered our attack by a fire of artillery from the citadel, and of musketry from the walls of the town.

From the shells which our artillery had thrown, a large building about the centre of the place was soon set on fire, which burned with great rapidity, and illumined the country. Presently afterwards a shout was heard, and it was said the gates of the town on this side had been forced, upon which we all hastened up to the walls. We had not been there, however, more than three minutes when it was discovered that the drawbridges were yet up; and we found ourselves exposed to so sharp a fire of musketry, as obliged us for the moment to fall back a little into some trenches for shelter, in doing which one poor fellow of our infantry was killed close by my side.

In the interim, however, our light troops on the other side of the town had escaladed the walls with a very trifling loss, and the gates on all sides were now thrown open, while the French soldiers who composed the garrison retired into the citadel. This they refused to surrender to the British; but intimated that they would be ready to treat with any French officer whom Louis XVIII. would appoint; in consequence of which His Majesty sent an officer from Le Cateau on the following day, when they accordingly capitulated, and marched out with the honours of war, shouting *"Vive le Roi!"*

As soon as the town had surrendered and the gates been thrown open, which I think was about 9 o'clock, we entered by the Valenciennes gate, expecting to see the houses closed and the streets at least deserted by the women: judge of our astonishment then to find the whole town illuminated and hung with white flags, in the same manner as on a jubilee day: this was certainly a spectacle altogether novel and unaccountable.

If these people were really so loyal, surely they might have influenced the conduct of the few rebels (only about 300 I believe) who kept the gates shut against us; and indeed the national guards of the town, I should imagine, might easily have opened them by force. Our troops were assembled in the square in the best order, and the greatest care taken to prevent any disorderly or irregular conduct. We went to the Hall of the Municipality to receive General Colville's orders respecting the military stores found in the town. The cavalry had taken up their quarters in the villages adjacent.

26th. The King having signified his intention of visiting Cambray, preparations were made this morning to give his Majesty a flattering reception. Our troops had all marched at daylight. At breakfast at the inn I met Lieutenant P—— of the 59th regiment, who had been sent back on a duty which places the discipline of our army in a very conspicuous light. Under the impression that some of the troops might have obtained something from the inhabitants on the night of the attack, they were this morning searched on the march, and every dollar and trinket found upon them, of which they could not give a satisfactory account, was taken away, and Lieutenant P—— was ordered to convey the whole to the Mayor of Cambray, from whom he was to obtain a receipt for the same.

Notwithstanding all this, however, the inhabitants have since complained bitterly to those who were not there, how much they suffered from plunder in the storm. From this time until the evening of the 30th, we continued advancing towards Paris. On the 28th we crossed the river Aisne at Pont de Maxence, and marched until late in the night, under a very heavy rain. On the 29th we passed the town of Senlis, and on the 30th put up in a little village near Louvre, where the quarters were so bad that I gave them up to my servants, and slept in my baggage-cart. On the march this morning we met a deputation from Paris, inquiring for the Duke of Wellington.

In the first carriage was a French general in full uniform, wearing the badges of several orders: he said he was come to arrest our progress, as the Emperor had resigned in favour of his son. I heard afterwards that he met with a very cool reception from our great and gallant Duke, who told him that he had no orders or leisure to treat, being only instructed to fight, which he was resolved to do until he should find himself in possession of Paris, where a proper answer would be given to proposals of this nature by persons duly authorized.

Lord Castlereagh was at this time on his way over, having left London soon after the arrival of the Waterloo dispatches, in order that in the political discussions and arrangements arising from these important events, Great Britain might bear that part to which she was so well entitled. When the army passed the frontiers on the 21st, the following Proclamation to the French people, and Order to the army made their appearance.

Proclamation.

I announce to the French that I enter their territory at the head of an army already victorious—not as an enemy, (except of the Usurper, the enemy of the human race, with whom there can be neither peace nor truce), but to aid them to shake off the iron yoke by which they are oppressed. I therefore give to my army the subjoined Orders; and I desire that everyone who violates them may be made known, to me. The French know, however, that I have a right to require that they conduct themselves in such a manner that I may be able to protect them against those who would seek to do them evil.

They must then furnish the requisitions that will be made by persons authorized to make them, taking receipts in due form and order; that they remain quietly at their houses; and have no correspondence or communication with the Usurper or with his adherents, All those who shall absent themselves from their houses after the entrance of the army into France, and all those who shall be absent in the service of the Usurper, shall be considered as enemies and his adherents; and their property shall be appropriated to the subsistence of the army.

Given at head-quarters at Malplaquet, the 21st of June 1815.

(Signed)   Wellington.

Extract from the Order of the Day,
June 20th, 1815.

As the army is about to enter the French territory, the troops of
the different nations now under the command of the Duke of
Wellington are desired to remember, that their respective Sovereigns are the allies of His Majesty the King of France, and
that France must therefore be considered as a friendly country.
It is ordered that nothing be taken either by the officers or
soldiers without payment. The commissaries of the army will
provide for the wants of the troops in the usual manner: and it
is not permitted to the officers or soldiers of the army to make
requisitions.
The commissaries will be authorized by the Field-Marshal or
by the Generals who command the troops of the respective
nations (that is to say, in case their supply is not regulated by
an English commissary), to make the necessary requisitions, for
which they will *give* regular receipts; and they must perfectly
understand, that they will be responsible for all that they receive by requisitions from the inhabitants of France, in the same
manner as if they made purchases for the account of their government in their own country.

(Signed)   John Waters,
Acting Adjutant-General.

July 1st The British and Prussian armies having reached the plains
of St. Dennis, Buonaparte who since his return to Paris immediately
after the battle of Waterloo, had resided chiefly at Malmaison, perceiving that all his schemes were disconcerted, fled, together with his
brothers Joseph and Jerome. Marshals Ney and Soult also having disappeared, the chief command devolved upon Marshal Davoust, Prince
of Eckmuhl, who collected from the wreck of the Waterloo army
about 40,000 men, with whom he appeared determined to dispute
with us the possession of the city.

Prussia having in Buonaparte's invasion been plundered and wantonly laid waste, the Prussians, by their hostile spirit, excited a degree
of terror wherever they moved. Considering the extreme misery and
desolation brought upon other countries by the French, one really
could feel but very little pity towards these people; far although they
were not perhaps the precise individuals who acted the scenes alluded
to, yet as they took an interest in that policy which produced them,

it was not very unfair that they now should feel the consequences resulting from it. It should also be observed that the Prussians in their march were not guilty of those wanton acts of cruelty which marked the route of the French army. In the evening we were ordered to Tremblé, a small town not very far from the forest of Bondy, and we began to extend ourselves round the modern Babylon, whilst Blucher and his Prussian warriors were passing the Seine to take the heights of St. Cloud on the other side of the city.

CAPTURE OF PARIS

AND

TERMINATION OF HOSTILITIES,

July, 1815.

Nothing had now for some days been heard or talked of in the camp but the fall of Paris; and the Duke of Wellington and Prince Blucher with their Waterloo-men were resolved to accomplish it without delay. In passing the Seine, Marshal Blucher met with some resistance, but having at length succeeded in establishing himself at St. Cloud, dispositions were made for the grand attack, when the French Marshal Davoust desired to capitulate, and on the morning of the 3rd, terms of capitulation were agreed to and signed, of which the following were amongst the leading articles.

Article 1. There shall be a cessation of hostilities from this date.

Article 2. The French army shall evacuate Paris and retire beyond the river Loire, until the affairs of the nation shall have been settled.

Article 3. The evacuation of the posts of Paris to be as follows:

On the 4th the French troops will resign to the allies the posts in the plains of St. Dennis and suburbs of the city; on the 5th, the heights of Montmartre; and on the 6th at noon Paris shall be entirely evacuated by the French army and occupied by those of the Allies.

The French army instead of quitting Paris altogether by 12 o'clock today according to the convention, held the bridge of Neuilly until late in the afternoon, and fired upon our troops as they came up. Two staff-officers with a flag of truce being sent into Paris, to inquire into these circumstances, they were fired at in the street, and one of them (Lieutenant-Colonel Stavely of the Royal Staff Corps) severely wounded, his orderly killed, and the other officer with his attendants escaped with difficulty.

7th. It was fully expected that the army would enter Paris in triumph this morning, as the general orders of last evening commanded the men to clean their arms and accoutrements and turn out in the best order possible fit to pass the Field-Marshal, and we marched from Tremblé at a very early hour, but the national guards who had received the regular troops at the gates still wearing the tri-coloured cockade, no one was allowed to enter the town on this side without special permission.

About noon I passed through St. Dennis, where Louis XVIII. was attending divine service in the cathedral, accompanied by Monsieur (the Count d' Artois), Prince Talleyrand, and the Marshals Victor and Marmont. In the Champ d' Elysees, which was full of British and Prussian troops, our infantry were close up at the Thuilleries gates, with their bands playing "God save the King," while tri-coloured flags were yet flying upon the column in the *Place des Victoires* and other public edifices, and the national guards were parading the town wearing the revolutionary colours. We were put up at Chatou, on the banks of the river Seine, near Malmaison, where I got into a *château* which had been pillaged by the Prussians; a few days afterwards the owner thereof came over—he was very civil and promised to send me a bed and a little furniture from Paris.

8th. Peremptory orders having been sent into Paris to take down the revolutionary colours and hoist the lily standards, the King entered Paris this morning, and took possession of his palace of the Thuilleries. Although the British army had been disappointed of its triumphal entry into Paris, it seems Marshal Blucher was determined that the Prussian should not, for he marched his whole array, upwards of 50,000 men, through the town this morning, placing himself at their head, with a full band of trumpets and bugle-horns sounding triumphal marches! The infantry had their bayonets fixed, the cavalry their swords drawn, and the artillery not only their guns loaded, but matches burning. A strong piquet of Prussians was now posted in the "Place Carousal," and field-pieces were planted at the heads of several streets and avenues.

This afternoon Lord Castlereagh arrived in Paris, invested with full powers to treat on the part of England upon the measures to be adopted to quiet or fetter this restless nation, The Emperor of Russia, the Emperor of Austria and the King of Prussia also arrived with their

Cossacks, and the advanced corps of their armies, which were now entering France by hundreds of thousands! In the meanwhile the British Navy having blockaded all the French ports, Buonaparte after several unsuccessful attempts to escape to America, surrendered himself to Captain Maitland of the Royal Navy, off Rochfort, and embarked on board the British man of war *Bellerophon,* which immediately sailed for the shores of Britain, and anchored in Plymouth Sound, where the once mighty Napoleon was now awaiting his destiny from the Prince Regent of England.

To the French, this event of their great Emperor having fled from the face of a British army into the hands of a British navy, appeared as well indeed it might) a thing altogether so extraordinary, that in Paris it was generally disbelieved, and even after it had been officially announced, many persons still persuaded themselves that we had been deceived and had got the wrong man. It seemed so impossible that the great Napoleon, who had made all Europe tremble, should at last fly for shelter into the hands of his bitterest enemies. Times were certainly much changed since the beacons of alarm were blazing along our own coast, lighted by his formidable threats of invasion, and even since the time when he affected to consider a British army as too insignificant to attract his notice.

The significant remark too which he made respecting the Duke of Wellington *(We have not met),* proved rather an unfortunate one, for they seemed now to have met to so much purpose as to render it unlikely that they should ever meet again. Paris at this time exhibited the scene of a grand European masquerade, from the wonderful variety in the dress and uniforms of the several armies; and the assemblage of monarchs, princes, statesmen and warriors from all parts of Europe was such as in all probability will never occur again. The British Waterloo-men from the late events had attracted the curiosity if not the admiration of all. Buonaparte was often heard to say that he would sweep those proud islanders from the earth, so that it should be said, "there goes an Englishman!" and certainly the latter part of this prediction was now fulfilled, though in a far different way from what he intended it should be: for no English officer or soldier could pass without being saluted as an *"Englander"* from Waterloo.

The Prussians in particular seized every opportunity of complimenting the British, in the same degree as they neglected none of mortifying the French; but the following anecdote is one among many instances of magnanimity displayed by them in their resentments. A Prussian officer on his arrival in Paris, requested the authorities to billet him upon the house of a lady whose, address he had. On his coming to the house he was shewn a regular billet of two rooms, with which he expressed himself dissatisfied, and desired that the lady would give up to him her own suite of apartments on the first floor: to this she reluctantly assented, saying, that she would retire to the second floor; but the officer informed her that he destined that and the rest of the house for his staff and attendants.

He then called for the cook, ordered a sumptuous dinner for six persons, and desired the lady's butler to take care that the best wines which the cellar produced should be forthcoming, charging them withal that it was at their peril to disregard these injunctions. All this was accordingly done: the lady and her family in the greatest distress retired to a friend's house, when the officer ordered her to be sent for into his presence, when he addressed her as follows: "No doubt, madam, you consider my conduct brutal in the extreme;" to which she replied that she did not expect such treatment from an officer.

The officer then said, "I only wished, madam, to give you a specimen of the behaviour and conduct of your son during six months that he resided in my house after the entrance of the French army into the Prussian capital. I do not however mean to follow a bad example; you will therefore resume your apartments, and I shall seek lodgings at some public Hotel."

31st Upwards of *seven hundred thousand* fighting men having been marched into France during the last three weeks, and most of them moving upon Paris, the British cavalry and some Prussian troops were ordered into Normandy, and we marched this morning from Chatou to Pontoise.

August 1st. We marched this day to Magnay, where I was billeted upon a French gentleman, who quite astonished me with his civilities. I had scarcely passed the threshold of his house before he pressed me to take some refreshment, and without my consent sent to an Hotel for some wine and liqueurs. He expressed extreme regret at having no straw for the stable, although I had not asked him for any, and in short quite embarrassed me with his attentions.

2nd. Before I had taken leave of my landlord this morning, he threw off the mask of civility, and developed his mercenary views, by putting into my hands a bill, the charges of which were enormous, for the entertainment which he had pressed upon me, and even for the wine which I had not drank, peremptorily insisting upon being paid instantly, or that he would report me to Lord Wellington.

We reached our cantonments in Normandy in the evening, and I was quartered at Romilly, a village in the valley of Andelle, about eight miles from Rouen. The brigade occupied Andely, Gisors, Fleury, &c. Here we remained until October, when we were marched through Rouen to Yvetot on the. road to Dieppe, and the Prussians who had been quartered at Caen and its adjacents, were ordered to Paris, preparatory to the final adjustment of affairs, and the formation of the army of occupation.

On their march thither, a corps halted for a few days at Rouen, during the time that I was there, and were billeted upon all the private as well as public houses in the town, where they of course lived at free-quarters as usual. My landlord, Monsieur Le M———e, was able to plead exemption on account of my being quartered upon him, a circumstance at which he rejoiced not a little, and I was far from being considered a nuisance in consequence; but in the confusion which occurred in billeting 20,000 men, the authorities it appears forgot this, for in the evening two Prussian soldiers rang the bell, and on the door being opened they walked in, and without asking any questions proceeded directly to the room where *Monsieur* and his wife and family were sitting, and without any salutation further than a smile and a bow, *"sans ceremonie"* seated themselves by the fire, placing their firelocks with bayonets fixed by their sides, and called for a good supper to be provided immediately, as they were very hungry and had marched a long way.

Monsieur of course flew to me for assistance, and we got the mistake rectified; but the two gentlemen thought they might as well make sure of their supper before they departed to their new billet, as by this time the cloth had been laid and things provided: the family, who were quite genteel people, stood up to wait upon these private soldiers, and *Monsieur* himself was very active in furnishing them with wine and such other things as they required, and at the same time affecting much politeness, he passed some high encomiums upon his, visitors, and said the Prussians were always *"bons enfans,"* in return for which they in broken French, which was almost unintelligible, gave him and his family a most tedious history of the operations of the campaign arid battle of Waterloo, during which?' they frequently mentioned the word Britannia, meaning thereby the British army, as they said Britannia marched by one road while they moved by another; and lest their host should not sufficiently understand them, one of them occasionally got up and pointed' his loaded musket at his head, to shew how things were done, which almost frightened the poor Frenchman out of his senses.

To this ludicrous scene I was an eye-witness from the window of my apartment, which was exactly opposite to the room where it happened, and so near that I could distinctly hear the greater part of what transpired. These two fellows drank plentifully of wine, and when supper was finished, instead of going away, they called for some tobacco? and brandy, with which they were willingly supplied in order that they might forget to pocket the spoons and forks, which were removed from the table by stealth. At last the farce being ended, these two pleasant fellows bade the Frenchman *"bon, soir"* and took their leave.

Rouen is a large old town, the ancient capital of Normandy, containing about 80,000 inhabitants: the streets are narrow, and the houses built chiefly of wood. The cathedral is a gothic building, something similar in appearance to Westminster Abbey. There is still remaining the house where the celebrated Maid of Orleans was tried for witchcraft, and a statue of her is erected upon the spot where she was burnt. During my stay here I met with a French colonel, who had reduced himself to great straits by meddling in the late events. This officer had formerly been a captain in the French navy, and was taken prisoner by Lord Nelson.

In England he married, and at the peace of 1814 returned to France with a little property of which he had become possessed. At the reappearance of Buonaparte he repaired to Paris, obtained an audience of the Emperor, and tendering his services for the army, offered to raise a battalion, of which he asked permission to take the command. At this interview, Buonaparte gave him and every one present to understand that all his future fortunes would depend upon his first enterprise, which was to be directed against those unyielding enemies of France—the English, and advised them, in the enrolment of men, to give a preference to such whose fortunes were as desperate as their spirit.

This officer accordingly raised his regiment, and posted off with his men to the frontiers, but not arriving on the Sambre until the evening of the 18th of June, they were then saluted with the cry of Waterloo and *"sauve qui peut!"* upon which they quickly dispersed, and hastening back into Normandy threw off their new uniform, put on their " bourgeois" coats again, and mounted the white cockade, with which he himself hasterfed to Paris to cry "*Vive le Roi!*" where he made a merit of not being at Waterloo, and demanded a pension for his loyalty and past services.

November 20th. A treaty of Peace, which promises to be permanent, was this day signed and ratified by all the sovereigns of Europe or their plenipotentiaries assembled at Paris, by which France was required to pay by instalments, in the space of five years, as an indemnity to the Allied Powers, the following sum of money: Seven Hundred Million *Francs,* French currency, or about *Twenty-nine Millions Sterling,* to be divided amongst the four great Powers, Russia, Austria, Great Britain and Prussia, in. equal parts, and amongst the smaller states according to the number of troops they had respectively furnished for the late campaign.

To ensure the payment of these contributions and give stability to the order of things established, an army of 150,000 troops was to remain in France until the 20th of November 1820; but in the event of all the sums being paid, or security given for the payment thereof, and the allied sovereign, satisfied as to the tranquillity of the country, this army of occupation might be withdrawn in the year 1818. During its stay in France it was, to be supplied and quartered entirely at the expense of the French government, according to a convention annexed to the treaty. This grand army of occupation was composed as follows, and commanded by Field-Marshal the Duke of Wellington.

ARMY OF OCCUPATION

Russia	30,000	Great Britain	30,000
Austria	30,000	Prussia	30,000
Bavaria	5,000	Hanover	5,900
Denmark.	5,000	Saxony	5,000
Wirtemberg	5,000	Small States of Germany	5,000
	75,000		75,000

FORTRESSES
In France held by the Army of Occupation.

Landreçy	Avesnes	Philippeville
Givet	Cambray	Marienberg
Charlemont	Valenciennes	Versoix

Condé	Montmidi	Fort Louis
Maubeuge	Thionville	Bietch
Rocroi	Bouchain	Le Quesnoy
Sedan	Longwy	Sarre Louis

The British Contingent of the Army of Occupation which remained in France, was formed as follows :

CAVALRY

Lieutenant-general Lord Combermere,

Mayor-General Lord Edward Somerset, K.C.B.

1st Brigade of Cavalry	1st Dragoon Guards
	2nd Ditto
	3rd Dragoons

Major-General Sir R. H.Vivian, K. C. B.

2nd Brigade of Cavalry	7th Hussars
	18th Hussars
	12th Light Dragoons

Major-General Sir C. Grant, K. C. B.

3rd Brigade of Cavalry	11th Light Dragoons
	13th Light Dragoons
	15th Hussars

INFANTRY

Lieutenant-General Lord Hill.

Major-General Sir P. Maitland, K. C. B.

1st Brigade of Infantry	3rd Battalion 1st Guards
	2nd Battalion Coldstream

Major-General Sir M. Power, K. C. B.

2nd Brigade of Infantry	3rd Battalion 1st Foot (Royals)
	1st Battalion 57th
	2nd Battalion 95th (Rifles)

Major-General Sir R; W. O'Callaghan, K. C. B.

3rd Brigade of Infantry	1st Battalion 3rd Foot
	1st Battalion 39th
	1st Battalion 91st

Major-General Sir Dennis Pack, K. C. B.

4th Brigade of Infantry	1st Battalion 4th Foot
	1st Battalion 52nd
	1st Battalion 79th

Major-General Sir Thomas Brisbane, K. C. B.

6th Brigade of Infantry   1st Battalion 5th Foot

1st Battalion 9th

1st Battalion 21st

Major-General Sir Thomas Bradford, KC.B.

6th Brigade of Infantry   1st Battalion 6th Foot

29th

1st Battalion 71st

Major,-General Sir James Kempt, K. C. B.

7th Brigade of Infantry   1st Battalion 7th Foot

23rd

1st Battalion 43rd

Major-General Sir John Lambert, K.C.B.

8th Brigade of Infantry   1st Battalion 27th Foot

1st Battalion 40th

1st Battalion 95th

Major-General Sir John Keane, K. C. B.

9th Brigade of Infantry   1st Battalion 81st Foot

1st Battalion 88th

The 1st Division of Infantry consisted of the 1st, 7th and 8th Brigades, under the command of Lieutenants-General the Hon. Sir Galbraith Lowry Cole, K. G. C. B.

The 2nd Division of Infantry consisted of the 3rd, 4th and 6th Brigades, under the command of Lieutenant-General Sir Henry Clinton, K. G. C B.

The 3rd Division of Infantry consisted of the 2nd, 5th and 9th Brigades, under the command of Lieutenant-General the Honourable Sir Charles Colville, K. G. C. B.

Two Brigades of Royal Artillery were attached to each Division of Infantry, and one Troop of Royal Horse Artillery to each Brigade of Cavalry.

Commanding officer of Royal Artillery, Colonel Sir George A. Wood, C. B.

Commanding officer of Royal Engineers, Colonel Carmichael Smith, C.B.

Extract from the General Orders of the 11th December 1815,

The Field-Marshal desires that it may be understood that no officers, excepting those attached to the staff, cavalry, the 1st, 2nd, and 3rd Divisions of infantry, as formed in the orders of the 30th *ultimo,* and the household brigade; and the artillery and engineers, as formed according to the orders given to the commanding officers of the artillery and engineers respectively, can receive rations or be quartered in Paris after the 24th instant; nor will any officer whatever, excepting those belonging to the newly-formed army of occupation, be allowed quarters or to draw rations in France after the troops to which he belongs will have quitted the French territory.

Lieutenant-Colonel Kelly and the Commissary-General are particularly charged with the execution of this order.

British Troops ordered to embark for England.
CAVALRY

1st Life Guards	2nd Dragoons
2nd Life Guards	6th Dragoons
Royal Horse Guards	10th Hussars
3rd Dragoon Guards	16th Light Dragoons
1st Dragoons	23rd Light Dragoons

INFANTRY

2nd Battal. 1st Guards	3rd *Ditto* 95th
2nd *Ditto* 3rd Guards	1st *Ditto* 90th
4th *Ditto* 1st Foot	16th Foot
2nd *Ditto* 12th	28th *Ditto*
3rd *Ditto* 14th	32nd *Ditto*
3rd *Ditto* 27th	33rd *Ditto*
2nd *Ditto* 30th	36th *Ditto*
2nd *Ditto* 35th	38th *Ditto*
1st *Ditto* 41st	51st *Ditto*
2nd *Ditto* 44th	54th *Ditto*
2nd *Ditto* 59th	58th *Ditto*
2nd *Ditto* 63rd	64th *Ditto*
2nd *Ditto* 69th	73rd *Ditto*
2nd *Ditto* 81st	92nd *Ditto*
1st *Ditto* 82nd	42nd *Ditto*

Upon breaking up the army which the Field-Marshal has had the honour of commanding, he begs leave to return thanks to the general officers and the officers and troops for their uniform good conduct. In the late short, but memorable campaign, they have given proofs to the world, that they possess in an eminent degree, all the good qualities of soldiers; and the Field-Marshal is happy to be able to applaud their regular good conduct in their camps and cantonments, not less than when engaged with the enemy in the field. Whatever may be the future destination of those brave troops, of which the Field-Marshal now takes his leave, he trusts that every individual will believe, that he will ever feel the deepest interest in their honour and welfare, and will always be happy to promote either.

The peace of Europe having been thus secured and fixed on so apparently firm a basis, the monarchs and princes, together with such troops as belonged not to the army of occupation, began to quit France; and the regiments composing this army prepared to march for the line of demarcation assigned them, between the Flemish frontiers and the river Somme. Buonaparte having in the meantime been conveyed to Plymouth as a state prisoner, was removed from the Bellerophon to the Northumberland, and with all convenient dispatch conveyed to the island of St. Helena, where a residence was provided for him as suitable to his rank as circumstances would admit. The 53rd regiment had the honour of being appointed to guard him. A strong fleet, under, the command of Admiral Sir George Cockburn, K. G. C. B. was ordered to blockade the island, the garrison of which had been augmented, and placed under the command of Lieutenant-General Sir Hudson Lowe, K. C, B.

MEMORANDA OF LORD WELLINGTON'S TITLES,
Taken from the Treaty of Peace, November 20th, 1815.

Le tres-illustre et tres-noble Seigneur Arthur, Duc, Marquis, et Comte de Wellington, Marquis de Douro, Vicomte Wellington de Talaviera, et de Wellington, et Baron Douro de Wellesley, Conseiller de sa Majesté le Roi de Grande Bretagne en son Conseil Privé, Feld-Marechal de ses armées, Colonel du Regiment Royal des Gardes à Cheval, Chevalier du tres-noble Ordre de la Jarretierre, Chevalier Grand-croix du tres-honorable Ordre du Bain, Prince de Waterloo, Duc de Ciudad, Rodri-

go, et Grand d'Espagne de la premiere classe, Duc de Vittoria, Marquis de Torres-Vedras, Comte de Vimiera en Portugal, Chevalier del' Ordre tres-illustre de la Toison d'Or, del' Ordre Militaire d'Espagne de Saint Ferdinand, Chevalier Grand-croix del' Ordre Imperial Militaire de Marie-Therése, Chevalier Grand-croix del' Ordre del' Aigle noir de Prusse, Chevalier Grand-croix del' Ordre Imperial de Saint George de Russie, Chevalier Grand-croix del' Ordre Royal Militaire de Portugal de la Tour et del' Epée, Chevalier Grand-croix des Ordres del' Elephant de Danemarck, de Guillaume de Pays-Bas, del' Annonciade de Sardaigne, de Maximilien Joseph de Baviére, et de plusieurs autres; et Commandant-en-Chef les Armées de sa Majesté Britannique en France, et celles de sa Majesté le Roi des Pays-Bas.

TRANSLATION

The most Illustrious and most Noble Lord Arthur, Duke, Marquis, and Earl of Wellington, Marquis of Douro, Viscount Wellington of Talaviera and of Wellington, and Baron Douro of Wellesley, a Privy Counsellor to His Majesty the King of Great Britain, Field-Marshal of his armies, Colonel of the Royal Horse Guards, (Blues) Knight of the most noble Order of the Garter, Knight Grand Cross of the most honourable Order of the Bath, Prince of Waterloo, Duke of Ciudad Rodrigo and a Grandee of Spain of the first class, Duke of Vittoria, Marquis of Torres Vedras and Count of Vimiera in Portugal, Knight of the most illustrious Order of the Golden Fleece and of the Military Order of Saint Ferdinand in Spain, Knight Grand Cross of the Imperial Military Order of Maria Theresa, Knight Grand Cross of the Black Eagle in Prussia, Knight Grand Cross of the Imperial Order of Saint George in Russia, Knight Grand Cross of the Royal Military Order of the Tower and Sword in Portugal, Knight Grand Cross of the Royal Military Order of the Sword in Sweden, Knight Grand Cross of the Orders of the Elephant in Denmark, of William in the Netherlands, of the Annonciade in Sardinia, of Maximilian Joseph in Bavaria, and of many others, and Commander-in-Chief of the Armies of His Britannic Majesty in France, and of those of His Majesty the King of the Netherlands.

1816

As soon as the troops ordered home had all embarked, which happened early in the month of February, we left Normandy by Forges, Neufchatel and Blangis, crossing the river Somme at Abbeville, and were quartered at Etaples, a small town situated amongst the sands at the mouth of the river Canche, between Montreuil and Boulogne. The head-quarters of the Duke of Wellington also marched from Paris, and were established at Cambray, as the most central or convenient point of the line taken up by the army of occupation, which extended from the sea-coast near Calais and Boulogne to the banks of the Rhine near Strasburg. By a late ordonnance of Louis XVIII, all the chief agents of Buonaparte's conspiracy had been proscribed, and were required to quit France altogether by the 11th day of February.

Marshals Soult and Grouchy were amongst the number. Marshal Ney and Colonel Labedoyere, one of Napoleon's *aides-du-camp*, who had been much distinguished in the late defection, and most active in the campaign of Waterloo, were selected for examples, and shot in Paris. Ney's execution took place on the 8th of December. The valuable trophies of Buonaparte's campaigns, amongst which were many beautiful paintings, busts and statues of great antiquity, were now restored to their original owners.

The celebrated Venetian gilt horses, said to be two thousand years old, to which Napoleon had affixed a triumphal car, and placed over the portico of the grand entrance to the palace, had been taken down by a detachment of British infantry, and conveyed to Venice. I fortunately got a peep at the Louvre before its valuable contents were removed, and saw that beautiful piece of workmanship, the celebrated Venus de Medicis, just as it was on the eve of being sent home to its proper country, to which it had been restored by the triumphs of Waterloo. In the month of May I was ordered to do duty with a troop of horse artillery, under the command of Colonel Bull, C.B, at Bailleul, and in July sent to join the 2nd Dragoon Guards in the brigade of Major-General Lord Edward Somerset, at Hazebrouck.

On the 22nd of October, the British army was reviewed before their Royal Highnesses the Dukes of Kent and Cambridge, upon the field of Denain, near Cambray, rendered famous by the decisive victory gained there by the French Marshal Villers over the Imperial armies of Germany, under Prince Eugene, on the 24th of July, 1712. A mansion is standing in the village of Denain, which (I believe) was given to Marshal Villers at the time, and a small stone obelisk is erected by the road side a little above the village, tearing the following inscription, taken from Voltaire:

Regardez dans Denain l'audacieux Villers
Disputant le Tonnere à l'Aigle des Caesars,
24 de Juliet, 1712.

After the review the army being ordered again to its cantonments, the cavalry marched back to the coast, and we were quartered at Guines near Calais, the Major-General, Lord Edward Somerset, being in a *château* at Hardingham, the 3rd Dragoons at Audreuick and adjacents, and the artillery of the brigade at Marquise. Guines was formerly a place of some importance. During the civil wars in England between the houses of York and Lancaster, the famous Earl of Warwick was warden of the marshes of Calais and Guines: it had then a castle which is now a heap of ruins; the remains of fortifications are still visible on the western side of the town. The Kings of France and England having in June, 1520, repaired hither with splendid courts, and attended by all the chivalric pomp of those times, they met in a field between Ardres and Guines, which (from the circumstance of its being covered with a golden carpet) acquired the name of the "*Champ du drap d'or,*" the field of the cloth of gold.

1817

Early in the spring the Allied Powers having agreed to withdraw one-fifth of the army of occupation, the following regiments of the British army were ordered home:

1st Foot (Royal)	27th Foot	81st Foot
21st Foot	40th Foot	88th Foot

In consequence of this the 3rd Division was broken up, and Lieutenant-General Sir Charles Colville, and Major-Generals O'Callaghan and Keane were struck off the staff of this army. In the autumn the army again assembled between Cambray and Valenciennes for a review, after which we returned to our cantonments for the winter.

1818

In the month of February in this year an attempt was made against the life of the Duke of Wellington: he was fired at one night in the streets of Paris by a *ci-devant* French officer. The people in general had submitted with a wonderful degree of cheerfulness to the burthen and inconveniencies imposed upon them by our presence, but they looked forward with impatience to the autumn of this year, when they hoped the liberation of their territory would be effected. In order to preserve tranquillity and good order, however, we had on our part been obliged to submit to many annoyances and difficulties, to which the inhabitants of the country were often glad to subject us.

In the cantonments bordering on the coast, especially near Montreuil, the people were particularly quarrelsome, and disturbances of so serious a nature had recently occurred in the villages occupied by the 18th Hussars near Etaples, that Lieutenant-General Sir Henry Fane judged it expedient to issue the following General Orders:

Cavalry Head-Quarters, Pont de Brique,
2nd June 1818.

In consequence of the circumstance which recently occurred in the neighbourhood of Longville, and the temper shewn by the inhabitants of that vicinity, Major-General Sir Hussey Vivian will close up the cantonments of the 18th regiment, and will occupy the village named and its vicinity as strongly as circumstances will permit, consistent with the convenience of the troops. In the occupation hereby ordered, if the Mayors refuse to make the required arrangement of quarters, reference is to be had to the Assistant Quarter-master-General's instructions contained in the letter dated 29th October 1816, and also to the paragraph of the Quarter-master-General's letter dated 24th November 1816; and he will act in conformity to those two letters both as respects the occupation of quarters, and the communications to be made to the magistrate. He will of course see the troops put into possession of the billets which will have been arranged for them.

For the future, in every village occupied by the cavalry, in which not less than twenty men are quartered, there is to be a guard regularly mounted, and the post of that guard is to be the alarm-post of the cantonment in case of riot of disturbance, all soldiers are immediately to repair with their arms to that alarm-post, and a communication is to be forthwith established with the alarm-posts of the troop: for this purpose one of the guard is invariably to have a horse accoutred and ready to be mounted in case of a guard being attacked they are to defend themselves like soldiers, and not hesitate to fire upon those assailing them, as long as a man remains opposed to them.

The officers and soldiers will understand that these orders are by no means to be considered as intended to diminish the good understanding which exists amongst the most of them and the people where they are quartered: on the contrary the Lieutenant-General cannot sufficiently express his desire that the utmost harmony should be maintained; but what has passed renders it necessary that a more military aspect should be assumed to suppress, in its commencement, the audacity of the peasantry, and to protect the soldiers from insult and injury.

(Signed)   John Elley,
Col. & Dep. Adjutant-General.

Early in the autumn the Duke of Wellington from Cambray, and Lord Castlereagh from England, repaired to Aix-la-Chapelle, for the purpose of meeting there in Congress the Emperors of Russia and Austria and the King of Prussia. On the 27th of September these three puissant Sovereigns arrived, and on the 28th the congress opened with the first grand question, as to the army of occupation being to remain or to evacuate France.

On the 2nd of October the discussions upon this subject were ended, with a declaration on the part of the four great powers, Russia, Austria, England and Prussia, that they were satisfied with the state of France, with the securities offered for her tranquillity, and for the payment of the sums yet due; in consequence of which, they agreed in the expediency and policy of withdrawing the army of occupation from the French territory, separating it altogether, and sending the troops home to their respective countries: a treaty was consequently drawn up and signed on the 10th of October, ordering the said evacuation of the French territory to commence forthwith, and to be completed by the 30th of November next ensuing; so that this service now approaching its close, we were all once more assembled in the vicinity of Cambray and Valenciennes, Lord Wellington having determined, previously to the final separation, to unite the Russian, British and smaller contingents of the army for a review, at which their Majesties the Emperor of Russia and King of Prussia were to be present; and as this was perhaps the most splendid military spectacle ever exhibited in Europe, a brief outline thereof may prove interesting.

GRAND REVIEW
ON THE
HEIGHTS OF FAMAR NEAR VALENCIENNES,
23rd of October, 1818.

Orders having been sent to the British, Russian, Saxon, Danish and Hanoverian armies to turn out from their camps and cantonments in such time as would enable them to reach the field by 9 o'clock, the whole of these forces were accordingly assembled by that hour in the fine open position near Villars en Couche, and soon afterwards fell into line as follows:

The Russian army	25,000	on the right
The Saxon army	3,000	in the centre
The Danish army	3,000	*ditto*
The Hanoverian army	3,000	*ditto*
The British army	21,000	on the left.

At ten o'clock the firing of the cannons announced the approach of the Sovereigns of Russia and Prussia, who were accompanied by the Duke of Wellington, and followed by a very numerous retinue of Princes, Generals and other distinguished personages which it was not possible to number, well mounted, in their full dress uniforms, and wearing the badges of the orders to which they severally belonged. Field Marshal his Grace the Duke of Wellington, K,G. Prince of Water loo, appeared in full-dress uniform as a Field Marshal of England, (scarlet) with the General's plume in his hat, the Bath star at his breast, and sky-blue scarf, as a Knight of the Garter: he wore also his old Peninsular distinction, a white cravat, and was mounted on a little chestnut horse, which he continued to ride throughout the day.

His Imperial Majesty the Emperor of all the Russias wore plain Russian uniform, (green with scarlet facings) the Russian plume, one star, and grey pantaloons over Wellington boots: he was mounted on a very beautiful grey English charger. His Majesty the King of Prussia wore Prussian uniform, (blue with scarlet facings) extremely plain and without embroidery or decorations, the Prussian plume in his hat, and grey pantaloons over Wellington boots: he was mounted on a fine black English charger.

As the firing of the royal salute commenced the bands all struck up God save the King, and the Russian army, which had been complimented with the right of the line, set up a loud cheering on the appearance of their Emperor. The Field Marshal now began to pass down the line, with the Emperor of Russia on his left (nearest the troops) and the King of Prussia on his right, saluted by all arms, colours, &c. as they passed, with bands playing and trumpets sounding. No sooner had the inspection of the line ended, than the movements and sham fight began, and were continued throughout the day. The supposed enemy, consisting of the Russian *Cossacks*, British staff corps, and some other detachments, under the directions of Colonel Sir George Scovell, according to the plan of operations, laid down, were driven from hill to hill, but not until several villages had been. with apparent earnestness won and lost, and the cavalry had made several dashing charges.

The whole affair ended about four o'clock in the afternoon by the Russian army having turned the enemy's left near Valenciennes, and the British infantry carrying by a grand attack the heights of Famar, where in the year 1793, a real engagement had been fought between the French revolutionary forces and the British army under his Royal Highness the Duke of York. All the troops now assembled and began to fall into solid squares of about 1,000 men each, for the purpose of marching past their Majesties, and the Duke of Wellington having drawn his sword and placed himself at their head, the bands struck up, and the march began,

Aides-du-camp to the Duke of Wellington.
Russian, Prussian, Austrian, British, Saxon, Hanoverian and Danish.
Field-Marshal the Duke of Wellington, K. O. mounted.
The Russian Infantry,
In nineteen solid squares, with their colours flying in

the centre of each, and fifty pieces of cannon.
Nineteen battalions of British Infantry, and
Forty pieces of Cannon,
Saxon Infantry,
Hanoverian Infantry,
Danish Infantry,
The Russian Cavalry, about 2,000, and
Horse Artillery,
Saxon Cavalry,
Hanoverian Cavalry,
Danish Cavalry,
Six Regiments of British Cavalry,
Three Troops of Horse Artillery.

The infantry marched past at quick time, with their bands playing and colours flying. The cavalry passed in full trot with their trumpets sounding. The day closed as the 11th Light Dragoons, the last regiment, was passing, and it was 10 o'clock by the time we reached our quarters at Abancourt. This review certainly surpassed in magnificence and military splendour everything of the kind I ever saw; indeed, one can hardly imagine a scene more imposing than it really was. The extreme fineness of the weather, too, conspiring to bring spectators to the field, every vehicle in Cambray or Valenciennes had been put in requisition, and not only those places but the neighbouring towns also were almost deserted by their inhabitants, and many families of distinction even came from England to be present.

The train of carriages (principally filled with ladies) was so numerous that in some places they stood five and even six deep down the line. It is impossible to say what number of imperial, royal, or military decorations were here at one view to be seen, the profusion of scarfs, stars, crosses and other honourary distinctions was so great In short, this was perhaps one of the most chivalric as well as princely fields ever seen in Europe, Amongst the most puissant and distinguished personages present were the following:

His Imperial Majesty the Emperor of all the Russias,
His Majesty the King of Prussia,
Their Imperial Highnesses the Grand Dukes Constantine and Michael, Brothers to the Emperor of Russia,
His Royal Highness Prince Frederick of Prussia (Son of the King),

232

His Royal Highness the Prince of Orange,

Field-Marshal his Grace the Duke of Wellington, Commander-in-Chief of the Army of Occupation,

The Russian General Beningsen,

The Prussian General Von Zeithen,

The Russian General-in-Chief Count Woronzow,

The Hanoverian General-in-Chief Count Alten,

The Danish General-in-Chief,

The Saxon General-in-Chief,

Marshal Lord Beresford,

The Spanish General Don Miguel d'Alava,

More than 300 Knights Commanders or Companions of the Bath, besides Officers wearing the Stars of Foreign Orders, and about 18,000 Waterloo-men,

The British army was now ordered to march to the coast for embarkation, by the following routes, *viz.*

The 2nd Division of Infantry (in two columns) to march from Valenciennes on the 24th of October to Douai, on the 25th to Lens, on the 26th to Lilliers, on the 27th to Blandeques, on the 28th to La Recousse, on the 29th to Calais.

The 1st Division of Infantry (in two columns) to march from Cambray on the 26th of October to Douai, on the 27th to Lens, on the 28th to Lilliers, on the 29th to Blandeques, on the 30th to La Recousse, on the 31st to Calais.

The cavalry to march to the following points, and there wait for orders. 1st Brigade to Guines, 2nd Brigade to Moulle near St. Omer, 3rd Brigade to Therouenne.

The Prussian army commenced its march for Prussia, the Austrian army for Austria, the Russian army for Poland, the Bavarian army for Bavaria, the Hanoverians and Saxons were ordered to pass through Belgium, and the Danes by way of Dunkirk.

In our marches to and from Cambray each year, we passed through the town of Arras, famous as the birth-place of the tyrant Robespierre, who acted so prominent a part in the bloody scenes of the French revolution. It is related of him, that he here beheld three hundred victims of his rage beheaded together in one morning from the window of his house, in the *Petite Place* and laid a wager with a man as devoid of feeling as himself, respecting the time which the executioner would take to perform his melancholy task. The hand of Heaven, however, was not slow in overtaking this monster of cruelty, for Robespierre and his associates, after a short reign of terror, fell by the hands of the very executioners they had commissioned to take the lives of others.

During one of these movements also I met with an officer of the medical staff of our army, who related to me the following interesting story, of an adventure which befell him in the Peninsula; and it is of a nature so singularly affecting, that I cannot refrain from inserting it here. In the retrograde movements made by the British army in Spain after the battle of Talaviera, this gentleman, who then belonged to the 23rd Light Dragoons, and some other officers, were surprised and made prisoners at Placentia, and conducted to Madrid, where by the exercise of his professional skill he rendered such service to the French wounded, that Buonaparte, upon his subsequent arrival in France, not only gave him his liberty without exchange, but presented him with a gratuity of *Twelve Hundred Francs* (fifty pounds sterling) from the public purse.

The prisoners, both Spanish and English, after remaining at Madrid two months, early in October 1809 marched for France, under a strong escort appointed to convey them to the frontiers. In passing over the Sierras de Guardarama by St Ildefonso to Segovia, the attention of this officer was attracted by the interesting appearance of a little boy, about six or seven years old, riding in a wagon apparently under the care of a Spanish woman, who appeared to act the part of a mother to him.

Observing, however, that there was something in the child's countenance and complexion which indicated that he was native of a more northern clime than Spain,—he asked it a few questions in Spanish, and to his surprise was answered in the same language; but upon further inquiry it appeared that he was under the protection of the French officer commanding the escort that he was the orphan child of a Serjeant McCullen, of the 42nd regiment (Highlanders), who fell in the battle of Corunna, and that the mother in the retreat from Salamanca upon Lugo, had died upon the road through excessive privations and fatigue, when the poor child fell into the hands of the enemy's advanced guard, fortunately commanded by this humane officer.

Upon learning this story, which was folly corroborated on every hand, the British prisoners unanimously petitioned the French officer to give up the child to them as its more natural protectors, that they might forward it to England, where its forlorn case would claim for it an asylum from some humane institution. The French officer, however, refused to part with the boy, but promised to take care of him and use him well, and the English in their own destitute situation as prisoners of war, had of course for the present no alternative but to submit.

On their arrival at Tolosa in the Pyrenees, an order met them which directed that the English prisoners should be marched into France, but the Spanish conducted to the fortress of Pampeluna, and the French officer herein alluded to being ordered upon the latter duty, the British officers with much regret parted from the little orphan. The author of the narrative having (as before mentioned) been recommended to the special notice of the Emperor Napoleon for the service he had rendered the French wounded, was ordered to Paris to receive his discharge; while he was there waiting for his dismissal, a Captain H—— of the 23rd Light Dragoons arrived in Paris, a prisoner also from Madrid, having under his care the little orphan boy, whom, on his passing Tolosa, he had there found in the most forlorn condition, forsaken by both his foster-father and mother.

The former it appears had found a difficulty in conveying his prisoners to Pampeluna as ordered, from the enterprising spirit of the Spanish guerrillas under Espozy Mina, who were resolved to liberate their countrymen; and the Spanish woman dreading their resentment for attaching herself to a Frenchman, had fled. Under such circumstances Captain H—— had, without hesitation, brought the child with him to Paris, where he now very providentially met the very officer who had been the first to identify and interest himself for it, just obtaining his passport for London: it was agreed therefore that the poor little. boy should go to his native land with him, and Captain H—— wrote letters to the War-Office, to the Duke of York, and also to the Marquis of Huntly (the colonel of the regiment), on the subject.

Arriving in London with his little orphan, Mr. —— immediately left the letters at the Horse Guards and Richmond House, and that same evening received a note, intimating that the Duke of York would be happy to see him and his little *protégée* on the following morning at 10 o'clock: accordingly they went to York House at that hour, and were very graciously received. The Duke of York condescendingly conversed with the child in German and French, both of which languages, as well as Spanish, he had learnt: the first he had acquired from his foster-father, the second from a Saxon servant, and the last from the Spanish woman.

His Royal Highness was altogether so much pleased with the child, and so affected with his interesting story, that he resolved to put him into the Military Asylum, under his own patronage. He had about this time resigned the office of commander-in-chief, but with that humanity and condescension for which His Royal Highness is distinguished, he wrote to Sir David Dundas, drawing his notice to the circumstance, with a view that the parties might, with the least possible delay, be furnished with the necessary certificates, and pursue their respective interests.

At length nothing was wanting for the admission of the child into the school for soldiers' orphans but a certificate from the Marquis of Huntly, when Mr. —— and the poor little fellow, in proceeding one morning to Richmond House for this document, overtook near the Horse Guards a serjeant of the 42nd regiment, with a letter in his hand addressed to the Marquis of Huntly. Under an impression that the man might give him some information which would assist him in his interview with Lord ——, Mr. —— inquired whether he had served in the late campaign in Spain, and being answered in the affirmative, then asked if he knew his comrade Serjeant M'Cullen, who was killed at Corunna.

The man, evidently much agitated, replied that he knew no comrade of that name killed at Corunna, but begged to know why the gentleman asked this question. Because, said Mr. ——, this is his orphan child, whom I found in Spain. He was soon interrupted with the simple but emphatic exclamation of, "Bless your honour, Sir, I am the man! it's my child!"

Then turning to the child, who had still a faint recollection of his father, he was deeply affected; indeed, we can well conceive that the feelings of each party may be better imagined than described. It afterwards proved that the unsealed letter which the soldier was carrying to the Marqius of Huntly, was from Colonel Stirling commanding the regiment then lying at Canterbury, informing him that Serjeant Mc-Cullen was not (as supposed) killed at Corunna, but wounded and got safe off, and that he had sent the man to London, that he might answer personally for himself any questions which might be put to him.

Thus ends this affecting narrative, which I conclude with the hope that this poor fellow has not since fallen in some one of the several bloody fields in which his regiment has subsequently been engaged in the Peninsula or at Waterloo. The child, I understood, was placed in the Military Asylum.

Such is the warrior's fruitage of acclaim,
His honours such: but, as for future fame,
The sons of battle are like autumn leaves,—
Fame like the gale their brittle stem that cleaves;
Leaf after leaf confused is seen to fall,
The gale one moment flutters with them all,
And ere they reach their brethren strewed around,
One little instant buoys them from the ground:
That instant over, each is left to fade,
Forgotten all their once protecting shade.

Zuillinam.

On the 29th of October the embarkation of the army commenced with the 1st column of the 2nd Division, consisting of the 4th, 6th, 29th, 71st and 79th regiments, which went on board the instant they arrived, and sailed with the first tide for Dover. As fast as they landed the troops the transports returned, and by the 3rd of November the whole of the infantry had been embarked, excepting the guards and 52nd regiment, which for the present remained in garrison at Cambray and Valenciennes.

The artillery and military stores were next conveyed over, and the embarkation of the cavalry commenced on the morning of the 7th, when we bade farewell to our old quarters at Guines. By 8 o'clock in the evening the whole of the regiment with the horses had been got on board, and all the vessels, about forty in number, were ready to weigh anchor. The scene which now presented itself from the pier of Calais was as beautifully interesting as any I can recollect having seen. It was a fine calm and moonlight night, and all the sails were spread with a gentle breeze.

At the instant the first vessel began to move, the band in the headquarters ship struck up, and the trumpets in several others began sounding "God save the King," which they continued as they together sailed majestically down Calais harbour, until the leading ship had passed the pier-head into the ocean, when the band struck up "Rule Britannia," and played until by the rippling of the waves we lost the sound. On the 10th of November at 10 o'clock in the morning I embarked at Calais in the *Thames* transport, and after a blowing passage of seven hours landed at Ramsgate at 5 in the evening.

Part of the 3rd Dragoons and 12th Lancers came over at the same time, and in less than six weeks from the commencement of the embarkation, all the army had quitted France. On the 13th I reported myself in London, and received the indulgence granted to the staff of the army of occupation, of retaining their full pay two months after their arrival in England; being placed on half-pay on the 11th January 1819.

Waterloo Prize Money allotted me, 4th class, as Lieutenant, £34 14s. 9d. sterling.

www.ingramcontent.com/pod-product-compliance
Lightning Source LLC
Chambersburg PA
CBHW032048080426
42733CB00006B/198